Catholic Education
in the Western World

Catholic Education

in the Western World

Edited by
James Michael Lee

Foreword by
George N. Shuster

Contributors:
Didier J. Piveteau
Franz Pöggeler
Jos. J. Gielen and W. J. G. M. Gielen
Vincenzo Sinistrero
John P. White
James Michael Lee

1967
University of Notre Dame Press

To All Those
	Laboring in the Catholic School Vineyard
The World Over

Preface

Today's world is an educational world. It was not always so. Before the twentieth century, the typical adult in the developed countries had spent only five years in a formal educational institution. But by the second half of our century, the typical child in these same countries could look forward to remaining in school for an average of thirteen to seventeen years, or about 20 per cent of his life. In many ways this 20 per cent of his life span spent in school constitutes the most formative period of the development of the person.

It is only natural, then, that the Catholic Church, in its unceasing efforts to mediate God with man, has been more and more investing its resources in the school apostolate. Now as never before the impact made on the personality during the years of *becoming* goes far in conditioning the existential self for the remainder of life.

The Catholic Church enjoys a deserved reputation for a coordinated, catholic organization in almost all its activities, missionary work, for example, or the parish-diocese-regional-national-international hierarchical network. Thus it seems all the more incongruous that the highly organized Church is unbelievably—and scandalously—unorganized in one of its most vital and influential spheres of apostolic activity, namely the schools under its jurisdiction. Despite the tremendous, indeed the staggeringly tremendous investment of personnel and funds in the Catholic school enterprise, the Church still does not have a central world office coordinating its educational activities. The Church does not even have as much as a central agency which disseminates information on Catholic schools in various countries.

This volume represents the editor's attempt to take the first step toward such coordination of Catholic schools the world over. That this attempt should constitute a pioneer effort is itself a withering indictment of the haphazard manner in which the Church conducts one of its most vital enterprises. Yet it is better to light a single candle, however feeble, than to curse the darkness. That is the purpose of this work.

Thus it is the goal of this book to give Catholic educators and educationists in various countries an overview of what their confrères in the educational apostolate in other lands are doing. As far as the editor and the contributors of this work are aware, this is the first book which affords such a comparative view of Catholic education in representative countries. Catholics in every nation wish their schools to become better and better. It is devoutly hoped that this first step toward disseminating knowledge of Catholic education in a variety of countries will lead to the improvement of Catholic—and indeed of government—education in every land. And perhaps the final fruit will be a full-fledged world office for coordinating Catholic education.

There are many books on comparative education, almost always written about government schools. But the present volume is unique in that instead of relying on one or two authors, it represents a team effort of separate educational scholars each writing about the schools in his own country. No educationist, however learned, can ever capture the true essence of schools in a foreign land; it is only by growing up in a country and having the milieu of that country penetrate one's very being that an education scholar can truly understand the unique character of the schools in a country. Every contributor to this present book is a native of his land and, further, is among the foremost of Catholic education scholars in his country.

All the chapters are written in parallel organization, so that the reader will have a book which is as fully comparative as possible. The subheads under each chapter heading in the table of contents indicate the broad areas of this parallelism. In the appendix will be found the detailed outline which each contributor used in writing his essay.

The six countries included in this volume were chosen because each represented a substantially different pattern of Catholic school "system" vis-à-vis the respective national government, and further that they embodied contrasting patterns of educational thrust. Thus a spectrum of Catholic schools is provided. Roger O. Parent, Sister Maryl Hofer, and Phyllis Adair assisted in the final stages of preparation of this book.

Didier J. Piveteau, Jos. J. Gielen and W.J.G.M. Gielen, John P. White, and the editor of this volume all wrote their chapters in English. Erwin Neumayer and the editor made some addenda to Franz Pöggeler's chapter. Cirian Tormey translated Vincenzo Sinistrero's essay, while Franz Pöggeler's contribution was translated by Manfred

Prokop. The editor subsequently edited all the manuscripts, and a second editor, D. Pobdowm, reviewed the manuscript once again.

Everyone connected with the writing of this short work ardently hopes that it will bring about an educational renewal in Catholic schools the world over. The lack of such authentic renewal will only result in the nostalgic yet fateful words expressed by the American poet:

> *Of the saddest words of tongue or pen*
> *The saddest are these: "It might have been."*

James Michael Lee
Notre Dame, Indiana
August 1, 1966

Foreword

That Catholic education is a going enterprise in nearly every country in the Free World should occasion no surprise, for as one of the contributors to this volume says, such education is based on the conviction that no sacrifice is too great which leads to the keeping of the Faith alive in the hearts of children. Still it is rather startling to discover how vast and complex an undertaking it is. Each country has of course its own extensive literature on the subject, but it has been very difficult for nonspecialists, as most of us are, to come upon even a portion of that.

Professor Lee, to whose prodding the contributors to this volume have responded so generously, and whose skillful scrutiny of the scene in the United States is included, occupies a special place in American educational scholarship. On the one hand, he is an ardent advocate of Catholic schooling, tens of leagues removed from the notion that maybe this schooling has outlived its usefulness and should perhaps give way to new experiments in making parish life the all-inclusive center of religious formation. On the other hand, no voice speaks more clearly for reform or *aggiornamento*, whichever term is preferred. All his writing and speaking clamors for the day when, to borrow from Blake, Catholics "will have built Jerusalem" in educational terms.

This book reflects that mood. Spokesmen for a number of European countries—not all of them, but even so a fair sampling—make it evident that they cherish Catholic education. They know what it is, understand the reasons why it came into being, respect its accomplishments, and yet are quite realistic about the problems it must confront and the changes which for the most part are long since overdue.

Some of these last are fortunately unknown to Catholic education in the United States. Primary among them is a rigid, unitary government control which holds all schools, public and private alike, in a vise. Whereas we are almost too free to experiment and to deviate, they cannot venture to depart as much as an inch from the prescribed educational routine. And even if the now widespread demand for some liberalization being voiced generally in Europe does bring about a change, it will be very difficult to implement it quickly or in significant ways.

Other problems we share, notably those of finance and adequate teacher preparation. The situation in French Catholic education is now much better than it was in the heyday of anticlericalism, but still newly granted forms of assistance do not answer the question as to where sufficient money is to be found. Even in Germany, where the tax collector does yeoman service to ecclesiastical establishments, one of the grave needs is for schools in rural areas. Whereas these areas were once safely in the credit side of the Catholic ledger, this is no longer the case owing to a variety of upheavals. How can they be financed?

Or we may consider the extremely important issue of how religion is to be taught effectively. Owing to a dearth of research no one really knows whether young people who have spent years in Catholic schools will do better in terms of their religious life than do others who have attended public schools. Still there have been diligent attempts to make the work of catechists such as Jungmann come into its own in terms of religious pedagogy, and even to transcend any particular style of teaching in the effort to help young people commit themselves to an active Catholic life.

The gravest problem of all, and it is one which we are confronting in this country, too, is the marked decrease in the number of vocations to the religious, in particular the priestly, life. If this continues, the character of Catholic education will be altered in ways which it still is quite impossible to predict.

At all events, this book will, one hopes, bring to a great many Americans valuable insights into what Catholic education in Europe is and thus an increased awareness of this central part of the Church's mission. It will also, let us hope, awaken a sense of solidarity across national boundaries. The American Catholic is not alone in shouldering responsibility for the religious education of youth. This he is doing in his way, while others are making the effort in their ways. Professor Lee's book does not discuss broad philosophic principles except in passing. It is down-to-earth pedagogy by men who know their trade.

George N. Shuster

Contents

Catholic Education in France

by Didier J. Piveteau

A Short History
of Catholic
Education in France

The Pre-Revolutionary Period

Catholic schools have existed in France from as early as the fourth century. To be sure, the Romans had established flourishing schools in Gaul at the time their legions occupied the country. But they disappeared gradually to the point where Sidoine Apollinaire was able to write in a letter "Nowadays very few are those who give themselves to culture, and fewer still those who do it with success." The Church therefore established a number of schools. In the beginning these schools existed together with classical schools. However, after the conversion of Clovis (510 A.D.), they rapidly developed; from the seventh century on they were the only schools existing in France.

By the onset of the Middle Ages, Catholic schools were of three principal types according to the religious authority which set them up. Abbatial schools, those founded by monasteries, constituted the first category. These schools were established to teach and prepare young aspirants to religious life. But it was not long before they were opened to other students as well. In abbatial schools the students were taught reading, grammar, rhetoric, singing, and sometimes astronomy and the elements of medieval science. Some of those schools left enduring reputations, one being the Abbey of Cluny. Such famous personages as Alcuin and Lanfranc claim the honor of having attended abbatial schools.

Cathedral schools formed the second chief category. As implied by their name, cathedral schools were founded and supported by local bishops. In the beginning, these schools were established for the formation of priests; however, their activities soon expanded to meet the educational needs of the community. The two most famous cathedral schools were those of Chartres in the eleventh century and of Notre Dame de Paris in the twelfth century. It was in the latter that Abelard was a student and later a teacher.

Presbyteral schools comprised the third and final category of medi-

3

eval schools. These, the equivalent of our contemporary parish schools, developed principally in rural areas. They were open to all children; in this sense they are often called public as opposed to some abbatial or cathedral schools which were available only to future clerics. There was no tuition in presbyteral schools.

In order to teach in any of these schools, teachers at every level had to obtain the *licentia docendi* or license to teach. This license was granted either by the local lord or by the local bishop. The teachers were entrusted with the care of their pupils, even to providing board and lodging for them. The curriculum comprised seven subjects, divided into two groups: the *trivium* (grammar, rhetoric, and logic) and the *quadrivium* (geometry, astronomy, arithmetic, and music). The methods used for teaching were either the *lectio*, which consisted in the teacher's delivering a commentary on the textbooks, or the *disputatio*, which was a kind of speech contest between students.

Foundation of Universities

The thirteenth century in France was marked by a strong resistance of rising bourgeois classes against all kinds of feudalism. This resistance, which eventuated in rights and privileges for the cities, had important consequences for the school system. Wishing to preserve their rights against the influence of bishops, the teachers and students united into a corporation which was soon acknowledged by the king (1200 A.D.) and by the pope (1215 A.D. and 1366 A.D.). Thus was born the University of Paris, symbol and model of all French universities before the French Revolution. The official title of the University of Paris was significantly *Magistrorum et Auditorum Lutetiae Universitas*. The University was a self-governing body by virtue of privileges granted to it by the king and the pope. On the other hand, it was a Catholic institution since only Catholic professors could teach there; yet it was established as a bulwark against the authority of the bishops. Consequently it may legitimately be disputed as to whether the University of Paris was a secular or a Church institution. This question would have puzzled thirteenth century people since politics and religion were so closely interwoven in that era. Suffice it to say that all candidates for the bachelor's degree had to solemnly declare: "I swear I shall live according to the precepts of the Catholic, Apostolic and Roman Church; were I to fail this promise I should be expelled and deprived of all academic privileges."

In order to offer the best conditions for study, there soon developed the practice of compelling students to reside within the precincts of the University. Such centers of residence became known as colleges; they could admit students as early as the age of nine. The most famous of those colleges was founded by Robert Sorbon. This college was later to expand greatly and eventually to give its name to the whole university, La Sorbonne.

Post-Tridentine Foundations

The foundations of universities and their right to accept nine-year-old boys had an influence on the abbatial, cathedral, and presbyteral schools which had previously existed. These schools gradually abandoned what secondary or higher education they may have offered as part of their curriculum and retrenched to a program which was to be the ancestor of present-day elementary schools. By the fifteenth century the situation had become resolved: primary education was given in purely and exclusively Catholic schools, and advanced education was offered in universities which were under papal control but were subject to the jurisdiction of the ecclesiastical authorities of the country. However, the need for Catholic education, made evident by the Protestant Reformation and by the Council of Trent, resulted in two major developments in Catholic schools in France.

The first of these developments was that certain religious institutes established colleges on the secondary school level to effect a breach in the all-powerful privileges of the rapidly secularizing universities and to provide the youths with a more religiously oriented education. Most famous of these colleges were those founded by the Jesuits, which number among their alumni Condé, Descartes, Corneille, and, ironically, Voltaire. By 1762 there were 124 such Jesuit colleges in France. It is noteworthy that tuition was free for day students in these colleges, so that they were actually open to boys from all socioeconomic classes. The idea that Catholic education in France is reserved to higher socioeconomic classes is a recent concept which developed only with nineteenth century capitalism.

The second post-Reformation and post-Tridentine Catholic educational development was the need for a new impetus to parochial schools, called *petites écoles*, which was felt urgently in the seventeenth century. In parochial schools, Latin was not taught, and indeed the vitality of the school had fallen into decay. Consequently the working classes and the rural population suffered from illiteracy. The best known Catholic educational reformer in this regard was St.

John Baptist de la Salle who founded a new religious nonclerical institute, the Brothers of the Christian Schools, whose sole concern was and still remains that of providing a Catholic education for the lower socioeconomic classes. Not only were new schools opened by the brothers but also new teaching methods were devised and utilized. These advanced pedagogical processes contributed greatly to the progress of modern education.

Thus at the eve of the French Revolution the Catholic Church in France had some 800 colleges of secondary school status for boys and at least 350 for girls. The historian Taine estimated that out of 37,000 parishes 25,000 had a parochial school. It must be noted, however, that girls' attendance at these parochial schools was relatively low (the proportion of wives signing their names after their husbands on official registers varies from one-third to two-thirds) and that the colleges enrolled only 75,000 students, only one out of fifteen boys of school age.

From 1789 to the Advent of the Fifth Republic

The French Revolution as such achieved nothing definitive in the field of education. Nevertheless this great social cataclysm did take several steps which were of great importance to Catholic schools and which influenced the French system of education down to the present day. Decrees of 1790 and 1792 transferred schools from the responsibility of the Church to that of the state, deprived religious of the right to teach, and attempted to suppress all freedom in education. Notwithstanding, as early as 1795 a step toward educational freedom from the *ancienne regime* was taken when the *Directoire* recognized the rights of "citizens to establish private institutions of instruction and education, as well as societies for the promotion of science and liberal arts" (22 Août 1795). The result of this decree of freedom was the multiplication of Catholic schools rivaling government schools. This mushrooming of Catholic schools forcefully demonstrated that the Revolution had not eradicated religion from the hearts of the faithful.

Indeed this welling up of Catholic feeling by means of Catholic schools did not escape the notice of Napoleon. Consequently he decided to provide a clear-cut solution to the problem. On May 10, 1810 he created the Imperial University, a self-governing educational corporation independent of both Church and state, entrusted with the monopoly of education throughout the country. According to

Napoleon's scheme, the Imperial University was not against the Church; rather it was separate from but allied with the Church, since all schools had the obligation to teach Catholic religion and to provide a chaplain for the spiritual welfare of the students. Lower, nonuniversity instruction remained outside the scope of the Imperial University and was again left to private enterprise and, therefore for all practical purposes, to the control of the Church. Further, the bishops were allowed to open Catholic seminaries independent of the Imperial University, thus affording the opportunity for the Church to develop Catholic secondary schools which could conveniently be called "seminaries." This breach in the law soon created problems; in 1811 the government *lycées* enrolled 35,130 students and the pseudo seminaries enrolled 32,400 students.

Indeed, the very success of the pseudo seminaries in the following years and well after the fall of Napoleon induced the civil authorities to promulgate some restrictive measures. One restriction made it difficult for seminaries to accept pupils other than seminarians. Chaplains were granted very few hours for teaching religion in *lycées*. As a counterpoise to the influence of the Church, the teaching in the *lycée* was often atheistic and antidogmatic. As a result, Catholic thinkers like La Mennais, Lacordaire, and Montalembert began campaigning for the abolition of the privileges of the Napoleonic university and for freedom in education. Two important laws attempted a final solution to these vexing problems. In 1833 Guizot created a public system of elementary education throughout France. Such a decision was made necessary by the development of industry and by the need for literacy which Catholic schools were unable to meet. However, the Church was granted the freedom to open elementary schools. In 1850 the famous *Loi Falloux*, while preserving the privileges of the university to confer degrees, granted freedom to anyone to establish secondary schools, even if such schools were not seminaries in the true sense of the term.

The aforementioned legislation resulted in a field day for Catholic education in France. In 1863 there were 3000 Catholic elementary schools for boys compared with 3500 government schools, and 14,560 Catholic elementary schools for girls versus 6500 such government schools. In 1875 there were no less than 370 Catholic secondary schools for boys. It is fair to say that in those days the Catholic school was the main, if not the only, instrument of Catholic pastoral action in France. Such Catholic schools also constituted the primary means for recruiting candidates to the many religious institutes which maintained schools in that era (there were eighteen such teaching institutes in 1870). If to these impressive statistics is added the fact that even in government schools the influence of the Church was frequently dominant, one can understand the various steps taken by the Third Republic to weaken this ecclesiastical impact. In 1879 the teaching brothers were expelled from their elementary schools in Paris. In 1880 crucifixes were removed from classrooms in the municipal schools in Paris. In 1902 teaching religious were no longer permitted to teach in any schools, even private schools. (These institutes maintained 3000 schools at that time.) However, freedom of education was not suppressed. Private elementary and secondary schools could still be operated. Consequently many religious became "secularized" and continued their work in officially Catholic schools.

This situation lasted until World War II. Strong and influential French Catholic opinion blamed the French military debacle on the type of education given to French youth during the preceding forty years. As a result the rather politically conservative government of Marechal Petain abolished the 1901 laws and permitted the religious institutes to teach again in private schools. But these private schools encountered more and more difficulties in their effort to survive. They relied heavily on endowments and real investment, which with the successive devaluations, preserved very little value; further, they depended to a great extent on the generosity of Catholics. Under the Fourth Republic, the Catholic Church strove vigorously to obtain government financial support for private schools. A new relationship was set up between Catholic schools and the government in 1958, when de Gaulle ascended to the presidency. This development will be treated later.

The Purpose of Catholic Education in France

In their Plenary Assembly of 1951, the French cardinals and archbishops conceded that in certain circumstances, even when Catholic schools do exist, it may be permissible for Christian parents to send their children to a government school. Underlying their concession was the fact that Catholic schools had been unable to admit all young Catholics—in an age when schooling is both general and prolonged.

This declaration of the French hierarchy proved a great relief for many a Catholic family. On the other hand, the declaration concomitantly gave rise to the question of the *raison d'être* of the Catholic school.

Perhaps the answer to this question may be found in the eighteenth joint declarations made by the body of French bishops between 1945 and 1962, in the more recent declaration of Monseigneur Veuillot, President of the Episcopal Commission for Schools, and in the statements of Monseigneur Cuminal, General Secretary of Catholic Schools. One answer is that Catholic schools render a service to the nation by providing education to more than one and one-half million French children. Second, Catholic schools are the concrete realization of the educational wishes of Catholic families. On March 12, 1962, Monseigneur Veuillot declared that he "was aware of being the echo of thousands of Christian families" when he defends Christian instruction and education of Catholic children. Recently another purpose has been assigned to Catholic schools. These schools act as symbols, as sacraments, so to speak, and thus reach and sanctify not only those students who attend them but all Catholic children, even those enrolled in government schools. Catholic schools thus serve, in the words of the Gospel, as the light placed on the hill and shining forth on all who look at it. Consequently Catholic schools have the supreme imperative to be educationally excellent and to be linked vitally to the general pastoral work of the Church. Catholic schools should manifest to all the charity of Christ and the care of the Church for *this* world. Such should be their distinctive character when compared with non-Catholic or government schools.

The purpose of French Catholic education was not officially conceived of so humanistically, so sacramentally, or so pastorally, until very recently, however. Well into the late 1940's, the prevailing official Church position held that however good they may be, government schools do not really conform to the educational rights of the Church and of the family, and consequently are not entirely suited for Catholic children to attend. The official position held that Catholic schools are necessary to stimulate and strengthen the faith of young Catholics; therefore, all Catholic children ought to attend Catholic schools. As was often said, "The only satisfactory school for a Christian is the Christian school."

Until the waters cleared in recent years, the entire question of the purpose of the Catholic school was muddied by its being involved in French politics. To be sure, it is widely believed in France that the

Catholic school question has been used as a political issue rather than as an educational or a pastoral concern by the Church, on the one hand, and by anti-Church forces on the other. It cannot be doubted that between 1945 and 1958 the Catholic school question was used by all sides as a political football to obtain various political advantages. Many politicians believed that this issue was necessary to keep politics alive and were not at all anxious to see the difficulties resulting from the 1901 laws resolved. Edouard Lizop, who played a prominent role on the Catholic side during this period could count on the mass influence of the one and one-half million members of the *Association des Parents d'Eleves de l'Enseignement Libre* (APEL). This group organized huge mass meetings and demonstrations to press its claims forcefully. On another level Lizop created the *Association Parlementaire pour la liberté de'Enseignement*, which acted as a pressure group to influence politics. Before each election members of APEL all over France were strongly urged to vote only for those candidates who had adhered to Lizop's Parliamentary Association. This zeal for the defense of Catholic schools went so far as to state the position that "It is not unwise to judge a candidate by his stand on the Catholic school problem." Of course the entire Catholic school question was also exploited for political gain by those politicians who were opposed to Catholic schools.

The Relationship of Catholic Schools with State Schools

Government Legislation Which Has Affected Catholic Schools

The present status of Catholic schools in France is principally delineated in the law of December 31, 1959, called *Loi Debré*. According to the provisions of this law, four possibilities were open to nongovernment schools. The first of these can be termed the status quo. Dating from 1836 with the *Loi Guizot*, nongovernment elementary schools may legally be established. When the law was first promulgated, Catholic school teachers enjoyed what was called the "privilege of obedience." This privilege meant that these staff members did not need to meet any professional qualification apart from the permission of their own religious superiors. But this privilege was cancelled in 1880, and from that time on Catholic school teachers have been required to hold the *Brevet d'Etudes élémentaires* in order to teach. On the secondary school level, the Falloux Law permitted the establishment of nongovernment schools. Any Frenchman who was at least 25 years old, possessed the *baccalauréat*, and had taught for at least five years could open a secondary school.

The second possibility of the Debré Law was to integrate all private school teachers and buildings into the national system of education.

The third possibility was to enter into an agreement called *contrat simple*. This is a temporary provision, set up for nine years and due for revision in 1968. Schools operating thus are subject to government control, examinations, and syllabi. The principal of the school is free to choose the members of his staff. The teachers are paid by the government, but the operating expenses are not.

The fourth possibility is an agreement of a closer nature called *contrat d'association*. Not all schools are eligible to participate; they must meet an "officially admitted educational need." The question remains open, however, whether this official government recognition of an educational need lies in the hands of the government or of the population. Fiscal subsidy from the government is greater in the *contrat d'association* than in the *contrat simple*; however, in schools under the *contrat d'association* the government can also exercise some control over pedagogical processes and the selection of teachers. Originally the *contrat simple* was intended to be adopted by elementary schools, and secondary schools were expected to enter into the *contrat d'association*. But a number of secondary schools proved reluctant, fearing the loss of their freedom. By 1963 the situation with respect to the two types of *contrats* was as follows:

	Contrats simples	*Contrats d'association*
Elementary schools	10,500	147
Secondary schools	509	344
Technical schools	176	92

All private schools, regardless of which of the four categories they chose to enter, are still dependent on the "privilege of the University" created by Napoleon in 1810, a control confirmed by the Falloux Law in 1850. This means that private schools do not have the authority to graduate their students. All French students, whether they be in government or nongovernment schools, must take their examinations on the same date, and the questions are exactly the same all over France. The members of the Board of Examiners are members of the University and/or government schoolteachers. In 1965 an important advance was made when members of private school staffs who had hitherto been excluded from becoming *agregés* to the University could sit for the competitive examination intended to select them, provided they had served for five years in a school under the *contrat d'association*. One side effect of this new policy is that the level of staffs in private schools having only a *contrat simple* is bound to become lower.

Comparison of Catholic Schools with Government Schools As to Quality

It has often been asserted that teachers in French Catholic schools possess less professional preparation than their government school counterparts. It is certain that the 1833 law granting the privilege of "obedience" in favor of Catholic schools operated by religious institutes, together with the lenient provisions of the Falloux Law with regard to the standards of the professional preparation of Catholic school teachers had created dangerous educational laxity during the nineteenth century. These laws were enacted at a time when the Church was challenged by evolutionism and modernism; as a consequence bishops looked upon science, and indeed upon education generally, as a peril to the faith. Very few priests or religious prepared the examinations which were required of their colleagues in government schools. In addition, most Catholic secondary schools offered only the liberal arts curriculum, neglecting the natural sciences. This unhappy development provided ammunition to those who claimed that Catholic schools were blocking progress.

Although the privilege of "obedience" was finally withdrawn in 1880, the standards required for teaching in a private school were always lower than those for teaching in government schools. The general theory prevalent in Catholic circles until 1940 was that competence should be the hallmark of government schools, whereas piety constituted the distinctive feature of Catholic schools. However, this is a simplistic dichotomy which gives justice neither to the piety frequently found in government schools nor to the actual competence of many Catholic school teachers even when that competence was not officially supported by a university degree.

The academic results of students from government schools compared with those of students in Catholic schools as far as state examinations are concerned are approximately equal. Yet there seems little doubt that the results in Catholic schools were often obtained through drill and repetition, so that in effect the secondary schools were operated after the manner of elementary education. One deleterious consequence of this is the difficulty often experienced by Catholic school graduates—a difficulty also observed by their university professors—when these graduates start attending an institution of higher learning.

Many Catholics were disturbed by the 1959 Debré Law because it required Catholic teachers to have the same preparation as their counterparts in government schools. Yet for the reasons given in the preceding paragraphs, it is apparent that the Debré Law proved extremely beneficial to Catholic schools since it impelled these institutions to maintain a high educational standard which doubtless never would have been accomplished were the Church to have total control of its schools.

A parenthetical remark should be made at this juncture. The status of Catholic schools is entirely different in the provinces of Alsace and Lorraine. These provinces were separated from France in 1870, a time in which the Concordat between Napoleon III and the pope which gave special privileges to Catholic schools was still in effect. When these two provinces were restored to France in 1918, they demanded to be governed by the laws which existed at the time of their separation. Consequently the Catholic schools in Alsace and Lorraine enjoy a special status quite similar to that prevailing in early nineteenth-century France.

The Present Form
of Catholic
Schools in France

The Organizational Level

It would be erroneous to speak of a Catholic school system in France, at least insofar as this would imply some type of highly structured and carefully integrated organization. There are Catholic schools of course, but in the aggregate they can hardly be called a "system" for three principal reasons. The first of these is that Catholic schools are spread over France in a very uneven manner. Thus, for example, the percentage of Catholic elementary schools ranges from 66 per cent down to 4 per cent of all schools at that level, depending on the particular province. To get a clearer notion of these differences, the following table will be of help.

Percentage of Catholic Schools According to Départements*

	Over 40%	40-20%	20-10%	10-5%	Under 5%
Elementary schools	7	7	25	38	9
Lower secondary schools	13	13	30	24	6
Upper secondary schools	11	8	34	30	3

* Numbers in table indicate absolute number of Départements; data are from the 1963–64 academic year.

Regions with a high percentage of Catholic schools are in the west and in the center of France. It has been impossible to determine comparable statistical data for technical schools because the available figures are contaminated by the existence of many private nondenominational technical schools supported by chanbers of commerce or industrial plants.

The second reason for the lack of a system in French Catholic education is that until very recently each of these schools enjoyed a great deal of autonomy. There was little or no articulation among Catholic schools. They were like independent castles, each with a protective moat, each a world unto itself, without any reference to what the other schools or colleges were doing. This was particularly true of secondary schools. In no way could Catholic schools be considered as a network or as bricks in a pyramid that would constitute a Catholic school system in France. This unhappy situation is changing; indeed, the specific type of unity that will be established among those separate entities is one of the problems which confronts French Catholic education at the present time.

The final reason for not being able to speak of French Catholic schools as a separate system is that the structure of these schools is exactly modeled on the structure of government schools. Less than ever, since the Debré Law of 1958, is originality in nongovernment education encouraged. Thus to study the Catholic school system in France is equivalent to studying the French school system in general.

The first level of French Catholic schools is the kindergarten, which enrolls children from three or four to six years of age. There are not too many Catholic kindergartens in France. What few there are are typically conducted in an excellent and rather original manner due to the efforts of Father Faure, of the *Centre d'Etudes Pédagogiques*, who since the end of World War II has trained a number of female teachers according to Montessori methods.

When they reach the age of six, children advance to the next educational level, the elementary school (*école élémentaire*) for a period of five years. The students progress through the following grades, remaining in each for one year: (1) preparatory grade (*cours preparatoire*); (2) first elementary grade (*cours élémentaire* 1° *année*); (3) second elementary grade (*cours élémentaire* 2° *année*); (4) first middle grade (*cours moyen* 1° *année*); (5) second middle grade (*cours moyen* 2° *année*). According to present legislation, a child must not repeat a grade during those first five years. At the end of the fifth year of elementary school, children must take an entrance examination to be admitted to the first year of what might be termed a lower secondary school, a junior high school, or a middle school (*enseignement secondaire du* 1° *cycle*). More precisely, a successful graduate is admitted to the sixth grade of the observation cycle (*le cycle d'observation*). He remains in this cycle two years, the sixth and the fifth, and then goes for another two years, the fourth and the third, to the orientation cycle (*le cycle d'orientations*). The two-year period of the observation cycle and the following two-year period of the orientation cycle constitute a single unit called *college d'enseignement secondaire* if Latin is taught, and *college d'enseignement général* if Latin is not part of the curriculum.

At the age of fifteen, students must pass another entrance examination to be admitted to the senior high school or upper secondary school (*enseignement secondaire deuxième cycle*). This lasts three years, at the end of which students sit for the *baccalauréat*. Those three years in the upper secondary school are called 2°, 1°, and *classes terminales*, respectively.

Children who when they were eleven years old failed the entrance examination to the lower secondary school (6° *du cycle d'observation*) are allowed to repeat the last grade of elementary school, the *cours moyen* 2°*année*, but only for one year. When they become twelve, they must enter the *college d'enseignement général* which, it will be recalled, is the upper secondary school whose curriculum does not include Latin. If after repeating the grade they pass the entrance examination to the upper secondary school, they join the normal stream in the 6° *d'observation*. If they again fail the examination, they are remanded into an "opportunity cycle" of two years, the 6° *de transition*, followed by the 5° *de transition*. The name opportunity cycle suggests that these two grades might open their minds so they might be able to join the regular stream. If they still remain below the standard level, instead of being admitted into the 4° *d'orientation*, they will go into a 4° *terminale* followed by a 3° *terminale* which will bring them to the point where they will have passed the compulsory school age.

It is to be noted that the numbering of grades in France is the opposite of that in the United States. French grades begin with the highest number.

Institutions of higher learning in France are of two types, the universities and the advanced schools (*grandes ecoles*), for example, Saint Cyr, Advanced Teacher-Training School (*Ecole Normale Supérieure*), the Polytechnic Institute (*Polytechnique*), School of Mines (*Ecole des Mines*), and so forth. Students who graduate from the upper secondary school can enter the university directly. However, two additional years are required to pass the very selective entrance examinations to the various *grandes ecoles*. These two years are generally spent in special preparatory sections attached to the upper secondary schools. The Catholics have established at this point a unique institution, which has no equivalent in France. It is a school called Sainte Geneviève, located in Versailles and conducted by the Jesuits. This school enrolls students with the *baccalauréat* and prepares them to pass the entrance examination to practically any *grande ecole*. Studies in a *Grande Ecole* customarily last from two to four years, as compared with three years required to obtain the first diploma (*licence*) from the university. University studies following the *licence* through the *maîtrise* and the doctorate are at present being completely reorganized; consequently it is not possible to give precise details as to what they will be. Of interest is the fact that Catholics have opened some *grandes ecoles* with an excellent reputation such as *les écoles supérieures d'électronique* in Paris, Angers, and Lille and *l'Institut Catholique des Arts et Metiers* in Lille. There are five Catholic universities, in Paris, Lille, Lyon, Angers, and Toulouse.

A French university is composed of the separate faculties of humanities, law and economics, science and technology, medicine, and pharmacy. The organization of the French curriculum was profoundly altered at the beginning of 1966. The aims of the teaching at the university level were then defined as threefold: (1) to spread existing knowledge on an advanced level; (2) to contribute to the furtherance of knowledge; and (3) to prepare future professors and men who would direct the nation in various spheres of major influence.

French universities have no entrance examination. The *baccalauréat*, which comes at the end of the secondary school studies, is all that is required for matriculation in a university. For those who failed their *baccalauréat* it is possible to take a special examination, the successful passing of which entitles them to admission to a university faculty. The number of matriculants in this category is very small.

The program of French universities is divided into three successive stages. The first cycle, which acquaints the student with the basic elements of higher learning, lasts for two years. In the second cycle the student begins his specialization on an advanced level. This cycle leads to the *licencié* degree after one year, and to the master's degree after two years. The third cycle is restricted to advanced research. Only students who hold the master's degree are eligible for the third cycle.

Outside the scope of the regular "school system" Catholics have established a number of orphanages, reformatory schools, and various types of schools for handicapped children. Indeed, for a long time the Church pioneered in these types of schools; however, the government recently began to make a large-scale effort in this area. Sooner or later the government will eclipse the Church in these areas of special education and residential education by virtue of financial resources far superior to those available to the Church.

No mention of technical schools has been made up to this point. The school reform brought about important changes in this domain. The most notable of these is that at present there is no differentiation at the lower secondary school level other than that previously mentioned between children attending the orientation cycle and those attending the opportunity cycle with the hope of gaining admittance into the orientation cycle. There is still, however, a minor distinction which takes place during the course of the first year: after three months' observation some pupils begin studying Latin and are thus placed in the classical curricular track, whereas others will be in the so-called modern curricular track. Real differentiation does take place when students are fifteen years old and are ready to enter the upper secondary school. They can be admitted either to the humanities track curriculum, to the scientific curriculum, or to the technical curriculum. Schools which offer all three curricula are called comprehensive secondary schools.

It is easy to see the problems which such a school organization creates for Catholic schools. In many areas, for lack of communication and for want of articulation, Catholic schools have developed in a way close to anarchy. It is not infrequent to find in a small town several schools offering the humanities curriculum but none offering the technical. The result, which is bitterly resented by Catholic families, is that a child is never sure of being able to have a Catholic education throughout his school career. In the regions and *départements* where the percentage of Catholic schools is very low, the Church does not cater to the needs of her children as far as Catholic schools are concerned. Consequently some Catholic families believe that inasmuch as their children are not assured of a continuous Catholic education, it is better to place them in a government school rather than in a Catholic school from the start. This anarchistic situation is all the more shocking since Catholic schools usually minister to the needs of the brightest pupils, neglecting or ignoring those practical or technical curricula which are necessary for less intellectually gifted pupils. To remedy this bizarre and dangerous situation, an effort is being made in every diocese to establish what is called *la carte scolaire*, which is to consolidate and tighten up Catholic schools in given regions. Thus, for example, small Catholic schools which duplicate one another will be closed, and new Catholic schools for which there is a demonstrated need will be erected. One of the most obvious consequences of this Catholic school reorganization is the introduction of coeduction into Catholic schools, since in some regions this practice represents the only way to obtain sufficient enrollment for a school which wishes to offer all the various curricula to its students. A formal motion was made in May 1966 by the education commission of the *Comité National de l'Enseignement Catholique* to that effect.

A very significant aspect of the status of French Catholic schools must now be introduced. As noted previously, all pupils are required to sit for several examinations throughout their school years immediately prior to enrollment in a new school level. In 1958 Catholic schools acquired the right to examine their own pupils without any interference from the state. Thus, for example, a pupil enters a Catholic school at the age of six. He will be examined by his or another Catholic school (if he transfers to another) when entering the 6° *d'orientation*. He will be examined again when he is fifteen, before entering the secondary school 2° *cycle*. And finally he will be examined when he is seventeen by his own school before entering the finishing year, to determine what sections he will join (A, B, C, D, or T).

However, the *baccalauréat* examination must be taken before an official government examining board. This is due to the "privilege of the University" dating back to Napoleon: the University alone has the power of pronouncing graduation so that even government school students have to sit for an examination before a board which does not come from their own school.

There are only five Catholic universities in all of France: *L'Institut Catholique de Paris*, enrolling 8500 students; *Les Facultés Catholiques de Lille*, enrolling 4200 students; *Les Facultés Catholiques de Lyon*; *L'Université Catholique de l'Oeust* in Angers; and *L'Institut Catholique de Toulouse*. Of all Catholic universities, only *Les Facultés Catholiques de Lille* has a complete school of medicine.

In addition to the *baccalauréat* there are two other principal types of examinations which students take under the same general conditions. For those pupils who leave school at the end of the $1°$ cycle of secondary school, there is the *certificat de fin d'etudes obligatoires*, and for those who successfully complete two years of vocational training, there is the *certificat d'aptitude professionnelle* (C.A.P.).

Control Structure of the Catholic School System

As previously noted, French Catholic schools were until recently very loosely coordinated. The question of control, therefore, remained very vague. Elementary schools are operated either by the parish or by a religious institute. In the latter the authority of the pastor is much less influential. The tendency now is for all elementary schools to set up a threefold authority: the pastor is responsible for catechesis and the religious education given in the school; a board of education, principally chosen from among parents, is responsible for the financial management; and finally, the principal—together with a group of parents—is responsible for the educational aspect, schedule, regulations, curricula, and so on.

Catholic secondary schools in France are never parish schools; they are conducted either by a diocese or by a religious institute. Every diocese has a superintendent of schools, as it were, called the *Directeur de l'enseignement chrétien*. However, there is a certain ambiguity attached to this post, since frequently there is also in each diocese a superintendent of religious instruction, a *Directeur de l'enseignement religieux*, whose role it is to govern religious teaching throughout the diocese. This latter post was created to initiate, coordinate, and supervise the pastoral care of Catholic children attend-

Chart Outlining French School System

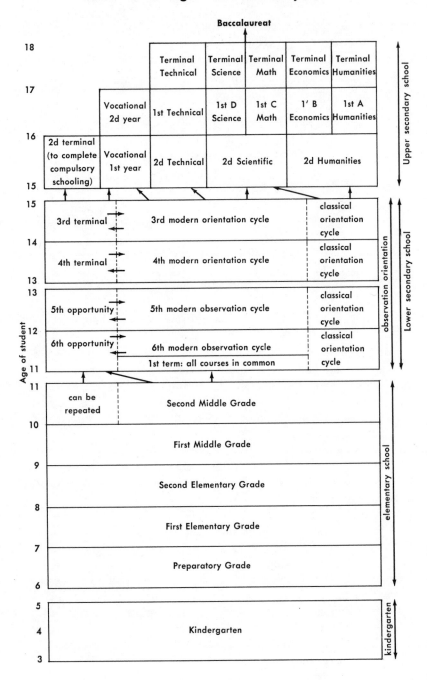

Baccalaureat

		Terminal Technical	Terminal Science	Terminal Math	Terminal Economics	Terminal Humanities
18						
17		Vocational 2d year	1st Technical	1st D Science	1st C Math	1' B Economics	1st A Humanities
16	2d terminal (to complete compulsory schooling)	Vocational 1st year	2d Technical	2d Scientific		2d Humanities	

Upper secondary school

15	3rd terminal	3rd modern orientation cycle	classical orientation cycle
14	4th terminal	4th modern orientation cycle	classical orientation cycle
13	5th opportunity	5th modern observation cycle	classical orientation cycle
12	6th opportunity	6th modern observation cycle	classical orientation cycle
11		1st term: all courses in common	

observation orientation — Lower secondary school

11	can be repeated	Second Middle Grade
10		First Middle Grade
9		Second Elementary Grade
8		First Elementary Grade
7		Preparatory Grade
6		

elementary school

5	Kindergarten
4	
3	

kindergarten

Age of student

ing government schools. The net result is that Catholic schools are not infrequently less organized than others in the strictly catechetical aspect, because each of the superintendents thinks this field is covered by his colleague. The *Directeur de l'enseignement chrétien* is always a priest. He is frequently assisted by one or two inspectors who sometimes are priests but often are laymen. His authority over elementary schools is rather well established, particularly since 1958. He has become increasingly utilized as a mediator between schools and the state in the establishment of the various contracts. However, the authority of the diocesan superintendent of schools is much less real over secondary schools, both diocesan and private religious. Indeed there are some Catholic secondary schools in which the inspectors never dare go for a supervisory visit. Here again things are changing because of an increasing awareness of the need for articulation and systemization, and because the post of *Directeur Diocesain* usually constitutes the initiating and mediating agency in the task of planification.

On the national level stands the Secretary General for Catholic Education (*Secretariat General de l'Enseignement Catholique*). The *Secretariat* is the executive arm implementing the decisions taken by the Assembly of French Cardinals and Archbishops on Catholic schools. The Secretary General and the Assistant Secretary General represent the interests of Catholic schools at appropriate government hearings, inquests, and functions. The Secretariat also attempts to coordinate the various efforts and activities undertaken by Catholic schools by disseminating information, organizing two or three annual meetings of the diocesan superintendents of schools, and so on.

Parallel to the *Secretariat*, more or less, is the National Committee on Catholic Education (*Comité National de l'Enseignement Catholique*) composed of the representatives of the various groups concerned with Catholic education. Among those represented on the *Comité* are pupils' parents, teacher associations, the union of teaching brothers, the union of teaching sisters, principals' associations, and so on. In theory this *Comité* is entrusted with the care of promoting professional and educational improvements in Catholic schools. In practice, however, the line of demarcation between the activities of the ancient and traditional *Secretariat*, with a fine past record of action, and the newly born *Comité* is not clear-cut. There has been a recent effort to establish similar more professional *Comités* parallel to the superintendent of schools in the various dioceses. But these *Comités* meet the same difficulty in defining precisely their respective duties. In reality this ambiguity of activities of the diocesan superintendent

and the broadly based *comités* illustrates the rather heavy clerical
influence over French Catholic schools, together with the resentment
which the clerical establishment harbors toward present efforts to give
more responsibility to laymen. However, one should not stone the
past with rocks from the present. The importance of laymen in Catholic education is a rather recent phenomenon. A few years ago, it is
true, laymen were less professionally prepared than priests or religious.
But this situation has changed; consequently the only blame that can
be placed on the past is that it should have changed more quickly
and more profoundly, because laymen should have been prepared
more decisively to hold positions with initiative and responsibility.
There are many signs indicating that laymen will soon be admitted
fully to assume their rightful share of the care of Catholic education
in France.

Some Statistics on Catholic Schools

The following table presents pertinent comparative data on government and Catholic schools in France.

Statistical Summary,
Catholic and Government Schools in France*

	1964		1960	
	Government schools	Catholic schools	Government schools	Catholic schools
Total kindergartens	n.d.	n.d.	n.d.	239
Total schools elementary	n.d.	n.d.	n.d.	10,145
Total schools secondary	1,222	1,292	n.d.	n.d.
Total schools technical	n.d.	n.d.	n.d.	n.d.
Total schools coll. ens. gen.	n.d.	n.d.	n.d.	n.d.
Total universities	19	5	19	5
Total students kindergarten	1,358,510	238,852	1,171,608	166,922
Total students elementary	4,808,654	859,560	4,910,801	788,312
Total students secondary	1,163,741	395,776	741,165	298,477
Total students technical	279,378	158,745	201,132	107,142
Total students coll. ens. gen.	875,424	n.d.	548,948	126,869
Total students university	326,311	20,000	n.d.	n.d.

* There are no data on the median student enrollment at any school level in government or
Catholic educational institutions. Nor are there data on the median class size or the percentage of Catholic students at each level in the government school system. No data are
available on the median school size in rooms at each level in government or Catholic schools.

The importance of French Catholic schooling might be realized in one sense by analyzing the percentage of French youth who attend Catholic schools. (Of course it must be remembered that there is a distinction between attendance at a Catholic school and having one's life transformed by the Catholic school.) Data gathered in 1964 by La Vie Catholique illustrée are presented in the table.

Attendance at a Catholic School (in percentages)

Catholic youth, age 14–20	Always	For a period of time	Never
Total persons	11	23	66
Boys	9	22	69
Girls	12	26	62
Boys, 14–16	8	13	74
Boys, 17–18	10	25	65
Boys, 19–20	10	26	64
Girls, 14–16	9	27	64
Girls, 17–18	12	23	65
Girls, 19–20	19	24	57

The tables show, among other things, that one-third of all French children and youth have spent some time in a Catholic school, a percentage which is higher than one might believe if one glanced only at the enrollment figures of students in Catholic schools as compared with those in government schools.

As a rule Catholic schools are smaller than government schools. A secondary school with an enrollment of 1000 is considered very large. There are perhaps no more than a dozen which have more than 1500 students. A primary school with 600 pupils is a large one. A simple example will give an idea of the average size of secondary schools. There are 1292 such schools (576 for boys and 716 for girls) with an aggregate register of 394,854 students, or an average roughly of 300 students per school. But the median number of pupils per classroom is very large. This is the result of the general policy in France: in order to pass a contract with the state, a classroom must have a minimum of 35 students in elementary and secondary, that is 1° cycle schools.

Catholic schools follow the same schedule as government schools and have the same vacation periods. The school year begins about September 15 and continues until the end of June. There are three terms (trimesters) in the French school year. The first concludes at Christmas, with a recess of two weeks. The second ends with a two-week vacation at Easter, and the third lasts until the end of the academic year.

On the elementary level school usually begins at 9 A.M. and ends at 5 P.M., with a two-hour break from noon until two o'clock. Homework is officially forbidden for elementary school. The pupils attend thirty class periods per week, each of sixty minutes duration. On the secondary level, the number of one-hour courses varies from twenty-five to twenty-seven according to sections. In some technical sections it can reach 35 periods. There is one fifteen-minute recess in the morning and another in the afternoon. It is customary for Catholic secondary school pupils to remain in school until 6 P.M. to study under supervision. This close supervision of studies has made Catholic schools famous all over France.

Because of financial difficulties which prevailed until 1958, Catholic school buildings are rather old and very traditional in architectural design. For the past seven years, however, new buildings have been erected which indicate trends in current Catholic educational thinking. Very little imagination has been used in the construction of schoolrooms; the outmoded tradition still prevails in which pupils are assigned to a room and their teachers circulate from room to room. Classrooms are rigidly built to accommodate a maximum of forty students. The furniture is very comfortable but suited only to lecture courses. Catholic schools do not yet include a central library in their buildings, but this is also true of most government schools. Laboratories, on the other hand, have been painstakingly included in all new Catholic school buildings; indeed Catholic school laboratories frequently compare favorably with those in government schools.

Many Catholic secondary schools are boarding schools (for example, the internationally famous French convent schools for girls); it is in these educational institutions that the greatest strides have been taken to create a homelike atmosphere for the boarders. The former long, barnlike dormitories accommodating some fifty boarders have been replaced by hotel-like residences where each student has her (or his) own private room with bed, desk, and washstand. Large refectories seating 200 pupils at two or three long tables are rapidly giving way to attractive dining rooms with small tables. In some instances, the school's food service is the cafeteria self-service system. Many schools have built lounges where students can meet according to age groups to read papers, listen to music, smoke a cigarette, or play cards.

Despite some notable exceptions, physical training facilities in Catholic schools are still very inadequate.

One important change in Catholic school architecture can be seen in the building of the school chapel. There was a time when Mass was more or less compulsory for all students, both boarders and "day hops." Chapels looked like so many churches or even grandiose minor cathedrals. Such pretentious chapels are no longer built; indeed, some have been converted into rooms of secular nature. Small, simple chapels are erected where a group of pupils can voluntarily have a Mass on occasion during the week.

The latest architectural development is to build secondary schools more or less on the campus style, with several separate buildings. Language laboratories are also in vogue. In this area Catholic schools seem to have boarded the train of progress as quickly as government schools. But the conception of the classroom itself remains rather traditional and constitutes one of the major obstacles to the progress of educational methodology in general and the teaching process in particular.

Financial Support of Catholic Schools in France

Fiscal support of Catholic schools constitutes the most sensitive and most critical of all French school problems. It must be noted that very few persons or groups actually oppose the existence of private schools or Catholic schools as such. Even after the secularistic 1901 laws, Catholic schools operated without restrictions. The only contention of persons or groups who are commonly regarded as opponents of Catholic schools is that nongovernment schools should not receive any state subsidies or aid of any kind. Their slogan is "Public funds to public schools." They believe that if the Catholics want schools of their own, they themselves should pay for such institutions. And it is true that from 1901 until the end of World War II, Catholics did indeed totally finance their own schools.

After 1945, however, the financial burden of maintaining Catholic schools became extremely heavy. It has been estimated that the operating expenses of Catholic schools in 1961 was 900 million new francs, or approximately 200 million dollars. The fiscal burden was made even heavier by the necessity of erecting new schools to meet the needs of a greater demand for more education, to repair old decaying buildings, and to modernize outmoded school equipment according to the advanced standards of modern education. The frequent devaluation of the French franc added to the difficulty by reducing ancient fiscal foundations to quasi nothingness.

These postwar years were heroic indeed. Some teachers did not earn more than $70 a month. It was a time commonly referred to as the "raffle period," because of the many devices used to get money from the faithful. One famous and frequently quoted example was that of General Leclerc, in whose diary after his death was found some money with the notation "money saved on tobacco expenses for Catholic schools." Not all Catholics, however, favored the principle of government funds for Catholic schools. The Paroisse Universitiare, a group of Catholics teaching in government schools, thought that the Church should come abreast of democracy and of the modern world by integrating Catholic schools into the French school system. This attitude is similar to the traditional attitude of Protestants in France. The Protestants have trusted the state, declared neutrality, and closed the 1500 schools they had in 1901.

The financial plight of Catholic schools became so severe by 1950 that in the west of France a resolution was passed to boycott a number of government taxes and even to refuse to pay the income tax. The bishops did not issue this resolution, but they did not dismiss it either. It took several months of prickly and heated discussions to come to an agreement. The issue marked a turning point, however, because since that time a few steps have been taken to give government monies to assist Catholic schools. Popular sentiment in that era was propitious for this move; a 1955 Gallup poll showed that 45 per cent of the population favored government fiscal grants to Catholic schools (as compared with 28 per cent in 1945), whereas 42 per cent were against such assistance (as compared with 51 per cent in 1945).

Before analyzing the financial aid which has been and is now given to Catholic schools, it might be well to note that statistics reveal how important this financial assistance has been to Catholic schools. When compared with the actual proportions of students in Catholic schools, the data showed that Catholic parents were frequently prevented from enrolling their children in Catholic schools because of the tuition. These data also point out that interest in Catholic schooling was slowly diminishing among the younger generation. A Gallup poll sponsored by *La Vie Catholique* asked: "If Catholic schools were free, would you send your children to them?"

French adult Catholics	Per cent Yes	Per cent no	Per cent no opinion
Both sexes	43	47	10
Men	38	52	10
Women	48	42	10
21–34 years old	40	49	11
35–49	42	48	10
50–64	44	45	11
over 65	47	45	8

The first type of post-World War II government fiscal aid came through the *Loi Barangé* of September 22, 1951. This law stipulated that every family having a child in any elementary school whatever—government or private—would receive a regular allowance for each such child. This allowance initially amounted to $2 per trimester for each pupil. The parents' association of each Catholic school was in charge of the management of these funds for Catholic schools. The grant money was to be used to increase teachers' salaries. Ten per cent of the funds could be used for educational purposes, such as purchasing instructional materials and so on. Six days after the passage of the Barangé Law, on September 28, 1951, the *Loi Marie* granted the benefits of scholarships to students of Catholic schools provided the schools met certain educational standards and the students passed a special examination. Finally, the previously discussed Debré Law opened a new and larger avenue for government fiscal assistance to Catholic schools. Catholic schools which passed a *contrat d'association* receive an annual stipend varying from forty to one hundred dollars per student to cover operating expenses. In addition, the teachers in these schools receive the same salaries as do their counterparts in government schools, with the exception of fringe benefits. Those Catholic schools which passed a *contrat simple* do not receive funds to cover operating expenses; however, their teachers are paid on the same basis as government teachers, with the exception of fringe benefits.

In Catholic schools, the parents pay tuition. The maximum tuition required in a school with a *contrat simple* is fixed for each Catholic school at the time the contract is signed. Schools with a *contrat d'association* are not supposed to ask tuition fees properly so-called, but they may request a "contribution" from the family to cover the expenses for building new extensions, buying materials, and so on. Paradoxically, these fees may thus exceed those asked in schools with a *contrat simple*, even though the latter receive smaller grants.

The consequence of all this government financial help has been that by the beginning of 1967 the average salary of teachers in elementary Catholic schools was $210 per month, and in secondary Catholic schools $230 per month, which is reasonably good compared with other professions.

The law provides that no government money can be allocated for new capital expenditures on school buildings, which are a critical need of Catholic schools at the present time. Some Catholic schools are located in the heart of old cities where the population has dwindled, whereas new suburban areas sorely need new Catholic schools. Catholic schools must rely on gifts or income to build or modernize; no provision is made even to assist them in getting loans from banks on special conditions.

The structure of government financial assistance to Catholic technical schools is different from the pattern described in this section. As early as 1920 and 1925, fiscal assistance had been granted to them through the *Loi Astier,* an act which organized technical schooling in France. This law stipulated that "every person or group engaged in an industrial or commercial profession is bound to pay a tax for the promotion of technical instruction." The tax rate is generally 2 per cent of the total salary paid to the workers. The employers or companies were free to allocate the revenues from this tax to the schools of their choice, even to a nongovernment school. The sums that Catholic employers could thus transfer to private schools was frequently fairly large. This explains why many Catholic schools pragmatically have opened a technical section during the past twenty years to be able to benefit from these tax receipts. A law passed in 1966 stipulates that the state guarantees bank loans made by technical schools for their extension or modernization. Thus Catholic technical schools or technical sections of schools can keep pace with modern educational developments, but elementary or secondary schools are fiscally mired in the difficult problems involved in expansion.

Children attending Catholic elementary schools cannot always benefit from the transportation facilities provided for students in government elementary schools. The basic principle is that each child should attend the school nearest his home. In some instances the government school is nearer a student's home than the Catholic elementary school, which cuts him off from use of the school bus. Students in Catholic secondary schools enjoy the same transportation facilities as government school students, provided the Catholic schools they attend have signed a contract with the state. The law will even permit a parents' association, for example, to establish a corporation which owns a school bus, thereby entitling it to government financial aid to operate it.

Before 1958, when Catholic schools were fiscally hard pressed, many of them established a number of revenue-gathering services which helped them to survive. Catholic schools would furnish meals at noon, for example, for a great number of pupils, or lodging for boarders, services which were operated at a neat profit. These services were, incidentally, a boon to families. These well-meaning Catholics gave the Catholic school great credit for providing these services, although the motivation of the school in providing the services was somewhat ambiguous. The current trend is to farm out the cafeteria system and gradually drop boarding schools whenever possible. However, many boarding schools remain, and they are a source of profit, although tuition is reasonable. Room, board, and fees vary according to the facilities offered, to the location, and to the "social class level" of the student clientele; on the average, room, board, and academic fees cost about $250 per year.

The five Catholic universities in France are assisted fiscally by the government in several different ways. First, a 1952 law stipulates that students attending Catholic universities can receive grants to continue their studies in the university. In addition, all students in Catholic universities are entitled to substantially reduced prices on meals taken at the students' cafeterias and to other advantages of this sort. The government also grants many scholarships to foreign students to enable them to attend courses in Catholic universities, particularly the famous summer courses on French culture given by the Institut Catholique de Paris. The government regards such studies as a means of fostering the spread of French thought and the French language. Budgetary provision was made for Catholic universities in a 1965 school finance law. This law does not supply a regular channel of fiscal assistance to Catholic universities; it is simply a stipulation in the budget which may be continued or cut off at any time. This budgetary clause allocates a fixed sum to be given to the *Institut Catholique de Paris*, which in turn assumes the responsibility for the allotment of the monies to the various schools and institutes. Other than these subsidies, French Catholic universities, as such, receive no additional government financial aid. However, French Catholic universities have created a number of special schools and institutes, as in engineering and electronics. These special schools and institutes are eligible to receive substantial subsidies from industrial firms. Consequently these schools and institutes have no financial difficulty in growing and developing, whereas the financial circumstances of the Catholic universities themselves are very hard. Thus, for example, a priest teaching in a Catholic university receives no more than $100 a month, a sum substantially lower than he would receive if he were teaching in a secondary school. Therefore, most professors in Catholic universities engage in additional teaching in secondary schools to supplement their income; as a result, they are unable to conduct research work in the serenity so necessary for such activity.

The Curriculum

Because of the close relationship created in 1958 between Catholic and government schools it may be said that, apart from religion, the curriculum of the Catholic school has no distinctive features. During the five years of elementary school, the curriculum includes reading, writing, arithmetic, history and geography, art, singing, and, of course, French grammar and composition.

In the first cycle of secondary education, the curriculum has become stabilized and hardened. All students take practically the same courses during these four years. The only area of differentiation is in languages: some take Latin, others do not. Students may choose from among several foreign languages. All students must take French, mathematics, history, geography, civics, one foreign language, science, and technology. The introduction of this last subject into the curriculum is rather recent. The purpose of the technology course is to explore the technical world in which we live and to express it in a universal code, namely, industrial drawing. Technology is compulsory for all. Art and music are also compulsory; unfortunately, some Catholic schools are woefully deficient in these areas for lack of qualified teachers. Gymnastics is also a required subject. Catholic schools ironically have a good reputation for their gymnastics curriculum, thanks to the National Catholic Teacher Training College, which prepares physical education teachers. In the first cycle of secondary school, religion is offered for three or four hours per week in Catholic schools. Pupils who have not been admitted into the regular cycles of observation and orientation drop such courses as foreign languages and technology in order to acquire a better foundation in the basic studies to be admitted into the next regular stage of the ongoing curriculum.

Differentiation into basically divergent curricular patterns begins at the age of fifteen, when students enter the second cycle of the secondary school. The four principal curricular patterns here are: (1) humanities (Latin, Greek, foreign languages); (2) modern (foreign languages, mathematics, and science); (3) technical; and (4) vocational. The first two patterns, and in certain instances the third, are university-preparatory curricula. In the second cycle of secondary school, religion is offered in Catholic schools for two periods per week. A characteristic of French secondary schools is that they offer philosophy (metaphysics, ethics, epistemology) on a rather large scale. Indeed, some segments of the curriculum include as much as nine hours per week of philosophy. Art and singing are no longer required courses, but they may be taken as electives. Electives may help to gain credits at the *baccalauréat* according to a rating system with which students are quite pleased. If a student decides to sit for the examination in music, for example, all points which he scores above the median will be counted in his favor; if he fails, it will have no influence on the general results. In the second cycle of secondary schools the mathematics curriculum comprises field mathematics, an area in which Catholic schools have been pioneers. Of interest is that an increasing number of schools are including field mathematics as early as the first year of the first cycle. In the language sector of the curriculum, the structural approach is rapidly gaining favor, even in the teaching of the native French language.

There is no unit system such as the American Carnegie unit in French schools. The only qualitative or quantitative difference between the various subjects lies in the official coefficient which is involved in the marking of the final examinations taken in the divers subjects. All papers at the *baccalauréat* are marked on the basis of number ten. But then the mark thus obtained is multiplied by a coefficient (two or three or even seven) according to the designated "importance" of the subject. This coefficient of importance has been constantly changing over the past twenty years, from the pressure of one or another teachers' associations promoting the interest of the subject area in which its members teach. Catholic schoolteachers can never officially voice their opinions on the question of the coefficient. They must accept the decisions made by the Ministry of Education. As would be expected, the subjects having a higher coefficient of importance are taught a greater number of periods a week.

The rather rigid framework governing Catholic schools shows that these institutions simply cannot inaugurate curricular innovations. Indeed, neither can government schools bring about substantial curricular change. Such innovations, paradoxical as it may seem, are not left to the schools but instead to the government "centers of decisions." Consequently each type of school in France, classical, modern, technical, and so on, has exactly the same curriculum; in fact, even the same calendar and schedule. Nonetheless, a few schools have attempted to put into practice some of the curricular recommendations suggested by the staff. But even these must receive special permission from the government. The most notable curricular change is found at St. Joseph's, a Catholic school conducted by the Jesuits in Rheims, where students take more courses in art than is the custom, and manual labor, even for the classical curriculum, is a required subject. Curricular plans and innovations are discussed and advocated in such Catholic educational journals as *Pedagogie* and *Orientations*. But even these do not constitute empirically validated research studies on curricular innovations, since the authors know full well that their efforts will come to naught and that their voices will be unheard.

A distinctive new development in most French Catholic elementary and secondary schools is that religion courses are no longer listed as academic subjects. Until the mid-1950's, religion was regarded as strongly entwined with the strictly intellectual life. Consequently the religion course was subject to examinations, rating, and the comments which were tabulated with the other subjects in the general evaluation of the student. The advances made by the catechetical movement have shown that courses in religion should primarily aim at fostering faith and charity in a youth's soul, an educational goal not subject to academic assessment. The preceding generation perhaps went too far in the assimilation of religion as pure knowledge; the pendulum of the present generation may be swinging too far in the other direction, but the result is that religion courses, although remaining part of the curriculum, are no longer treated as lifeless academic subjects. In any event, definite and real progress has been made in the methodological processes of teaching religion. It is fair to say that even in schools which follow the hidebound, rock-ribbed, traditional curriculum, the teaching of religion has changed greatly. Religion as a course is no longer subject-centered, nor is it a compromise grafting of catechetics onto theology. Rather, the religion curriculum is student-centered, starting from the students' needs as expressed through questionnaires or informal conversations.

Apart from innovation in the religion curriculum, teachers in Catholic schools have engaged in educational experimentation in extracurricular activities rather than in formal academic subjects. This timidness is easy to understand, since even if teachers in Catholic schools wished to innovate, they believe experimentation might cause their students to fare poorly on the official, nonflexible examinations, evidence from research in the United States to the contrary notwithstanding. There is a rich extracurricular activities program in Catholic schools including sports, dramatics, photography clubs, cine-forums, and so on. In the field of cinema, Catholic schools have achieved prominence. Not only do these schools introduce the students to sophisticated film criticism, but they also foster in the youths a creative attitude toward films. One of the features of extracurricular activities in Catholic schools is that they are usually undertaken by the teachers themselves, rather than as a formal school program. Government schools frequently offer similar extracurricular activities, likewise independent of a formal school program. In Catholic schools there is a well-established tradition encouraging teachers to spend time with their students outside of the regular school periods. This teacher-pupil contact has done much to create a fine educational atmosphere, in affecting easy interpersonal relationships which tend to offset the rather harsh discipline which is quite characteristic of Catholic schools. Thus Catholic schools present a curious and paradoxical mixture of awesome discipline and friendly atmosphere. This unusual situation possibly accounts to a great extent for the permanent attachment which usually links alumni to their alma maters. All Catholic schools have flourishing alumni(ae) associations which meet for prayer, action, and recreation. On the national level, there is even a federation of all Catholic alumni associations which has done much to defend and assist Catholic schools in times of pressing circumstances. The federation publishes a magazine called the *Haut Parleur.* However, the new situation brought about by the contracts might endanger the teacher-student bond. Teachers are obliged—if they want to be paid—to devote more time and attention to purely academic activities. Many of them have the tendency to drop their extracurricular responsibilities to the extent that a separate educational staff is being organized whose work will be to take care of the students during all those periods they spend at school outside the "regular" class day.

The French school curriculum is widely known as abstract and subject-centered, but it would appear that this unhappy situation has come to a dead end. Signs of change are already in evidence. The traditional situation may be described as follows. A curriculum is enacted by the Ministry of National Education. It is accompanied by an official syllabus compiled by some government general inspector of schools. Such syllabi leave some room for the teacher to exercise instructional imagination and creativity. But then textbooks are an impediment. France is perhaps the country where school textbooks are at once excellent and the main obstacle to sound educational methods. Financial competition in a capitalistic economy is boundless, and the textbook industry is one of the most lucrative in an age of democratization of education. All publishers wish to put out the best books. This means that to be on the safe side they will enlarge on the official syllabus, and consequently students must wade through 500-page books when 250 pages would be adequate. Moreover, most teachers would feel humiliated at being satisfied with commenting merely on the book; their students, in turn, would feel slighted if they thought their teachers have nothing to tell them other than what appears in the textbook. Therefore the teacher frequently dictates notes on tangential matters which the pupils are required to study. Finally, supposedly to be more concrete and in contact with life, all textbooks are wonderfully illustrated; indeed they seem to be art volumes rather than schoolbooks. This latter approach is perhaps a backward step because it prevents teaching from being a social encounter. It is very difficult for a teacher to utilize documents and other similar reading for collateral study and observation, because these will appear shabby and dull compared with the more opulent and pictorial textbook. What is needed are educationally oriented collective material, portfolios, and records which will supplement and expand on the syllabus and textbook. Some books of this description do exist, but they are never prepared in cooperation with educationists to be used for specific parts of the curriculum. There is a strong outcry against this regrettable situation, but so far no one has been able to alter it. Catholic teachers, compelled as they are to a tutioristic attitude, are reluctant to experiment with other methods, although doubtless they would willingly adopt ancillary materials if they were readily available.

There appears to be scant, if any, teacher-pupil planning of the curriculum in French Catholic schools.

Instruction

A common accusation levelled at the French Catholic schools is that in the era of their freedom, that is before they signed contracts with the government, they failed to utilize their freedom to conduct research in educational methods. Unfortunately, this charge is true, but there may be some excuse for this regrettable inertia. In the days when the government did not assist Catholic schools fiscally, they had to prove their worth in order to get students. Catholic parents would have hesitated to place their children in Catholic schools if these institutions had been seriously below the level of government schools. The tragedy is that instead of asserting their worth by discovering new paths in instruction and education, Catholic schools adopted the tutiorist way of rivaling the government schools, that is in the educationally infertile field of examination-passing. The sole ambition of Catholic schools was to have more students graduating from elementary schools (*certificat d'études primaires*) or from secondary schools (*baccalauréat*) no matter what pedagogical method was used to obtain those results. With the post-1958 contractual arrangement, the opportunities for innovation, experimentation, and invention in the teaching process are drastically reduced so that the methods of teaching used in Catholic schools are largely the same as those used in government schools. Another obstacle to experimentation and utilization of a wide repertoire of teaching methodologies in both Catholic and government schools is the large number of pupils in each class. There are commonly thirty-eight, forty, or even forty-four students per class not only in elementary but also in secondary schools. The teaching methods used in French Catholic elementary schools are basically variations of the traditional lecturing and telling. These variations include the teacher's commentary on the textbook (referred to by derogators as "rehashing the textbook"), lesson-hearing, exercises, and so forth. More sophisticated teaching methodologies such as role-playing, panels, group work, six-six discussions, and the like are almost never utilized. One ray of hope is the growing influence of the *Centre d'Etudes Pédagogiques*, which since the end of World War II has been organizing workshops and institutes to introduce teachers to the more advanced methodologies. Disciples of Father Faure, S.J., small in number but scattered all over France, are developing workbooks, implementing small-group discussion methods, and introducing individualized teaching processes.

In French elementary schools, the self-contained classroom situation prevails so that all subjects, with the occasional exception of gymnastics, singing, and art, are taught by the same teacher. Catholic schools boast of having developed singing instruction via the Ward method more intensely than have government schools. The teaching of art is disgracefully poor, despite the Catholic philosophy of beauty as a vehicle for carrying one to God and despite an excellent methodological approach called *L'enfance de l'art* developed by Father Boulers, S.J., and Sister Benjamin.

In secondary schools the teaching methods are also very traditional. Lecturing and telling are the undisputed pedagogical czars, sweeping all before them. Catholic schools have made a remarkable effort to equip their science laboratories, and in this they compare favorably with government schools. In the early 1960's, Catholic schools developed language laboratories in a proportion that is doubtless greater than that of government schools. Regrettably, such libraries in Catholic schools are in a deplorable state; however government schools have done little in this field. The Barangé Act gave Catholic schools the opportunity of purchasing audiovisual aids in an era before private schools were subsidized. Consequently the audiovisual equipment in Catholic schools is relatively advanced. But evidence points out that audiovisual materials and methodology are still used only in an occasional way and only rarely are woven into daily educational practice. One exception is that of film education, a field where Catholic schools have achieved originality. Catholic schools have not been content with introducing their students to the understanding and appreciation of films in previously mentioned extracurricular cine-forums. The teaching methodology underlying the Catholic school's approach to cine-instruction is that motion pictures constitute a language parallel to speaking and reading and must therefore be studied in connection with all forms of language. Courses in filmology are woven into courses in grammar, syntax, and literature. There is a national commission studying these problems and introducing teachers to their apprehension; they issue a magazine of great value, *L'Ecran et la Vie*.

Traditionally there has been a difference between Catholic schools and government schools in the methods of teaching on the first cycle, secondary school level. Teachers in government schools have typically been primarily subject-centered—they have been specialists trained in and actually teaching their separate subjects. Teachers in Catholic schools, on the other hand, tended to be more pupil-centered, since they taught several subjects and hence were more concerned with the manner of teaching than with the subject taught. This practice may well have originated in the insufficient number of subject-matter specialists in Catholic schools. Ultimately, what in one sense was an inadequacy in Catholic schools turned out to be beneficial to students who are unable at that age to hear the lectures of several teachers in one day, to adapt themselves to too many methods of thinking or teaching. Government schools are more and more adopting this view despite violent opposition from the subject-matter specialists. Another common practice in Catholic schools is that of a homeroom teacher even on the second cycle level. It has proved influential, if not in instruction at least in education.

There is a rather general practice in Catholic secondary schools to send students abroad during summer vacations to study foreign languages. This exemplary practice has tended to remedy the deficiencies of language teachers, deficiencies which were notorious some years ago in Catholic schools. Every possible effort is made to send students from fourteen years of age on either to England, Germany, or to Spain, and even to the United States, thanks to the efforts of the National Parents Association, to improve their foreign language skills. Finally, there is an increasing tendency to foster extended educational field trips for students in the upper grades. Catholic schools use routine field trips or visits to museums less than other schools; nonetheless, they are active in setting up extended educational excursions with geographical, artistic, political purposes. It is not infrequent to see Catholic school students working on their educational excursions to Germany, Russia, Morocco, or Israel.

Catholic schools in France have the reputation of requiring more homework than do government schools. The reasons for this are at least threefold. First of all, Catholic schools are often boarding schools, and homework provides a simple solution to the problem of keeping students busy during the long study periods. These study periods are typically supervised by university students who are unable to help the boarders in their schoolwork and hence simply exercise tight surveillance over them while they are supposedly studying. Second, for day students, homework is regarded very favorably by parents because it helps the parents keep their children quiet when they are at home. Finally, homework conveys the impression that the school is a serious enterprise and that teachers spare no effort in promoting the education of children. For some empirically unverified reason, heavy doses of homework are popularly believed to be the best means to stimulate student progress. Further, as everyone is aware, assigning large quantities of homework requires commitment and effort of the teachers, who must mark so many papers, and such effort and commitment do not go unnoticed by a teacher's superiors.

Until recently Catholic schools were famous for their tightly structured evaluation system. In some Catholic schools there was what is called a "blank examination" as often as every fortnight, at least in courses which feature a regular major examination at the end of the year. The philosophy underlying this practice is that frequent tests keep the student in a high state of motivation. The present trend is to become more fluid in testing students; nonetheless evaluation via achievement tests still takes place at least once a month. In order to be more objective, the achievement tests used in Catholic schools are often obtained from one of the four or five Catholic agencies which compose tests and later mark them. These tests are not formally standardized examinations. Another frequent practice often adopted is for one Catholic school to exchange tests with another, a device quite popular because it is inexpensive. Evaluation is done after learning rather than concomitant with it; the various results are tabulated to be used for admission to an upper grade at the end of the year. At least three times a year a more formal evaluation procedure is carried out, the results of which are announced in a more or less official way, sometimes at an assembly program, occasionally with parents present. The trend, however, is to abandon this practice as it is both of dubious educational value and out of joint with the mentality of modern youth. The tradition in French Catholic schools is to mark papers very strictly, particularly where marking is subjective, such as essay examinations. Here again the theory is that if students are marked more strictly than they should be, they will be motivated to greater effort and will have a pleasant surprise when they confront the official examining board on the day of the major examination. The validity of an examination seems to have escaped these Catholic school educators.

Catholic schools have an excellent reputation for reporting student evaluation to parents because of the frequency of reports. Both in elementary and in secondary schools the common practice is to issue a report card each week. In elementary schools report cards are often subjective; they contain principally a summary of the teacher's personal assessment of the efforts of the pupil in the various courses. In secondary schools the report cards contain both objective and subjective elements. Parents must sign the report cards and return them to the school; frequently parents are requested to make comments in a special section reserved for this purpose. It is customary in Catholic schools to encourage parent-teacher conferences about the evaluation of the children, a practice of which parents many times avail themselves. Consequently Catholic schools are usually regarded as paying greater attention to a child's progress than are non-Catholic schools.

Despite the arguments of educationists and psychologists, Catholic schools persist in listing the pupils according to their scholastic achievements. Since percentile or letter grading does not exist, a pupil will be publicly categorized as the first, or eighth, or twenty-ninth in his class. Although this is very gratifying for the scholastically superior students, it is rather discouraging for the others. The same can be said of the frequent report cards. Report cards are better received by parents whose children are doing well than by those whose children lag scholastically. It is salutary to show parents that the school cares for their children, but teachers do not seem to be aware that frequently it diminishes the warm home atmosphere by introducing scholastic standards into what should be only a sanctuary of love. Many parents appear to pay more attention to the rank of their son or daughter than either to the actual educational results or to the effort their child has made. Another regrettable consequence is that there is a glaring discrepancy between what the Catholic school teaches and what it actually practices. The main motivation accruing from the ranking system is competition, which impedes teamwork, cooperation, and the like. The marking system is so strict and rigid in some Catholic schools that any type of cooperation is viewed as cheating. Apropos of this, however, it must be remembered that this entire attitude is a reflection of the basic mentality of hyperindividualism prevalent in France. Moreover, this practice is so anachronistic in our age of cooperation that many Catholic schools are beginning to realize the need for a change and are starting to minimize such meticulous rating, if they cannot eliminate it entirely.

The problem of supervision of classes and establishing educational standards for Catholic schools has been very much simplified for Catholic schools since 1958. All schools that sign a contract with the government must submit themselves to government supervision and inspection. Official inspectors come to judge the physical facilities, the relevance of the instructional material, the value of the laboratories, and so on. This supervisor tends to be traditional rather than modern, in that supervision is regarded more as a measure to make sure that teachers meet government requirements than as a learning experience whereby the teacher learns how to improve instruction by conferences with a nonpunitive specialist. An interesting development has emerged from the existence of government supervisors. Catholic supervisors no longer must serve as judges and evaluators as in previous years. They have kept their posts, but they come to schools more as helpers and advisors than as inspectors. They are now playing a large role in the improvement of teaching methods, especially among the younger generation of teachers. Indeed, Catholic supervision currently is much closer to true supervision in the sophisticated sense than is that of the punitively oriented government inspectors.

The Program of
Religious Education

On the elementary level, Catholic schools normally devote one-half hour a day to religious education. On the secondary level the number of lessons offered in religion decreases to one hour per week, depending on the age of the students. Further, there is also a marked distinction between Catholic schools conducted by laymen or by diocesan priests compared with those operated by religious institutes. In the latter, the tendency is definitely to offer a greater number of religion periods. On the university level, religion courses are not compulsory except for students in theology.

The important catechetical renewal which started after World War II under the guidance of Canon Colomb has brought about great changes in the traditional approach to teaching religion. In the early 1950's, religion was just another academic subject. To be sure, it was an academic area in which teachers were urged to prepare more carefully; fundamentally, however, there was no great difference in the methodology of teaching religion from that of other courses. Lecturing, telling, and lesson-hearing prevailed. The catechetical renewal resulted in the publication of superior and sometimes even excellent textbooks. These textbooks were adapted to the findings of child psychology and were also carefully geared to the object of religious instruction, the growth in faith and charity. The teaching of religion no longer consists of the question-answer rote approach which conveyed the impression that faith is simply a treasure to be kept in one's memory. Religion textbooks and teaching methods cater to various student-centered activities, self-expression, and group discussions through which children can give their personal answers to the message of God for which every lesson aims. Religion teaching and textbook orientation offer frequent opportunities for organizing a celebration instead of engaging in a traditionally formal lesson, thus linking the celebration of the Word of God to its proclamation. On the elementary level the renewal has even resulted in creating new methodological structures for teaching religion. Thus in some Catholic schools parents are invited to come one period a week and conduct small group discussions in which the Word of God can be concretely applied to the daily lives of the students.

Religion textbooks for teen-agers have not been modified so successfully. A great deal of discussion on catechetical curricula and textbooks had been going on in the early 1960's but to little avail. However, the pedagogical methods of catechesis have been profoundly altered, partly due to the influence of the catechetical renewal in general, and partly to the influence of Catholic Action. Observing the efficiency of small group discussions and of the "inquiry method" of Catholic Action cells, some teachers have attempted to utilize them in religion classes. There is some controversy whether these two activities of Catholic Action and classroom instruction are compatible, that is whether religion classes should not be more purely traditional in instructional thrust. Nevertheless some very interesting innovations are spreading rapidly. One of these curricular innovations is called the "self-service system." Instead of assigning one religion teacher to one class, a choice of courses is offered to all juniors in a secondary school. One course may have a purely doctrinal syllabus; another might be termed a course in Christian culture; still another, a course to meet the personal problems of students; and so forth. Through this differentiation in religion courses, the religion curriculum hopes to minister to the varying needs of the students, since not all the boys or girls at the same grade level are living the same degree of Christianity. Another attempt at curricular restructuring is to repeat the course twice in the same trimester, thus halving class enrollment and greatly facilitating group discussions, socialized lessons, and questions and answers. Finally, there is the trend to abolish the traditional course in religion for students ready to graduate from secondary school. This course is replaced by an "afternoon of Christian life" given every three weeks, starting at 5 P.M. and lasting until 10 P.M. This course aims at avoiding the tragic dualism of learning religion in the isolated classroom and living it in real life. During these five or six hours, there are a lecture by a visiting professor, personal study, group discussions, testimony by a convert or a member of one group or another, a common meal, and celebration of Holy Mass. There is great probability that endeavors of this kind will become the general practice in the near future.

There are at least three major French Catholic journals specializing in the improvement of catechetical instruction: *Catéchistes*, *Verité et Vie*, and *Catéchèse*. These publications exert influence among the more professionally minded teachers of religion in France.

It is difficult to ascertain definitively whether the preparation of religious instructors is as good as the preparation of teachers in the strictly academic areas. Preparation of religion teachers varies widely according to places, schools, religious institutes, and so forth. It is safe to say, however, that the intellectual and financial investments of Catholic schools in the teaching of religion is, ironically, considerably less than in the more academic curricular fields. The budget percentage devoted to the religion department is often shamefully low. This is a result of the situation created by the new legislation; in order to cope with government requirements the first and greatest efforts have been made for laboratories, libraries, and sports facilities. It is also safe to assert that the need for solid professional preparation of teachers of religion is deeply appreciated and that positive steps have been taken to meet this need. This is particularly true of religious institutes. In 1965, for example, there were 371 participants in summer school courses devoted to teaching catechetics to adolescents; most of the participants work in Catholic schools. The five Catholic universities have set up an undergraduate curriculum leading to the bachelor in catechetics degree.

The integration of religion into other areas of the curriculum has been affected by the government's financial aid to Catholic schools. When they began to receive government monies and to be subject to government inspection and regulations, Catholic schools were confronted with the danger of becoming replicas of government schools with the mere appendage of a few classes in religion. As a result, an agonizing reappraisal was undertaken to define the specific character of the Catholic school. Perhaps the main conclusion of this reappraisal has been the renewed attempt of Catholic schools to integrate religion into all areas of the school program. This was called "Christian teaching of secular disciplines." Unfortunately this concept when translated into practice too often consisted merely in using special textbooks, in replacing readings about cats and dogs with texts selected from the lives of Christian heroes, and in adding a small conclusion in praise of God after a course on nature or astronomy. There is a movement afoot, however, which places the burden of integration of religion in the school program on the minds and hearts of the teacher. This new approach demands that every teacher in a Catholic school must possess a sound theology of secular realities. Sophisticated and empirically proven curriculum integration, such as the "Core Curriculum" tested in the United States, is relatively unknown in French Catholic educational circles.

Supervision of religious instruction is not very effective at any school level. It never reaches beyond the walls of the school. In schools conducted by religious institutes the principal sometimes coordinates and supervises religious teaching. In elementary schools the local pastor also exercises a kind of supervision. At all school levels there are services set up to help teachers who are willing to get information or formation. Each diocese has its own Bureau of Catholic Doctrine. It might be noted that this Bureau also has charge of the religious teaching given outside Catholic schools. There is also the National Center of Religious Teaching, located in Paris, which issues special publications and organizes workshops, conventions, and courses.

Formal religious instruction is not regarded by French Catholic schoolmen as sufficient to develop a living faith and charity. In secondary schools it is common practice to supplement religious instruction with retreats given in all classes, particularly for students who are about to graduate. These retreats are customarily free. As late as the mid-1950's there was compulsory Mass attendance on weekdays for all students. The liturgical renewal has triggered great progress in this entire area. Thus by the mid-1960's in the large majority of Catholic schools the desire to attend Mass had been initiated by small groups of students. Finally, at all school levels a great effort is made to insert Catholicism into daily living, chiefly by means of Catholic youth movements. Many of these are organized around the methods of the Jocist cell adaptation of Catholic Action which has flourished in France. Student youth movements are commonly regarded as reservoirs for Catholic Action leaders in adulthood. On the elementary school level, this is the M.E.J. (Eucharistic Movement of Youth). For teen-agers there is the Legion of Mary. The Young Christian Students (J.E.C.) are also very active. The Companions of St. Vincent de Paul devote themselves to corporal works of mercy.

A very important but controversial issue concerns the benefit which Church and state have derived from Catholic schools in France. Some research findings are available although they are not as plentiful or as definitive as might be hoped.

Certain sociologists have tried to determine the relationship between attendance at Catholic school and the number of vocations to the religious life. A 1948 survey by Canon Boulard pointed out that for eighty-four dioceses, nearly 92 per cent of the seminarians came from Catholic schools, even though the number of Catholic students attending government schools is much higher. Making the necessary corrections, this survey indicated that out of one thousand students attending Catholic schools, twenty-two enter the seminary, whereas out of the same number attending government schools only four enter the seminary. Canon Boulard also asserted that the decline in the number of religious vocations in France was felt fourteen years after the laws of 1882-1886. A 1957 survey conducted by Monseigneur de Bazelaire came to the same conclusions as the Boulard study. Of course, students in Catholic schools tend to come from families that are more religious, a factor of great importance in the nurturing of vocations.

Research investigations have been launched to correlate the number of priests in a diocese with the number of Catholic schools in the diocese. The figures have been parallel, as would be expected. In the diocese of La Rochelle, for example, in which 12 per cent of the children are in Catholic schools, there are 6.2 priests for 10,000 inhabitants, whereas in the diocese of Rodez, with 45 per cent of its students in Catholic schools, there are 25.6 priests for 10,000 inhabitants (*Famille Éducatrice*). However, these statistics do not permit clearcut conclusions, since it can be mooted whether it is the Catholic school which fosters Catholics or Catholics who sustain Catholic schools. Most probably there is a reciprocal influence here which is very difficult to measure.

Another area of research investigation is the influence of Catholic schools on the value system of those who attend it. A 1965 survey by *La Vie Catholique Illustrée* revealed that 79 per cent of those who attended only Catholic schools were regular church-goers as compared with 47 per cent of those who had Catholic schooling for only part of their education and 25 per cent for those who were never enrolled in a Catholic school. On the other hand, only 1 per cent of those who went only to Catholic schools declared themselves nonbelievers. But it would be a mistake to assume that regular church attendance is the unequivocal mark of a bonafide Christian. Nonetheless, it is probable that there is a significant correlation between the two, and so this survey has merit. An extensive 1963 study by Duquenne found that the differences between students who attended Catholic schools and others were apparent in three areas. First, students from Catholic schools appear to be more open to community values. Thus, for example, when mentioning the various motives for choosing a profession they put a greater emphasis on the social service dimension. Second, there seems to be a difference in the way students from Catholic schools evaluate and appreciate sexual relationships. The question of premarital intercourse, in particular, is more roundly condemned by students from Catholic schools (51 per cent) than by students attending government schools (31 per cent). Interestingly, however, there was no difference between their respective attitudes toward divorce. Finally, students from Catholic schools seem to be more satisfied with their schools than were the others. Whether this reflects the greater docility of Catholic students is difficult to say. However, it is important that apart from these three areas there is no marked difference in values between students in Catholic schools and those attending government schools.

One may raise the question of what are the academic results in French Catholic schools. One general answer can be given by quoting the number of prominent men in the nation, especially in the political field, who attended Catholic schools. In the 1965 presidential elections, all five major candidates were Catholic school alumni. Notwithstanding, the scholastic value of Catholic schools is sometimes questioned on two grounds. First, the proportion of graduating students in liberal arts curricula exceeds those from the science curricula, a fact which implies that Catholic schools are not resolutely pointed toward the future. Second, the chronological age of students in Catholic schools exceeds that of those in government schools at every grade level. Father Dainville has noted in this regard (*Études*) that although Catholic schools have a greater proportion of students in liberal arts curricula courses, this is true only in respect to all students. If applied to boys only, the percentage is about the same as in government schools (48 per cent compared with 52 per cent). Further, Catholic schools are established mostly in rural areas where the environment is less socioeconomically advantaged; consequently students in these schools tend to be older. It is doubtless that their concentration in rural areas is at once most significant and most perilous for Catholic schools; as France is becoming more and more urbanized, perhaps Catholic schools may be said to be inserted in the past rather than the present, to say nothing of the future.

Catholic schools have established relationships with the parishes only on the elementary level. Yet even this is not always true. A number of elementary schools are operated by religious institutes, and until Vatican Council II these religious tended to live in as close a circle as possible. It was not uncommon at one time, for instance, for Catholic schools to be reluctant to send their pupils to the parish youth movement or to supply altar boys for liturgical functions. These schools wanted to keep their students exclusively for their own liturgical, apostolic, nonparish services. The usual practice, however, is for the local pastor to deem himself responsible for religious instruction in the elementary schools located within the boundaries of his parish, even if the school is conducted by brothers or nuns. Thus he examines young students and instructs them at least one hour per week during the three years preparatory to what is known in France as *Solemn Communion*, a ceremony which takes place when children are 10 or 11 years of age, and which incorporates a renewal of the baptismal vows.

Secondary schools are never parochial; consequently their bonds with parishes are considerably looser than are those of the elementary schools. Secondary schools usually have a chaplain, directly appointed by the bishop. Frequently the chaplain is not one of the priests from the local parish. The attitude of secondary schools is rapidly changing, nevertheless, and many of them are now eager to have their students participate in the life of the parish either liturgically or in the various apostolic movements. As far as the five Catholic universities are concerned, their relationships with parishes is absolutely nonexistent.

Student Personnel
and Guidance Services

The services offered by French Catholic schools are not limited to instruction alone. One of the chief assistances which French Catholic schools give to the full growth of the personality of their students is the celebrated boarding system. There are no reliable statistics on this educational sphere, but it is safe to say the proportion of boarders in Catholic schools is much greater than in government schools. (Parenthetically, the boarding school system has a sizable impact on the instructional service because it is the means for many students in rural areas to obtain a Catholic secondary education.) The nature of the boarding situation induced these schools to develop various extracurricular programs to occupy the leisure time of the boarders—sports, cine-forums, dramatics, bands, and so on. Until recently extracurricular activities were entrusted to untrained personnel. However, a national center for the professional preparation of these moderators is now in operation in Paris. In any event, the very nature of boarding schools as "total institutions" requires them to have a rather complete program of student personnel services. Another service known as "snow schools" was developed in the late 1950's and early 1960's. Catholic schools have entered this educational sphere under certain pressure from the state. In the large metropolitan cities, children breathe such foul air and are so deprived of contact with nature that the government grants subsidies for eight-to-ten-year-old pupils to journey to mountain resorts with their teachers for a full month. The urban gamins are given courses all morning, and their afternoons are spent relaxing on the ski slopes. Scholastic results are reported to be better during that month despite the reduced time devoted to academic activities—a finding borne out in American and Canadian researches. Nearly 20,000 pupils in that age group have benefited each year from the snow schools.

Until 1958 there was no such thing as a formal guidance program in French government or Catholic schools. Indeed, students did not even have much choice in the school's curriculum. There were private organizations, and in the big cities a representative of the semi-official guidance agency, the *Bureau Universitaire de Statistiques*, to help students enter a profession. The 1958 school law required schools to establish testing and guidance. It was some time before Catholic schools realized the significance of this. Little by little, however, school psychologists began to be trained; now there is a national Association for the Development of School Psychology in Catholic Schools. This association also publishes a quarterly bulletin. The tendency is to have a team of psychologists for a group of schools or even for a diocese in preference to having one psychologist attached to one school. The work of these school psychologists is diffuse. They administer collective tests at the end of elementary school to assist the parents in making the wisest possible decision about the type of further education which should be selected for the child. The same is done at the end of the first cycle of the secondary school. School psychologists administer private tests (intelligence tests, aptitude tests, personality tests) during interviews with "problem" children. Finally, they act as counselors to the teachers themselves to help them analyze their relationships with their students and eventually to revise their methods of education. This last activity is looked upon as a distinctive feature of Catholic school psychologists. By 1967 twenty-five dioceses had a psychology and guidance bureau.

A major need is to establish libraries or sections in school libraries devoted to guidance materials, including educational and occupational information. There are still very few Catholic schools which have a special room where the books and literature published by universities, teacher-training colleges, industrial unions, or the state are at the students' disposal.

The practice of a homeroom teacher has always been the rule in French Catholic schools. Government schools are gradually adopting this system. The homeroom teacher has in the past compensated in one sense for the absence of trained psychologists. A major defect of the system is that the homeroom teacher has offered a kind of "spontaneous guidance" based on intuition rather than on the findings of the new science of guidance. Nevertheless the efforts of the homeroom teacher have been deeply appreciated by the students and by their parents. Catholic schools owe much of their success to the homeroom teacher.

Of course the French schools, government and Catholic, have a long, long way to go before they reach the level of organization and sophistication of guidance services which characterize American schools.

Catholic schools have always enjoyed the reputation for maintaining good discipline among their students. The good discipline results from their application of the well-known theory which holds that it is easier to prevent than to cure. Consequently close supervision of boys and girls is given very careful attention. The current rule is that students should never be left alone and that the "friendly" presence of teachers or other staff members will automatically keep them quiet. It is also commonly held that tight organizational control and the lack of individual student initiative substantially assist in keeping students quiet and in their place. This explains why Catholic schools have the habit of requiring their students to file in silence when moving from one place to another. Students must maintain silence in the dormitory, in the dining-room before grace is said, and so on. Of course these disciplinary practices appear more and more anachronistic to boys and girls of the present generation. Therefore some Catholic schools are attempting to implement a more liberal type of discipline. Indeed, some are experimenting with methods of self-government. Such forward-looking schools are very few. But it must be admitted that these liberalizing attempts are not easy in buildings which were not meant to facilitate student government and control, buildings which were conceived to handle very large groups in a military-like style of life. Nevertheless everything points to a trend toward a more supple type of discipline; in the newer plants such discipline is more readily attainable.

The post of chaplain has been rather neglected in French Catholic schools. Paradoxically, this situation was the result of the confidence which the hierarchy had in Catholic schools. Because these schools were run by priests, brothers, or sisters, the bishops had full trust in the religious training and atmosphere of those schools, and they too frequently appointed infirm or retired priests to the post of chaplain. Many have realized the long-range dangers of such policy and have adopted different attitudes. Nonetheless there still is no general policy on school chaplains, nor is there any national association of chaplains of Catholic schools which would develop a program of pastoral work and scientific religious guidance. Professional training for this sensitive post is also virtually nonexistent.

The Staff of the Catholic Schools

The following tables give pertinent data on the composition of the staff of Catholic schools in France.

Catholic School Staff by School Level

School level	Lay teachers	Clerical and religious teachers
Elementary schools	27,344	11,712
Secondary schools	18,750	10,117
Technical schools	5,703	2,417
Country schools (agricultural and home-keeping)	1,873	1,100

By canonical status, there were in French Catholic schools as of 1966 5310 priests, 4593 brothers, 17,353 sisters, and 51,427 lay persons (of whom 11,883 were men and 39,544 were women). The figure for each category exceeds the comparable figure in the preceding table because these figures also include the staffs of seminaries, novitiates, universities, and special schools.

Catholic School Staff by Age

	% Under 40	% 40-50	% Over 50
Priests	30	36	34
Brothers	35	26	39
Sisters	n.d.	n.d.	n.d.
Lay persons	n.d.	n.d.	n.d.

Up to 1958 Catholic schools were totally private along the lines of nineteenth-century liberal train of thought. Consequently until 1958 Catholic schools enjoyed an immunity which was not conducive to a high standard of professional preparation of their personnel. The state required only the bare minimum from persons wishing to teach in a private school. For elementary schoolteachers this minimum was the Brevet Elémentaire, a diploma granted after three years of post-elementary education; for secondary schoolteachers only the baccalauréat, the secondary school diploma, was required. No specific professional preparation in education was demanded. Of course not all teachers in Catholic schools have simply the bare minimum; some have more training. In government schools, however, a much higher level of professional preparation has always been required. Elementary teachers received a professional preparation in government teacher-training schools for at least one year. Secondary school teachers in government schools had to have a university degree, and many of them sat for the Agrégation, a competitive examination on the post-graduate level.

The contrats signed by Catholic schools perforce put an end to the immunity of Catholic school teachers in the matter of professional preparation. Hence while seemingly restraining their liberty, the contrat has forced Catholic schools to have better qualified teachers than was true in the pre-contrat era. All teachers now entering the Catholic school system must have the same degrees required of government schoolteachers. Elementary schoolteachers must have a professional degree, the Certificat d'Aptitude a l'enseignement. Upper secondary schoolteachers must hold a university degree, the licence, and teachers in the first four years of secondary school, that is the first cycle, need only two years of university education. No specific preparation in professional education courses is required of secondary schoolteachers.

There is a great demand by teachers for inservice education; this demand is perhaps greatest among Catholic schoolteachers. Inservice education is given in summer school courses, forums, workshops, seminars, and so forth. In 1965, for example, over one-third of all Catholic schoolteachers participated in inservice work.

There is no specific professional preparation for administrators in government schools. Most principals and directors of studies are priests or religious who are appointed by their religious superiors. This lack of professional administrators in Catholic schools is most regrettable, and educationists and alert administrators are deeply aware of the problem. In the summer of 1966 steps were taken to correct this situation. In that summer the principals of Catholic secondary schools met in convention and took courses in administration and public relations.

There are several professional associations for teachers and administrators in Catholic schools. One is the National Association of Catholic Secondary School Principals. Other principals' associations include the Association of Catholic Technical School Principals and the Association of Catholic Agricultural School Principals. There are three labor unions which school teachers can join, an independent union which is a purely professional union and two unions affiliated with national labor unions. However, membership of Catholic school teachers in unions is very low. Until recently membership of a Catholic school teacher in a union was vigorously discouraged by employers and even by the hierarchy. Although the atmosphere has become more permissive in this regard, still by 1967 only one-tenth of all teachers in Catholic schools were union members.

Three other professional associations should be mentioned. One is *Action Catholique du Mouvement des Enseignants Chrétiens* (ACMEC), which is the Catholic Action movement formed by Catholic lay teachers. ACMEC boasts of a membership of about 7000 militants. Indeed, ACMEC's influence is growing. The various male nonclerical religious teaching institutes are grouped in the Union of Teaching Brothers, and the different institutes of teaching sisters form the Union of Teaching Sisters. Both unions are active in organizing conventions and in working toward a solution of common problems. Both are represented in all national associations concerned with Catholic schools.

In one way Catholic teachers enjoy a much greater freedom than do their counterparts in government schools, since the latter are civil servants and hence not free to choose their assignment. Government schoolteachers can be shifted from one town to another unless they are *agrégés*. Catholic school teachers, in contrast, are employed by a specific school and will not be transferred or dismissed unless they are guilty of professional misconduct. It is difficult to assess with precision the degree of academic freedom for teachers in Catholic schools versus those in government schools. However, it is safe to say that teachers in both types of school labor under various kinds of restrictions.

The teaching load for an elementary schoolteacher is thirty periods per week; for a teacher in the first cycle of secondary school it is twenty-four periods per week; for a teacher in the second cycle of secondary school, it is eighteen periods per week.

The Parents
and the
Catholic School

The contact between parents and the Catholic school is one of the areas in which great progress has been made since 1950. Every Catholic school has its parents' association. All these local associations are federated at the national level with the powerful Association of Parents of Private School Students, the *Association des Parents d'Élèves de l'Enseignement Libre* (APEL). The political influence of the national association has been considerable, particularly in furthering the interests of private schools. APEL is represented in various national political committees. However, the activities of the national and local parents' associations tend to be more educational than political. For this purpose, the national association issues a monthly publication, *La famille Éducatrice*, which has the largest circulation of any French educational magazine (700,000 by 1967). Local parents' associations in Catholic schools have widely adopted the various techniques of adult education to get parents interested in the education of their children. This undoubtedly represents one of the most outstanding and conspicuous achievements of French Catholic education, and indeed one of its most evident contributions to the educational needs of the nation. As late as 1950 it was the custom for parents to come to the Catholic schools and listen to lectures given by one of the teachers or by a visiting lecturer such as a physician or a psychologist. Such activities of the parents' associations were very passive and did not bear much fruit. Nowadays the dynamism of parents' associations is apparent. A number of moderators have been trained in group dynamics; consequently the dialogue between parents and school takes the form of small group discussions, parent-directed workshops and the like. These parent-school encounters arouse great interest and have completely transformed the mentality of parents. By 1966 more than 150,000 meetings of these small groups were held in the various Catholic schools throughout France.

The growing importance of parents' associations is also felt in another direction. Formerly the parent-school contacts were largely individual and were always established through the principal. It was sometimes very difficult for parents to talk about their children with the teachers themselves. Collective contacts were made only when the school organized a garden fête or a fund-raising drive. At present there is a definite trend toward direct, personal parent-teacher contacts. In the newer school buildings, small rooms are set aside for parent-teacher interviews. School-parent contacts are no longer held solely at the discretion of the prefect of studies. In the old days parents could "cooperate" with the Catholic school only when and how the school wished. Now parents have more of a voice; for example, they can express their wishes about the homework assignments. A representative of the parents' association is required to be present to express the views of the parents at all faculty meetings in which the orientation and guidance of the students are discussed.

In the early 1960's APEL launched still another service. In face of the wide demand for international exchange of young Catholic students, and in view of the lack of moral support which these students receive in some of the existing student-exchange organizations, APEL has established a student-exchange program with Germany, England, and even with the United States. In 1965 APEL was able to receive and send 5000 such students from and to Germany, 400 from and to England, and 400 from and to the United States. APEL's effort has culminated in the organization of a joint pilgrimage to a shrine of the Blessed Mother in southern France, a pilgrimage in which young German and French students shared.

Special Educational Problems Facing Catholic Schools in France

The November, 1965 convention organized by the International Association for Freedom in Education (*L'Union Internationale pour la Liberté de l'Enseignement*) was entitled "Challenging the School." The various speeches and panel discussions expanded on that topic and studied the following: the school challenged by the state; the school challenged by parents; the school challenged by the students; the school challenged by industry; and so forth. These topics nicely summarize the very uncomfortable situation in which Catholic schools in France find themselves. They are questioned and challenged by all these various persons and groups. Indeed, it might be added that French Catholic schools are challenged and questioned by an important segment of the Church itself. The main solutions proposed by the various schools of thought working on educational problems will be presented; the present writer will also give his own solution to the various problems.

The first problem which Catholic schools in France must solve is their rather ambiguous existential situation. The government has signed *contrats* with most of them; yet the *Comité National d'Action Laïque* (CNAL), together with one of the government schools, has violently objected to this permissive attitude of "public funds for nonpublic schools." These opponents dispute the right of Catholic schools to receive government assistance and further accuse them of fostering divisiveness in French youth. The short-range aim of this hostile group is to let Catholic schools struggle on their own resources. Because of the Catholic schools' paucity of fiscal resources, these groups hope such a step will result in the eventual collapse of Catholic schools and bring about the association's long-range goal of uniting all French boys and girls in one national school system. Added to this are objections to the existence of Catholic schools emanating from Catholic circles. Until the early 1960's such demurrers were not too vocal; however, by 1965 the rumble grew louder. Thus, for example, *Témoignage Chrétien* (November 11, 1965) stated that the Declaration of Vatican II on Christian Education will be "one of the great weaknesses of the Council. It will be received in France, in particular, with some sadness by many of the most fervent and devout Christians." Similarly the association of Catholic teachers working in government schools in their bulletin *Vie Enseignante* (December, 1965) expressed regret that Vatican II has urged on Catholic parents the obligation to help Catholic schools and to send their children to them whenever possible. A year earlier a number of priests and Catholic laymen in western France sent to their bishop an open letter in which they asked for clarification of their position relative to the reception of the sacraments since they had decided not to support Catholic schools. Finally, in July, 1965 *Parole et Mission*, an influential Catholic quarterly, printed an important article written by Michel Duclercq entitled *"L'Eglise dans le Monde scolaire."* Duclercq's thesis argued that it is impossible for the Church in France to preach the Gospel to some groups of people so long as she maintains separatist Catholic schools. Such strong statements encountered vigorous opposition, but they show the precarious and difficult position of Catholic schools in contemporary France.

It is fairly certain that spectacular decisions concerning Catholic schools will not be made. Catholic schools cannot revert to the former system under which they were entirely free, receiving no fiscal assistance from the government. Such a step backward would mean their death, because French Catholics are unable to pay for their entire support; nor do they seem willing to do so. But on the other hand, precluding the very unlikely development of a sweeping political change in the country, there is no evidence that the government will move to suppress Catholic schools. Therefore it is reasonable to assert that the status quo will be maintained, evolving according to the exigencies of the times. That is to say, it is highly probable that an increasing number of private schools will shift from the *contrat simple* to the *contrat d'association*, which involves simultaneously greater financial advantages and greater control and conformity. Hence it is legitimate to ask whether this situation will not create an ambiguity in the long run. Will it not blur the difference between government schools and Catholic schools, a difference which eventually will be erased with the distinctiveness of Catholic schools being completely lost in the state? Some Catholics fear this possibility and fight to stop progress; others plead for Catholic schools to take care of educational areas which are underdeveloped either geographically, or sociologically, or psychologically (handicapped children, for example), areas in which government schools are poorly represented. Whatever solution is adopted, it is clear that a clarification of the distinct nature and role of the Catholic school is one of the main problems facing French Catholicism today.

The second major problem is somewhat related to the first. It is essential for the Catholic school to define its position in the post-Council pastoral work of the Church. It can no longer constitute an apostolate of protection; it must cease being a shelter institution. The modern world is pluralistic, not ghettoistic. Besides, not all Catholic boys and girls can attend the too few Catholic schools in France; nor can it any longer be maintained that the Catholic school is the normal educational milieu for Catholic children, since such a position would lead one to admit that two-thirds of French Catholic children are in an abnormal situation. There has been a good deal of reflection on this subject since the end of the Council; the answer generally given is in terms of mediation. The Catholic school should aim at being a privileged place for a twofold mediation. First, it should bring to the Church the needs and cares and hopes of the world of youth and the world of thought. It should be a privileged place for the Church to listen to this world, to get in touch with flesh and blood problems, to become acquainted with the world which through the youth is coming daily into existence. Second, the Catholic school should bring to this world in formation the assurance of Christ's love for this world. The Catholic school should be a privileged place for the Church to show to this world who she is, what are her features, and to give evidence of her vital role in this world. These goals can only be achieved by way of signification and symbols, a way which could be called sacramental if it were not for the *ex opere operato* aspect of sacraments. But the Second Person of the Blessed Trinity made flesh cannot directly reach all people living in the various parts of the world and at different centuries; rather this person-in-flesh reaches them through the mediating powers of the sacraments. So likewise, contemporary Catholic schools cannot reach all Catholic children living in France. Nor can these schools reach the non-Catholic children; yet it is the missionary duty of the Church to reach non-Catholics in some way or other. Hence it would seem that the work of promotion and love which Catholic schools ought to achieve can become a living sign to the whole nation that in those schools the salvation of God has come to pass. For this reason Catholic schools in France are thought more in terms of quality than in quantity, more in terms of signification than of immediate efficiency. For this reason, too, the French bishops can at the same time defend Catholic schools and ask them to think in terms of all Catholic students living in France, a request which would be nonsense in a different view of the Catholic school. This new view has important implications concerning the very location of Catholic schools; as the Gospel states, a light should not be placed under a bushel but should be placed on the hilltop so that it can be seen by everyone. Thus it appears that French Catholic schools will have to shift their position in the total pastoral work of the Church. This does not mean that Catholic schools will have no place in the Church at all; rather it means that the schools' role will be a different one.

These first two problems are somewhat abstract, but they lead us to a third critical problem which is much more immediate and practical. If Catholic schools have to find a new niche in the Church and in the state, they must be stimulated to realize the necessity of changing their aims, their structures, and their methods; in other words Catholic schools are confronted with the imperative duty of mutation. Not all so-called Catholic schools will survive; further, not all of them can rightly be called Catholic in the sense in which the Church needs them in the modern world. It could even be said, perhaps, that the number of post-conciliar Catholic schools which are assured of being kept in existence is frightfully low. In any event,

Catholic schools will have to devise new types and new styles of education to avoid mere duplication of government schools and thereby prove by their unique presence their utility to the nation. It is rather sad to have to admit that, in spite of long years of complete freedom, French Catholic schools have not made a substantial contribution to the progress of teaching methodology. As noted earlier, Catholic schooling has been quite satisfactory as far as examination results are concerned, but these purely scholastic achievements have been attained with a rather conservative mentality. (This does not mean that absolutely no contributions have been made by Catholic schools. There are some very fine pedagogical innovations as stated earlier. Moreover, this lack of originality is not so striking when one remembers that government schools in France are themselves very conservative and traditional.) Further, if the Catholic school apostolate does not appear clearly connected to the work of the Church, *Mater et Magistra*, to the Church who is the mother of all men, then Catholic schools will not enlist the support of progress-conscious Catholics who tend to form both the majority and the most militant religionists in France.

The question may be raised, therefore, whether French Catholic schools will be able to effect this bold transformation. The task is a difficult one because it involves thousands of teachers who have worked with certain methods for years; besides, it affects structures which have been in existence for more than half a century. There are hopeful signs, however, that Catholic schools may be gearing to the challenge. First of all, there is a large number of young men and women desirous of joining the teaching profession and who have begun to enter the various institutes attached to universities for the preparation of Christian lay teachers in Lille, Angers, Nancy, Lyon, Paris, and so forth. Second, a great effort has been made to provide inservice work for experienced teachers to improve their methodology and skill in the teaching process. Each year more than 150 centers offer summer inservice workshops. Notwithstanding, this effort is still much too small because it does not reach more than 12,000 teachers and, above all, because the workshops are much too short, usually not exceeding one week. However, the need for such refresher workshops is now clearly seen, and in all probability something more effective may be initiated soon on a national scale. There is less hope for success in the necessary evolution of structures; finding proper basic structures for the Catholic schools in France constitutes a fourth and last important problem in itself.

The first aspect of this structural problem lies in the avenues which should be chosen to achieve unity. In the past Catholic schools have suffered from lack of communication, from complete isolation, even from anarchy. Since 1958—when the state decided to give financial help to Catholic schools—the need for greater unity was felt, the need to establish a Catholic school system. More pragmatically, there was a strong desire to unite in order to affect the official decisions on the mode of application of the law vis-à-vis Catholic schools. There were two ways of achieving this defense of common interests: one through free, corporate associations and the other through hierarchical centralization. The latter finally eventuated in the creation of a sort of ghost Catholic ministry of education, paralleling the official government ministry. This Catholic "ghost ministry" has nearly the same bureaus as does the government ministry. It operates at the highest levels with the government ministry to promote Catholic school interests. The reason for the creation of this centralized ministry is that in 1958 the various local teachers' and principals' associations were not sufficiently organized to take such a mature course of action. Consequently centralization was imperative. However, the time has come to foster the first proposed avenue and restore to every unit of the Catholic school system the maximum responsibility and initiative. This is crucial because it is the only way to put into practice the principle of subsidiarity, enacted again and again during Vatican II. Pope Pius XI defined subsidiarity in *Quadragesimo Anno:* "Just as it is gravely wrong to take from individuals what they can accomplish by their own initiative and industry, and give it to the community, so also it is an injustice and at the same time a grave evil and disturbance of right order to assign to a greater and higher association what lesser and subordinate associations can do."

Further, giving power to the local level is vital because it is the only way to grant the laity that full part which it should play in the apostolate of Christian education. In spite of their numbers, the laity still play a minor role in the Catholic school system in France. Most secondary school principals and all diocesan superintendents of schools are priests or religious. The only minor exception to this rule is found among the corps of school supervisors and inspectors, positions which are being increasingly filled by laymen and by the mid-1960's directed by a very capable lay staff. This clerical and religious monopoly in French Catholic schools must be changed for many reasons, at least two of which merit attention here. First, when dealing with Catholic schools, government officials meet only priests or bishops; conse-

hey receive the impression that they are dealing with the
al Church acting as such. For this reason government school-
school dialogue is seldom open and never develops along
al lines. Second, the work of education in the modern world
;er a work of cramming curricula into children's heads, of
)ns, or of marks. Rather, education is a work of dialogue:
f the school with parents, of the school with all kinds of
il agencies, dialogue of teachers with students, and so on.
ialogue which must be at the very heart of the Catholic
l which must constitute the very signification of what the
s to say to this world is the dialogue between the various
......)f the staff as symbolic of the dialogue between the various canonical states in the Church. Consequently there has evolved
the increasingly prevalent opinion that Catholic schools can no longer
be conceived as operated and staffed entirely and exclusively by priests,
or that Catholic schools would be conducted by nuns only or by lay
teachers only. The Church has to be presented to the students in the
variety of its states of life, and each of these states should be called
into responsibility according to the criterion of professional ability
only. There should thus be laymen who testify that Christianity is
lived from day to day amid the worries and cares of this world. There
should be religious testifying that hope for the celestial Jerusalem
does not lead Christians away from the present secular city. And there
should be priests testifying that the mediations between God and
men are to be made in the human idiom.

The fact that all the problems touched on are so clearly seen and
formulated in many spheres is the best indication that Catholic
schools in France are aware of the changes taking place in the world
and that they intend to become in the future what the world and the
Church expect them to be.

Selected
Bibliography

Aigrain, R. Histoire des Universités. Paris: Presses Universitaires de France,
   1949.
Bur, Jacques. Laïcité et problèmes scolaires. Paris: Bonne Presse, 1959.
Coutrot, Aline, and François Dreyfus. Les forces religieuses dans la société
   française. Coll. U. Paris: Colin, 1965.

Fourrier, Charles. *L'enseignement français de l'antiquité à la Révolution.* Paris: Institut Pédagogique National, 1964.

Megrine, Bernard. *La question scolaire en France Coll. Que sais-je?* Paris: Presses Universitaires de France, 1963.

Ozouf, Mona. *L'Ecole, l'Eglise et la République (1871–1914). Coll. kiosque.* Paris: Colin, 1963.

Ponteil, Felix. *Histoire de l'Enseignement en France (1789–1964).* Paris: Sirey, 1966.

Riche, Pierre. *Education et culture dans l'Occident barbare, VI–VIII° s.Coll. Patristica Sorbonensia.* Paris: Seuil, 1962.

Rigault, Georges. *Histoire Générale des Frères des Ecoles Chrétiennes,* Vols. 1 and 2. Paris: Plon, 1937 and 1938.

Simon, Pierre-Henri. *L'école entre l'Eglise et la République.* Paris: Seuil, 1959.

Catholic Education
in Germany

by Franz Pöggeler

A Short History
of Catholic
Education in Germany

The twofold meaning of the term Catholic school bears great significance on the history as well as on the present structure of Catholic schools in Germany. The first sense of the term is that of a "free," independent, Church or private school; the second sense is that of a public, that is government-operated or communal, school. Catholic schools of the second variety are a German peculiarity which at present can be found only in very few countries of the world—Spain, Portugal, and Italy, for example.

Contrary to the effect in most other countries, the French Revolution did not result in a secularization or neutralization of the government-operated schools in Germany. Rather, as a consequence of the Napoleonic occupation at the beginning of the nineteenth century, Germany, starting with Baden and Hesse, established government-operated nondenominational schools (*Simultanschulen* or *Gemeinschaftesschulen*). These schools are public, Christian, or neutral schools open to pupils and teachers of all religious beliefs and persuasions. After the French Revolution, in many parts of Germany (Bavaria, Westphalia, the Rhineland, and Württemberg) the government-operated or the communal, denominational school (both Catholic and Protestant) remained the principal school. In the Prussian *Landrecht* of 1784 it was decreed for the first time that schools and universities should be under the direction of the state; they were no longer established, controlled, and operated by the churches. No parity between denominational and nondenominational schools was achieved in most German *Länder* in the nineteenth and twentieth centuries. Either the denominational school or the nondenominational school comprised the principal school; the alternative type was the so-called supplementary school, the private, independent (nongovernment-operated) school.

Until the end of the nineteenth century, when most Catholic schools in Germany had become government-operated schools, the Church retained the right of school supervision ("spiritual supervision") in such schools. By state authority, the local clergyman was entitled to visit teachers and pupils regularly and to report to the state authorities on the progress and the conduct of teachers and pupils. However, throughout the nineteenth century this spiritual supervision was opposed by the majority of teachers in the Catholic schools, chiefly on the ground that the clergyman was not qualified pedagogically to undertake such supervision.

In those parts of Germany where nondenominational (neutral) schools were the rule, a relatively small number of Catholic schools were established. After the establishment of the first German Republic in 1918, a struggle ensued for several years to enact a *Reich* school law. But such a bill never became law because the political parties were unable to agree on the structure of Catholic and Protestant schools. Indeed, after 1918 there was an increasing tendency to recognize Catholic (and Protestant) schools only as private schools rather than as public denominational schools as formerly. During the Nazi regime (1933–1945) all public Catholic schools were dissolved, one after another; in the end only those private Catholic schools which for the most part were conducted by religious institutes were able to continue instruction. Even Catholic religious instruction began to be prohibited in the public schools.

The inception of the renewal of the Catholic school system occurred after 1945. Despite the initial resistance of the British and French occupation forces, government Catholic schools were established soon after the end of World War II in North Rhine Westphalia, Lower Saxony, Rhineland-Palatinate, Bavaria, and Württemberg-Hohenzollern; however, none were established in Hesse, Baden, Hamburg, Bremen, or Berlin. No Catholic school has been founded in the Soviet-occupied zone of Germany, not even as a private school.

The number of private, "free" Catholic schools in the Federal Republic has increased considerably since 1945. These private schools were generally accorded equal recognition with government schools. Most government Catholic schools, however, are elementary schools (*Volksschule*). As a rule there are no government Catholic high schools (*Gymnasium*), intermediate schools (*Realschule*), or part-time vocational schools (*Berufsschule*). Since 1945—as also between 1926 and 1933—a number of teacher-training colleges (*Pädagogische Hochschule*) were established as denominational (Catholic or Protestant) institutions. For many decades the Catholic Church in Germany has contended that a Catholic government school presupposes a professional preparation of teachers in government-operated Catholic teacher-training colleges.

Since 1850 the steady increase of institutions for extracurricular youth activities and for adult education has had great impact on the Catholic educational system in Germany. German Catholics have concentrated much of their major pedagogical effort on these two areas in the twentieth century, both between 1900 and 1933 and subsequent to 1945. Today there is an unwritten law that the government does not set up separate institutions for youth activities or for adult education. When it is absolutely necessary for the government to establish such schools, these institutions have the status of subsidiary schools. The reason for this unwritten law may well be a consequence of the strong involvement of German Catholics in this educational area. The German school system is largely under government control and supervision, and is communalized.

The Purpose of
Catholic Schools
in Germany

Catholic German educators define Catholic education in the Catholic school as that education in that school in which the center of interest is Christ. Christianity in schools is not a result of the mere fact that teachers and pupils alike have a baptismal certificate; rather, instruction and school life must be penetrated by the spirit of the Catholic faith. It is the aim of the Catholic school to initiate the Catholic pupil to a Catholic view of the problems of life and to familiarize him with the Catholic archetypes of the world and the Catholic ideals of life. In a Catholic school a unity of the educational and the religious communities should be particularly concretized in the ethos and the atmosphere of school life.

The purpose and the goals of Catholic schools in Germany are characterized by the actualization of three cardinal principles. The *principle of doctrinal conformity* orders the entire school program around the teachings of the Catholic Church. Thus the Stuttgart Memorandum of 1946 states that "the education of Catholic children is best achieved in a Catholic school." The *principle of pluralism* causes the school experiences to be so structured that the children learn to live fruitfully in a world of varying ideologies while maintaining the opportunity of growth necessary to nurture the one ideology to which each child personally adheres. The *principle of freedom* is that element whereby the state gives the Church total freedom in the educational sphere to prescribe curricula, instructional methodologies, and the like within schools operated by the Church.

The Relationship of
Catholic Schools
to State Schools

In many countries government-operated schools are neutral schools. This is not the case with the German Catholic school system in which most Catholic schools are operated by the government or by the local community. (In the so-called "German Democratic Republic," that is the Soviet-occupied zone of Germany, there are no Catholic or Protestant schools.)

Government Legislation
Which Has Affected Catholic Schools

The legal status of Catholic schools in Germany is determined either by special public school laws or by laws for private (free) schools. The legislation differs among the twelve German *Länder* and Berlin only with respect to the financing of Catholic schools. The Constitution of the Federal Republic explicitly grants the right to free and private schools in all *Länder* including West Berlin.

The best and most representative school law in Germany is the First School Organization Law of North Rhine Westphalia of April 8, 1952. This law provides for the parents' right to have three types of schools established by the government, denominational (Catholic, Protestant), nondenominational (for children of all denominations), and secular (neutral, non-Christian). These three types may be founded as public (government or communal) schools or as private (fee) schools. Similar school laws in other *Länder* entitle the parents to choose from among various denominational schools for their children; however, in some *Länder* (notably in Hesse, Hamburg, Bremen, and Berlin) Catholic schools may be established only as private schools.

One overarching legal-political fact is important in this context: in the Federal Republic and in West Berlin, schools are a *Länder* affair and are not subject to the *Bund*. This *Länder* control over schools flows from the principle of "cultural federalism," of "cultural autonomy" of the *Länder*.

The *Elternrecht*, the parents' right to select a school as well as to have a voice in its policy-making, is provided for in the Constitution of the Federal Republic. The right to establish Catholic schools in Germany is not only guaranteed by the *Elternrecht* but also by the right to freedom of education, especially religious freedom in education.

Comparison of Catholic Schools with Government Schools As to Quality

In Germany the government requires from all Catholic schools, both private and government, a quality of instruction, teacher-training, and standard of examinations comparable to those of non-Catholic schools at the same level. Curricula usually are the same in Catholic and non-Catholic schools. The primary distinction between Catholic and non-Catholic schools lies merely in the different interpretation of teaching materials and the dissimilar school atmosphere.

The relationship between the government schools and the Church schools warrants special explanation. Because of the "condition zero" after the victory of the Allies over the Nazis, as well as the concurrent increase of Church activity in spiritual life, the Catholic Church in Germany took advantage of the opportunity to proclaim its ideas about setting up an educational system. Contrary to Protestant churches, German Catholics have based all their educational arguments on the natural law, not only in the area of *Elternrecht*, as is often erroneously surmised, but also in the area of delineation of authority. In accordance with the principle of subsidiarity, the Catholic Church in Germany maintains that each social group should undertake on its own the sphere of education which it is capable of doing and to which it is ontologically entitled, instead of heaping the entire educational burden on the state. Consistent with this line of reasoning, the government school is neither the original nor the only type of school. Since the state, because of its democratic nature, is neutral in *Weltanschauung*, it is neither capable of creating ideals which are significant in education nor of defining the goals and content of education. It is in this axiological zone that the several religious groups come in. (See Wilhelm Geiger in the Arndt, Geiger, Pöggeler volume.)

The principle of subsidiarity is accompanied by the principle of solidarity, according to which Christians recognize and appreciate the moral authority and dignity of the state. The authority of the state is determined in cultural policy by the dictum: "The State shall be the guardian of the common good."

In the area of culture, the State should exercise wise restraint and should guarantee freedom. Freedom of conscience must be guaranteed wherever philosophies enter the picture. The fostering of culture is primarily the task of the people and, to a large extent, of the Church. The State should limit itself to preventing harmful abuses, to helping with its greater means, and to providing the necessary institutions. If the State makes itself the founder of schools and of other cultural institutions, it has to avoid claims to sole determination. (From *Aufgaben und Grenzen der Staatsgewalt,* 1953.)

From that train of thought, some groups, such as the Association of German Catholic Teachers in their "educational program" of 1964, deduced that public schools include not only those which are conducted by the state but all those educational institutions which are operated by public corporations. Consequently Church schools are also public schools. This far-reaching conclusion is one at which no group other than the Catholics in Germany have previously arrived. The state as a democracy is basically neutral, but it is erroneous to conclude "that it could establish only 'neutral' schools—neutral in the zones of ideology and creed." (From the educational platform of the Association of German Catholic Women teachers.)

In German Catholic thought, the role of the state in education is, in Father Hartmann's words, to provide "a minimum of education for the citizens of the future." The range of authority of the state in educational affairs may, if compared with the Protestant viewpoint, appear minimal. The German Catholic position nevertheless presupposes a strong active state which should not direct its initiative to the determination of the pedagogical act proper but to the coordination of the various pedagogical activities. The state is vital for this task; no other institution is able to cope effectively with this gigantic undertaking. Again, it is not the structuring, but the organization, promotion and safeguarding of the educational system which constitutes the state's province in education. (Cf. Marian Heitger, *Staat und Kirche im Problem der Bildung,* 1956).

The Present Form
of Catholic
Schools in Germany

The Organizational Level

There is no Catholic school system as such in the Federal Republic of Germany. It is more accurate to speak of relatively independent

German Catholic schools existing at certain levels of education rather than to speak of a "system." It is only with government schools that a "system" can be found.

The position of *Reichsminister* of education does not exist in the Federal Republic. Rather, the control of education in Germany has been given to each *Land*. Each of the *Länder* has set up its fundamental school code; consequently it is usually not possible to make any one statement about German schools without qualifying that statement to admit of modifications given to it by each *Land*.

Preschool institutions—principally kindergartens—are largely operated under private auspices. To be sure, Catholics and Protestants are the chief ones engaged in operating kindergartens. For the present, at least, Germans do not appear eager to convert kindergartens from private to government control. Nursery schools are rather rare in Germany.

The *Volksschulen*, or *Grundschulen* (primary, or basic elementary, schools), are almost exclusively operated by the government, or to be more exact, by the community. This same holds true in the case of Catholic elementary schools. There are almost no private Church-related elementary schools, though there are a few for the education of the physically and mentally handicapped. The majority of all Catholic schools in Germany are government-operated schools at the elementary level. The *Grundschule* lasts for four years, from the ages six to ten, although in one *Land* it lasts for six years. All German students pass through this type of school; upon completion of this level, students are streamed into that type of postprimary education which is felt to be best suited to their interests and abilities. Students of high academic ability go to the *Gymnasium* (university preparatory secondary school). The *Gymnasium* is an eight- or nine-year secondary school designed to prepare students proximately to enter the university and ultimately to become the intellectual, cultural, and political leaders of the country. There are three basic types of *Gymnasium*: the *Realgymnasium* which emphasizes the natural sciences and mathematics, the *Humanistich Gymnasium* which emphasizes the classical languages and the traditional humanities-oriented curriculum, and a third type of gymnasium which emphasizes modern languages. Students who could not pass the entrance examination for the *Gymnasium* go instead to the *Mittelschule* (intermediate school). There are several curricular tracks in the *Mittelschule*. The first track is intended for students of academic promise and proclivity who were not able to gain admission to the *Gymnasium*. If by the end of two years in the *Mittelschule* these students have demonstrated definite scholastic growth so that they might be possible university students, they can transfer to a *Gymnasium* (sometimes called *Gymnasium Kurzform*). This system is promotive of horizontal articulation between the schools. The second track in the *Mittelschule* leads to matriculation in the *Berufsfachschule* (commercial high school). In this school the students are prepared to be lower-echelon white-collar workers in the business world, such as secretaries, clerks, and so forth. The student in this track remains in the *Mittelschule* for two years, and in the *Berufsfachschule* for an additional four years. The third track in the *Mittelschule* is usually the one opted by students of low academic potential. Students in this track customarily remain in the *Mittelschule* for four years. Then they may decide to continue their education in a *Fachschule* (technical high school) where the curriculum prepares the student to enter such professions as architecture, agriculture, mining, or forestry at less than the upper-echelon levels. Other students in the third track of the *Mittelschule* decide to discontinue attending school on a full-time basis. These students then go for a period of four years to the *Berufsschule* (work-study high school) in which they attend school for part of the week, while the rest of the time they work as apprentices to some tradesman or in an industrial enterprise. There are a few Catholic *Berufsschulen*. Catholic secondary schools of all sorts exist only as private schools, which in the postwar terminology are increasingly called "free schools" after the French and Dutch terminology. The term "free school" is more appropriate than the term "private school" because the Catholic Church in Germany is recognized as a public corporation rather than as a private institution.

Only students who attend the *Gymnasium* (either *Langform* or *Kurzform*) are eligible to enter the university. Entrance to the university is gained automatically by the student who, upon graduating from the *Gymnasium*, passes his *Abitur* examination. The *Abitur* is not an entrance test for the university, but rather the comprehensive examination given at the end of the *Gymnasium* to ascertain the level of scholastic attainment achieved by the student who is ready to leave. There are several forms of higher education in Germany. First there is the university, each with its separate faculties. A student does not enroll in the university as such, but rather in a *Fakultät* (faculty) in which he or she intends to specialize. The *Technische Hochschule* (higher technical school) prepares students to be the leaders in science and industry. A series of special-purpose institutions of higher education prepare students to enter various professions at higher levels, for example, a *Welthandelschule* (college of commerce) prepares its graduates to assume positions of leadership in the business world. The *Pädagogische Hochschule* (teacher-training college) prepares students to staff the nation's elementary school system. The university itself is oriented toward preparing students to enter the learned or classical professions. In some cases German universities have denominational *Fakultäten*, such as a Catholic faculty of theology or a Protestant faculty of theology. There are no Catholic universities in Germany, however. German Catholic intellectuals have objected to the establishment of a Catholic university on the ground that such a university would lead to a withdrawal of the relatively few Catholic professors from the government universities and thus deprive the Church of witness and influence in these universities. In addition, the German Catholic Church does not possess a sufficiently large number of qualified personnel to staff a Catholic university either as faculty members or as researchers.

The system of Catholic adult education is very well developed in Germany. It has often been stressed that the highly differentiated system of Catholic adult education in Germany floats in a vacuum, that is, it has no contact with the Catholic schools on the kindergarten, elementary, or secondary levels. But this same charge holds true for all aspects of the German Catholic school enterprise. Almost no vertical or horizontal articulation occurs among Catholic schools in Germany. To be sure, German Catholics have thus far rejected the concept of a unified school system because they feel that a system would bring about uniformity and choke that diversity which they prize so greatly.

The control structure of German Catholic schools conforms entirely to the state's requirements for schools at the appropriate level. In matters of religious education legal agreements have been made between the state and the Church.

Each principal is in charge of his school. Both in German government schools and in Catholic schools the relationship between the principal and the teachers is a very congenial one. Private Catholic schools have priests or sisters as principals; in other types of German Catholic schools laymen are customarily the principals.

Clerical control of education is forbidden in the government-operated Catholic schools in Germany. Nor is clerical control of education customary in German private Catholic schools. In the latter case there is no legal distinction between priest-teachers and sister-teachers on the one hand and lay teachers on the other. (The state requires equal rights and equal status for all teachers, lay, clerical, or religious).

Some Statistics on Catholic Schools

There is a paucity of available statistics on government and Catholic schools in Germany. However, it is interesting to note that less than 5 per cent of all secondary schools in Germany are operated by private or nongovernmental groups such as the Catholic Church.

In contrast to schools in other countries, the academic day in German schools does not continue from morning through the afternoon; rather, classes are held only in the morning from 8:00 A.M. to 1:00 P.M. (in the first four years of elementary school from 8:00 A.M. to either 10:00 A.M., 11:00 A.M., or 12). The school day is usually divided into definite time periods as follows: 8:00 A.M. to 8:45 A.M., class; 8:45 A.M. to 9:30 A.M., class; 9:30 A.M. to 10:00 A.M., recess; 10:00 A.M. to 10:45 A.M., class; 10:45 A.M. to 11:30 A.M., class; 11:30 A.M. to 11:45 A.M., recess; 11:45 A.M. to 12:30 P.M., class; and from 12:30 P.M. to 1:00 P.M., class.

Classes are in session six days a week, that is every day except Sunday. The five-day school week has not yet been introduced into the German school system. In the afternoon, pupils do their homework assignments, which in Germany are more extensive than in countries whose school day is considerably longer.

The competition engendered since 1945 by many government-operated Catholic schools which were given new and suitable buildings caused a considerable number of nongovernment Catholic schools to modernize their buildings or to erect new ones. The older nongovernment Catholic schools have been housed in abbeys or similar buildings. Today, however, there is a large number of lavishly equipped new buildings for private Catholic schools. A chapel, a residence hall, an athletic field, and a park are customarily included as part of the total school plant. There is an ever increasing tendency in Catholic boarding schools to eliminate the oversized, barrack-like dormitories and to replace these with single, double, and triple rooms.

Financial Support of Catholic Schools in Germany

The state and the local community assume complete financial responsibility for the government-operated and communal schools, both neutral and Catholic. Consequently the Church does not incur high costs for this type of Catholic school. The financing of the "free" or private Catholic schools, moreover, is also regulated in such a way that the fiscal burden on the Church is relatively small.

The government's subsidy for these private Catholic schools is provided for in the Private School Laws of the various *Länder*. At present the subsidies in the several *Länder* vary between 50 per cent and 90 per cent of the total cost of the Catholic educational system. Since 1945 continuous improvements in the government's financial aid programs have been achieved. In 1963 the Episcopal Center for Schools of Religious Institutes and Catholic Free (private) Schools published a report on the "financial aid of the German *Länder* to the private schools." (Cf. M. Heitger, *Staat und Kirche*.) This report reveals clearly the marked differences for the various *Länder*.

In Baden-Württemberg the subsidy per pupil in private high schools (*Gymnasien*) and regular elementary and secondary schools constitutes 40 per cent of the basic salary of the highest rank of high school teacher. In 1966 this amounted to $133 per year.

In Bavaria the subsidies are granted on three levels: operational compensation, equalization compensation, and subsistence grant. The operational compensation is given in all cases. It is computed by multiplying 50 per cent of the salary of teachers for each class by the number of all classes in participating schools of the *Land*. The teachers' salary expenditure is determined as being one and one-half times the salary of a married teacher in a secondary (*Gymnasium* or *Mittelschule*) government-operated school. A married teacher is paid according to level seven of seniority with locational compensation, class A. Each half of this amount is distributed over the two school types mentioned in proportion to the number and size of the classes. All schools which are entitled to subsidies receive approximately 50 per cent of the outlay for teachers.

In addition to the operational compensation, an equalization compensation may be given in special instances when the Catholic school seems to need the subsidies in view of the deficit of the previous year. The *Land* provides 30 per cent of the total amount of operational compensation paid the preceding year, as the fund for the equalization grant. The allocation of monies for the individual schools is carried out on a point assessment system; this, ironically, may bring about the deplorable situation whereby some schools are not eligible at all. The operational compensation, either by itself or in conjunction with the equalization compensation, must not exceed 85 per cent of the aggregate operational cost of the school. On the average the operational compensation together with the equalization compensation accounts for approximately 65 per cent of the gross cost of personnel; this amount represents about 50 per cent of the entire operational cost. In larger schools the subsidy may approximate $175 per pupil per annum. Under certain circumstances a subsistence grant of 50 per cent of the school's outlays for its lay teachers may be added; however, there is no such compensation for members of religious institutes.

Teachers in government-operated Catholic schools may take a leave of absence to teach in private Catholic schools. In such instances the private schools pay the salaries and in *Land Bayern* have to refer 30 per cent of the gross income to their credit as a subsistence compensation. Under the Private School Subsidization Law, compensation for a deficit and for expenditures on teaching materials is prohibited.

In Berlin there are subsidies for all recognized private schools. The grant must be renewed each year. Depending on the budget, a uniform percentage is computed for the school's fixed costs. The maximum amount allocated is 50 per cent of these costs. The subsidy must neither exceed the deficit of the school nor the comparable expenditure of a government school. The school budget is the basis for the calculation of subsidies. Operating expenses of the kind and size of comparable government schools are the only ones considered; the same holds true for rent expense. For members of religious institutes, 65 per cent of the salary of a comparable lay teacher may be put down to offset accommodation, living costs, and pension contributions. Restricted gifts and revenues from boarding schools are excluded from consideration. The subsidy may not exceed the predetermined percentage of recognized expenditures.

In 1962 the Berlin Senate appropriated approximately 43 per cent of the total expenditure of legally recognized private schools. Since 1961 efforts have been made to increase the subsidization. Thus far, regrettably, all efforts have been unsuccessful.

In Bremen all legally recognized supplementary schools which are nonprofit organizations receive subsidies. These subsidies amount to 50 per cent of the expenditure for teachers' salaries in a comparable government school with normal class size and number of teachers. If the school is pedagogically outstanding in some way, the full number of pupils—not the comparable one—is the basis for computation. Recently an increase in subsidies has been requested on several occasions. The budget of Bremen provides that $145.36 per student per year be used for subsidies of private schools.

In Hamburg there are no legal stipulations on subsidization. In point of fact, 90 to 95 per cent of the operating costs are defrayed by subsidies. In the Catholic districts of Hamburg there are approximately twenty elementary schools and three high schools (one *Mittelschule* and two *Gymnasien*).

In Hesse, 50 to 70 per cent of the comparable expenditure for staff salaries is covered by subsidies amounting to $150 to $245 annually per pupil. The first figure is the customary subsidy; the latter is an additional grant for experimental or pilot schools, or schools of special pedagogical significance.

Calculations for subsidies are based on the per pupil cost in a comparable government school (outlays for salaries and subsistence) of the previous year. As a rule this subsidy amounts to approximately $150 per pupil per year in the high schools. Factors which might increase costs, salary increments and higher prices, for example, are not considered in the same year's computations.

Only those nonprofit supplementary schools which received government grants of money until January 1, 1962 under Section 7, paragraph 2, of the Private School Law of April 27, 1953 are awarded subsidies. This law provides for exceptions of newly established schools only if these were classified by the Minister of Education as experimental or pilot schools, or schools with special pedagogical significance, and if the budget makes provision for the necessary funds. Aid to private special schools may also be given if the *Land* provides teachers for those schools. The private school financing law does not make any stipulation about tuition fees.

In Lower Saxony subsidies absorb 80 per cent of the average teacher's salary paid by a private school. For members of a religious institute, 56 per cent of the average salary may be allotted. The aid is increased by adding the expenditures for fringe benefits to the teachers, such as the employer's share of the employee's insurance, but only to a maximum of 10 per cent of the subsidy.

In North Rhine-Westphalia all types of recognized supplementary schools receive financial assistance to cover deficits. Basically, supplementary schools with a preliminary license are not excluded.

The budget forms the basis of the computations of subsidies. The *Land* supplies the amount to cover the deficit which is reflected in the annual balance sheet after the school has deducted its own expenses. These (including the lump sum rates of 7 per cent and 2 per cent, respectively, for school-owned real property and school equipment) are always 15 per cent of the comparable total operating expenses. In hardship cases this amount may be reduced to 2 per cent of the total expenses. Gifts from outside patrons and friends of the school, even those used to pay the school's own outlays, do not reduce the financial aid. According to established norms, expenses other than for salaries are considered in a lump sum arrangement without any additional audit by accountants. Revenues from boarding schools are not considered. For members of religious institutes, 70 per cent of the average salaries of comparable lay teachers are subsidized; the equalization of pension payments is taken care of similarly. If a supplementary school is dissolved, the *Land* assumes the liabilities of that school as well as the full salaries of teachers who cannot be transferred immediately to other schools. For this purpose the budget of another supplementary school is used as a model.

In Rhineland-Palatinate only private elementary schools, special schools, vocational, and high schools are subsidized. These schools receive grants according to so-called "class units." The number of class units is computed by dividing the number of pupils in a high school by thirty (in intermediate schools the divisor is thirty-five; in elementary schools, forty; in special schools, twenty; in home economics schools, thirty-two) and by increasing—according to the need of teachers—by fifty per cent (intermediate schools, 35 per cent; all other schools, 10 per cent). If the result is lower than 0.5 it is dropped; otherwise it is raised to the next highest integer. Thus the aid is principally computed for class units in accordance with the average need of teachers.

The subsidies amount to 75 per cent of the average salary of a comparable teacher in a government school. In addition, the *Land* pays up to 20 per cent of the average salary into the pension fund of the teachers.

In Saarland all recognized supplementary schools are eligible for fiscal assistance. The formula for the subsidy is similar to that of North Rhine-Westphalia for covering the deficit. In Saarland, however, the subsidies amount to 90 per cent of the deficit, or more accurately, the excess of expenditures over receipts after deducting the school's own payments up to 10 per cent of the operating costs of a supplementary school. The salaries of the teachers assigned to the private schools by the *Land* are included in the budget as income and expenditure; subsidized schools may, on application, obtain from the state teachers whose salaries are paid by the state. A leave of absence to teach in a supplementary school is permissible; these periods carry full salary and pension credit.

In Schleswig-Holstein there is no legal basis for fiscal assistance. However, subsidies increase annually (approximately $200 per year per pupil). The Diet of the *Land* has anounced an impending private school law.

All German universities are operated by the government. Hence all teachers, whether or not in Catholic faculties, receive a salary based on the same scale.

The Curriculum

Usually the curriculum in German Catholic schools is the same as in all other schools. Moreover, there is no difference in curriculum between the government-operated and the free Catholic schools. The curriculum, that is the subjects to be taught, are the same for all corresponding types of schools because all schools, Catholic or non-Catholic, are bound by government regulations to the all important final examinations. Therefore the curriculum is patterned after the examination requirements. The only topics taught are those which are required for the final examination. The variations with regard to the distribution of curricular materials over the school year are very minor indeed.

Only very few private Catholic schools (namely those which are recognized by the government as experimental) have developed a distinctive curriculum. There are, for example, several Catholic secondary schools for girls in which artistic handicrafts are taught, so the curriculum contains elements over and above those found in comparable schools.

In the kindergarten the curriculum is centered around playing and games. Thus German kindergarten education is considered an ontological entity in itself, unlike the American emphasis of kindergarten as primarily a vehicle to prepare the student for his future elementary school experience. As a general rule students from the upper socioeconomic classes tend not to go to kindergarten. Kindergartens cater to the children of working parents who must find a place to deposit the children while they are at work.

In the *Grundschule* (primary school) there is a rigid curriculum; each subject studied is customarily allocated a specific number of minutes a week. The subjects taken by the students in the *Grundschule* include reading, writing, basic arithmetic, geography, history,

German, and the basic elements of the physical sciences. The study of religion is compulsory for two hours a week.

The basic core for all the three types of Gymnasium is much the same: German language and literature, geography, history, mathematics, natural sciences, music, art, physical education, as well as religion for two hours a week. Students in each of the different Gymnasien also take additional course work in the areas of basic thrust of the Gymnasium he is attending. In the Realgymnasien (sometimes called the Mathematisch-naturwissenschaftliche Gymnasien) students study a great deal of mathematics and natural sciences along with two foreign languages. In the Humanistich Gymnasien (sometimes referred to as the Altsprachliche Gymnasien) emphasis is placed on the study of classical languages and literature, with Latin and Greek required in addition to one modern language. In the third type of Gymnasium the study of modern languages is emphasized. Courses in the upper levels of the Mittelschule tend to be general academic, with an emphasis on relating school studies to real life.

On the university, or Technische Hochschule, level the student studies principally from the courses offered by his Fakultät. He does not have to study other liberal arts courses if he does not so desire.

In Catholic elementary schools only required courses are offered. There are no electives. Only in the more advanced classes of the secondary school may a number of electives be taken. Extracurricular activities, such as are found in the United States, are not customary in German Catholic schools because the mandatory curriculum contains a heavy syllabus. Moreover, additional activities would result in a great burden on both pupils and teachers. An exception to this is the Catholic boarding schools which have extracurricular programs.

The curricular design in German schools of all types—government and Catholic—is typically subject-centered.

There is some, but not extensive, curricular experimentation in German schools. Much of the impetus for this experimentation comes from the example of the United States' schools in this regard.

Since the end of World War II no curricular innovations in government or Catholic schools have been introduced, except elective courses in the upper grades of secondary schools. The usual source of curricular innovations is the government educational authorities. Teacher-pupil planning is most unusual.

The syllabus is rigidly regulated in all German schools. Tight curricular structure is a hallmark of German education. Each school year a certain number of topics must be covered. Catholic educators see no reason to draw up a special Catholic course of study for Catholic schools. They regard the customary interschool course of study as good, but they stress the fact that where it is appropriate and meaningful the topics covered are interpreted from the Catholic point of view. Thus there are no specific Catholic curricula and no Catholic course of study; however, there definitely is Catholic interpretation of the subjects studied, as well as the development in the pupils of a Catholic *Weltanschauung*.

The curriculum is revised frequently; this is the task of the government authorities. There is no reason to consider the curriculum "bookish"; it is always adapted to reality and to the problems of life.

Instruction

In Catholic schools the same instructional methods are utilized as in non-Catholic schools. Lectures, discussions, and self-activity are the most heavily stressed. Since the teacher is the repository of knowledge, the students customarily learn by listening to him. Role-playing and panel discussions are rarely utilized. In most German schools, audio-visual media are available but are used very infrequently.

A new instructional methodology, biblical games, has been introduced and developed in German Catholic schools. In the lower grades of the primary school (from six to ten years of age) selected biblical actions are dramatized. Another innovation is the great variety and pictorial presentations for religious instruction.

In Catholic secondary schools the "open" discussion of problems is receiving more and more attention and popularity. Such discussions originate in pupil interests and, when utilized, often deal with controversial issues.

In the course of one class period and one school day, the teacher as a rule varies the instructional method several times. After a teacher-led discussion of approximately thirty minutes, the results are written down by the students. Or a five minute lecture by the teacher may be followed by a thirty minute discussion. And again, after an hour of discussion work, a period is devoted to individual student activity.

The specific distinctiveness of the Catholic school can be clearly seen from its textbooks. These are selected in such a way that the Catholic point of view becomes readily apparent.

A pupil in the lower grades of primary school spends about one hour on his homework. As he progresses in his grade level, the amount of homework increases so that by secondary school the typical pupil spends up to three hours and more. Because there are no classes in the afternoon, the pupil has much time at his disposal for his homework assignments.

Field trips, educational excursions, and so forth play a very minor role in a German school. There is only one Wandertag per trimester, and one or two one-day excursions per year. Just a few schools (especially secondary schools) have Schullandheime. In these rare instances each class has one week of instruction per year in this type of school.

Catholic schools in Germany have not yet developed their own unique methods of teaching and learning. Inasmuch as most Catholic schools are government operated, they take the prevalent government school methodologies as their models. One specific method, the Ganzheitsmethode (integrative approach), is especially emphasized in the Catholic schools. This method endeavors to present the teaching materials not in a systematic deductive way but in the form of Lebensganzheiten (totality of life). (To some extent these may be compared with the projects of the American project method.) The most important reason for the application of the integrative approach is the desire for universal continuity of curricular subjects. In this way a disparity in subject matter and philosophy is avoided, a dichotomy so typical of instruction in most non-Catholic and nondenominational schools where, for example, the biology teacher is a Materialist, the history teacher a Marxist, the geography teacher a Relativist, the German teacher a Christian, and so on. Integration of instruction, as Catholics understand it, can be guaranteed only by the Catholic faith of the teachers.

Motivation in German schools is not highly developed. What there is generally occurs in the lower schools, which students must attend under the compulsory education laws. Since students do not always go to these schools voluntarily, some German teachers believe that motivational devices are in order. Admission to the Gymnasium and the university is greatly desired by the students; hence at these levels the teacher does not utilize motivational devices to any noticeable degree, since attendance is prima-facie evidence of the student's inner motivation.

Social academic competition is not stressed in German schools. There are no honor rolls, dean's lists, and so forth in German schools. Rather, German students are encouraged to work as hard as they can to actualize their full academic potential.

Evaluation in the elementary school is left up to the teacher. In the Gymnasium, evaluation is carried out first by the teacher's impressionistic assessment of the student's learning achievement and second through formal tests. These tests are not standardized tests, nor are they given by the state, but they are teacher constructed. The *Abitur* examination, given at the end of the *Gymnasium* studies, is a state examination. If the student passes the *Abitur*, he at once receives this special kind of high school diploma and also gains automatic entry into the university. At the university level there are no major examinations at the end of each course. The only examinations are those which come at the completion of one's university studies. To be eligible to sit for these examinations, the student must have participated in selected seminars and received a seminar certificate indicating successful completion of seminar work. Critics of the German university system believe that evaluation should be more continuous, since under the present system a student stands or falls on the basis of only one set of examinations, and that given at the very termination of his university studies. These critics note that such continuous evaluation would eliminate the present sorry state of having German university students spend much of their first two years or so in the beer halls, while they reserve the last years for cramming their studies so as to pass the final set of examinations.

Report cards are given at midyear and at the conclusion of the academic year in all schools below the university level. There are no report cards or the like at the university level, since there are no major examinations until the completion of one's university studies. The marking system is customarily on a 1 to 6 scale, with 1 being the highest mark. The marks 5 and 6 are customarily considered as failing marks. Rarely are there any teacher comments on the report cards.

In the private and government-operated German Catholic schools, supervision of instruction is generally performed by specially designated government school inspectors. The reason for and the goal of this supervision are the guarantee of a level of equality of all schools of the same type. If school inspectors from the government visit non-government-operated Catholic schools it is not to ascertain the extent of Catholicity in these schools, but to determine the effectiveness of the teaching and the general educational progress. The school supervision by the government is particularly geared to preventing the hiring of incompetent teachers for such private schools. In former times, when the teachers in private schools were paid less than their counterparts in government schools, the private schools often accumulated a "negative selection" of teachers. Today the government is attempting to obviate such a deplorable situation.

School supervision by the government is, in the main, quite liberal for government and Catholic schools alike. The school inspector does not consider himself a detective sleuthing for mistakes; instead he regards his position primarily as an adviser to the school and the teachers. The German Catholic Church is quite satisfied with the present government supervision of instruction. From a practical standpoint, supervision is more of an indirect control than a direct one. Government supervision is performed principally on two occasions: (1) at the final examinations; (2) at the examinations of young teachers who have not yet been given permanent status and who still must pass their second (practical) state board examination (the first examination is mainly theoretical).

The Program of Religious Education

Elementary school children (six to ten years of age) have about four hours per week of religious instruction, and intermediate and high school pupils (ten to eighteen years of age) have from four to six hours weekly. In the course of the twentieth century a very vivid methodological innovation has been introduced into Catholic religious instruction in Germany. This methodology is characterized at present as follows. Religious teaching must have a kerygmatic orientation. In this way the pupil gains a clear understanding of the Word of God; at the same time he grasps the fact that religious instruction is not unrelated matter but rather a knowledge of life which should integrate all branches of instruction. Whereas a few decades ago bible and catechism instruction were rigidly separated, today's methodology attached great value to the bible-oriented approach to the teaching of catechism. Thus religion is not an abstract and deductive subject; it proceeds from the pupil's life. In the German type of catechesis, illustrations have come into great vogue. Much is being done to shape religious instruction according to the pupils' needs and desires.

There are various forms of catechesis—song catechesis, picture catechesis and liturgy catechesis, for example. Biblical games also form part of the pedagogics of religious instruction, particularly for pupils in the ten to fourteen age bracket. The older the pupils, the more the open, all-class discussions of religiolife problems become a part of the program of religious instruction.

Classes for First Holy Communion and Confession as well as for

Confirmation are held in close cooperation between school and parish. Usually every Catholic teacher in a Catholic school has received the *missio canonica* from the bishop and hence is approved by the hierarchy to conduct classes in Catholic religious instruction.

Religion teachers in German Catholic schools are of three distinct types, regular classroom teachers, parish priests, and full-time religion teachers of both sexes. The professional preparation in religion teaching of these three groups—and thus the level and quality of religious instruction—differs widely. A teacher at a Catholic elementary school takes courses in Catholic theology and catechistics (one to two hours weekly per semester) at a teacher-training college (*Pädagogische Hochschule*) for six semesters. Following this he takes an examination. If he passes the examination, he receives the *missio canonica*. A *Gymnasium* teacher studies Catholic theology for about ten semesters at a university. In addition, he takes four semesters of pedagogy, including methodology of religious instruction. Training for full-time female teachers of catechetics is being offered at various institutions, either at a university or in seminaries for pastoral assistance.

In theory the Church requires the same quality from all religion teachers. In practice, however, the professional preparation for the *missio canonica* lasts only a few months for many religion teachers. Parish priests working as part-time teachers of religion usually have a background of only two semesters of pedagogy and catechetics, and a practical training of but a few months before they teach religion in school. At present the professional preparation of religion teachers is considered generally inadequate.

In some German dioceses the regular classroom teacher conducts the class in bible, and the priest teaches catechism and liturgy. The current trend is toward having merely one catechist for each separate class.

The state of religious education in German Catholic schools can only be understood if it is constantly kept in mind that in these schools religion is considered not merely as a subject like all others, but rather as an integrating element for all classes, even for the so-called "neutral" subjects.

After the Nazis came into power, denominational schools were abolished. A few years later religious instruction was largely forced out of the regular curriculum in government schools in order to purge them of the Church's influence in the educational system. It is small wonder, then, that after 1945 the Catholic Church (as well as the Protestant) gave top priority to the reestablishment of conditions as they existed before the Nazi regime. The occupation forces were agreeable to the reintroduction of religious instruction into the curriculum. Difficulties arose in several zones, however, when the Catholic Church proposed to center the entire curriculum in specifically Catholic schools around the religious principle. The *Fundamentals of School Organization*, published in 1956 by the Association of German Catholic Teachers, stated: "In spite of the rapidly changing times, the entire educational system must be geared toward providing the pupil with a solid attitude toward the truth." (Cf. Bochum.) Further, "The Catholic faith as the power which instills meaning into all aspects of life is the motivating element in all educational work." (Cf. *Grundgedanken.*) Such statements are of great significance for educational policy, inasmuch as the Church alone is entitled to determine the content and goals of all subjects in a denominational school; there are no "neutral" zones in the curriculum. *Episcopal Principles for School and Education* (1956) elaborates on the principle of totality and unity:

The treasures of Catholic faith and morals in the history of the Church and of the saints, in the liturgy, in the cycle of the ecclesiastical year, as well as in Catholic tradition—these treasures must be extensively conveyed to the pupils. The continuous nurturing of sacramental life and of prayer ought to constitute the primary task of education. Every child should be under the religioeducational and formative influence of the school as a community. This Catholic educational ideal can be realized only in a Catholic school.

If this concept is carried to its logical conclusion, then Catholic parents may not in good conscience send their children to a nondenominational school. Notwithstanding, many parents, teachers, and politicians have not declared themselves in agreement with the exclusiveness of the principle of religious entirety. But the Church cherishes the hope that each of the faithful will arrive at this conclusion about education; after all, no one is compelled to be a member of the Catholic Church.

If this concept is applied to the elementary school as the common school, then the Church could not be content to operate a school as a *res profana*. Indeed, a Catholic elementary school is truly, on the one hand, a school for all the children of the state; on the other hand, it is at the same time a school for those who will grow to be the children of God, and inasfar as its educational happenings transcend the zone of politics (acclimating to the good of the commonwealth) into the zone of metapolitics. Some persons, Adolf Heuser, for instance, stress the importance of the "indwelling" of God in the Catholic school. (Cf. his *Die Katholische Volkschule*.)

This line of reasoning is an impressive example of the Church's claim to primary authority over the school whereby the former powers of the state are greatly curtailed. Here also the supranational and global structure of the Catholic Church reveals itself, a structure which can be criticized only for its isolationism if the national community is considered as the highest form of community.

The influence of ecclesiastical, that is divine, power in the Catholic schools can best be illustrated by the modern Catholic view of religious instruction. Religious education is an integral part of the curriculum and is thus subject to pedagogical-didactic laws and to the art-science of education; simultaneously it is part of metapedagogy since it is a form of direct pastoral care, the proclamation of the Word of God. God imbues powers and intentions into the school which, for the most part, cannot be grasped and controlled by man, and which reduce greatly the significance of the political aspect of the institution "school." (Cf. R. Padberg, "Religionsunterricht," in *Staatslexicon*.)

Catholics around the world and in Germany have become aware of the problem of whether infusion of relgion into all aspects of the school can be achieved at all in accordance with the principle of comprehensiveness, *if* the existence of the "Church as diaspora" in a democratic society is held as a value. Further, if such religious penetration is possible, how can it be achieved in the concrete? The existence of totalitarian regimes, in East Germany, for example, has brought many theologians and educationists to the conviction that a distinction must be made between a maximal ideal (penetration by religion) and a minimal standard for a Christian living in the secular order. It is possible to live a Christian life if the young people are educated not only in purely Catholic or Christian schools, but also in those which bear the mark of secularization. Be this as it may, the desired educational goal remains the proclamation of the Word of God, spiritual counseling, pastoral care, and a sacramental life. (On this point, see articles by Wilhelm Weskamm and Gustav Siewerth in *Kirche als Diaspora*.)

Since permission to teach religion is granted by the bishop of the respective diocese, he or an episcopal advisor on schools and religious education retains the power to supervise and control religious instruction. As a rule the *missio canonica* given to an individual teacher is valid only for a few years. After the expiration of this period, the teacher is invited to attend a short inservice course in catechetics, usually lasting for a week. If at the end of this inservice course the teacher is adjudged ready to continue teaching religion, he receives a permanent *missio canonica* appointment.

Until a few years ago, several dioceses in southern Germany required a special practical religion examination in which a deputy of the bishop would visit a teacher to observe him conduct a class period in religion. By this device the quality of the teacher's instruction was ascertained; if the quality was deemed less than adequate, the supervisor indicated the weak points and offered suggestions for improvement. Today, however, such supervision is no longer exercised because it is believed to be a violation of the basic principle that the teacher works independently with the Church's trust. This confidence, it is felt, might conceivably be destroyed by inspections which are not properly motivated and implemented. Supervision via observational visits of religion classes has been replaced by annual workshops lasting a week or even a day. During these workshops the Catholic teacher of religion receives information about new developments in theology and catechetics. Virtually every diocese releases a full-time catechetical expert to organize and implement these workshops. This type of voluntary inservice education is utilized by government-operated Catholic schools as well as by Catholic private schools usually conducted by religious institutes.

Religious instruction in a German Catholic school is not an isolated entity; rather, there is a close connection between catechesis on the one hand, and religious exercises on the other. Once or twice a week teachers and pupils attend Holy Mass as a body or as a class. Both private and government-operated Catholic schools have at least one obligatory Mass during the week for all pupils and teachers, from 8:00 A.M. to 8:45 A.M., which is part of the school day. On another morning during the week (usually before school starts) a special Mass is held for the faculty. School begins and ends every day with a prayer. Several years ago it was the custom at many private Catholic boarding schools to have compulsory daily Mass for all pupils; at present voluntary Mass attendance prevails in all Catholic boarding schools. Monthly Confession is provided for all pupils. The traditional pattern of having separate school Masses on Sundays is fast becoming obsolete because it is felt that on Sundays the child should attend Mass with his family.

Religious exercises in a German Catholic school constitute an integral and essential part of religious instruction. However, many pupils no longer attend Mass once their compulsory schooling is completed. Such a lamentable state of affairs is clearly an indication of the narrow correlation between pressure to participate in religious exercises and actual attendance at Mass. The problematic nature of this correlation is gradually becoming widely recognized. Indeed, at the age of fourteen, a pupil in Germany has the right to choose his own religion; he cannot be forced to retain the religion of his parents.

Unfortunately no research data are available on the effectiveness of Catholic school education in Germany. Only very few attempts have been made to determine the number of pupils who voluntarily go to Sunday Mass after they have finished school (from fourteen to sixteeen years of age). In the opinion of specialists, the percentage would seem to be the same as that for the Church attendance of their age group in general. It is highly probable that only 20 to 40 per cent of nominally Catholic youths regularly attend Sunday Mass and receive the Sacraments after age fourteen to sixteen. Thus the impact of Catholic schooling, at least on this area of their lives, may be questioned.

Nevertheless, this does not adequately describe the results of a Catholic school system. It must be noted that a certain residual ethical formation remains. Certainly it is difficult to say how this ethical foundation may be concretized; thus, for example, despite their Catholic school experience, the majority of Catholic youth regard premarital sexual relations as normal.

It cannot be maintained that graduates from Catholic schools in Germany are better prepared for college or for white-collar professions than those from other schools. Nor can it be proved that graduates from Catholic schools are better Catholics than those from non-Catholic schools.

In former decades the educational standards of private Catholic schools conducted by religious institutes were regrettably lower than those of government-operated schools. At present, this charge is no longer valid.

Private Catholic boarding schools are still criticized as allegedly ghettoistic rather than broadened in their educational thrust. It is also alleged that these schools present a one-sided view of the world since they purportedly indoctrinate their pupils only with the official Catholic viewpoint, sheltering them from other modes of thought. Many of the graduates from these schools, it is claimed, completely sever their relationship with the Church.

The so-called "parochial school principle" is still valid for the

government-operated Catholic primary schools in many German dioceses. School district and parish are identical, and the school building
is usually located close to the parish church. For several years the principle of parochial schools has been regarded as in jeopardy. A major
explanation for this is that in rural areas many primary schools with
one to three grades are being abolished and replaced by central, consolidated primary schools serving pupils from several parishes. In some
places the founding of new central schools is leading to the disappear-
ance of Catholic schools because central schools are often financially
viable only if pupils from various religious denominations attend them
together.

In certain large cities the parochial school principle is also being
discarded in the upper grades of primary schools because these grades
also are being centralized; the reason for this is that a majority of the
pupils do not remain in the elementary school after the fourth grade
but switch over to secondary schools.

At the elementary school level there sometimes occurs integration
of the religion class with the activities of the parish. However this is
not true at the secondary level. The alleged reason for this is that
students at this level come from different parishes, and hence it is
difficult to relate the activities of the religion class with parish life.

It is still customary for the teachers in Catholic elementary
schools—if they are parochial schools—to play an active role in parish
organizations. However, the number of these teachers is continually
dwindling. Further, a large proportion of Catholic teachers are not
convinced that school and parish districts should be identical.

Student Personnel
and Guidance Services

Pupil personnel and guidance services such as are prevalent in
American schools do not exist in German Catholic schools. In this
context the following facts bear mentioning. First, in private Catholic
boarding schools (principally secondary schools) the priest does not
only fulfil his immediate tasks as a priest, but also serves as mentor,
tutor, and adviser. Second, many pupils in government operated
Catholic schools (which are not boarding schools) belong to Catholic
youth organizations. These pupils participate in the activities of the
club at least one afternoon or evening per week. During vacation periods they often make trips and go camping with their group. Members
of Catholic youth organizations are primarily secondary school stu-

dents; only a very few are from the elementary schools. A mere 15 per cent of all Catholic secondary school pupils belong to Catholic youth organizations. This percentage is distressingly low. Third, an important element in school discipline, especially in secondary schools, is shared student responsibility. This constitutes a special German variety of pupil self-government. In this area there are no differences between Catholic and non-Catholic schools. Fourth, the influence of priests on the religious guidance of the pupils is not very significant, probably because most Catholic schools are not immediately under the direction of the Church and are government-operated schools. Religious guidance is purposely considered nonobligatory in the private and government-operated schools. Religious guidance is in the nature of an invitation open freely to all, an invitation many pupils do not accept.

There is no standardized testing program in the German school system.

Corporal punishment is forbidden in German schools. Suspension or expulsion from school is permitted; in practice, however, these punitive measures are seldom used. Because of the strong obedience to parents which characterizes the typical German schoolchild, overt misbehavior in the school is not particularly widespread. Where it does occur, however, the pupil might be detained after class to do some punishment. In more severe cases warning slips are sent to the parents, who in turn administer their own form of punishment to their offspring. The teacher is a powerful authority figure in the community and consequently commands the respect of the students. In Germany the teacher is considered always right and the student always wrong; consequently misbehavior in class is at a minimum.

Shortly before pupils graduate from elementary school they engage in a "religious week," a sort of retreat during which they are prepared for their future religiolife decisions. Similar programs are followed for graduates from secondary schools (*Primanerakademien*) to prepare them spiritually and intellectually for their study at the university. At Catholic, and also at many neutral secondary schools, a "religious week" is held almost every year in which, among other things, problems in sociosexual development are treated.

The Staff of the Catholic Schools

Priests, brothers, sisters, and laymen are on the staff of private Catholic schools in Germany, chiefly in secondary and vocational schools. Catholic teachers are on the staff at government-operated Catholic schools; with virtually no exception these are lay teachers.

Some private Catholic schools are finding it very difficult to hire a sufficient number of lay teachers. Since there are not enough clergy or religious to staff these schools, laymen must be employed. To be sure, some private Catholic schools have a preponderance of laymen on their faculty.

The same government-regulated preservice program governs the professional preparation of teachers and other staff personnel at all German schools, Catholic and non-Catholic. Candidates for elementary school teaching attend a teachers' training college (at the university level) for three years after having passed the high school graduation examination (Abitur). (The Abitur is required of all students who wish to matriculate at a German university.) After three years at the Pädagogische Hochschule there is another three years of preparatory internship training during which the young teacher conducts some classes. Concurrently he attends professional pedagogical seminars one afternoon per week, or one or two days per month, to improve further his professional skills. Secondary school teachers receive their education at the university for about four to six years. Following this, there is a two-year internship period during which the candidate teaches half the regular teaching load. Prälat Dr. Hubert Fischer, like others, contends that during their professional preparation at the university the prospective secondary school teachers are imbued with the spirit of a liberalism which does not do justice to the Catholic ethos of freedom. Many educators who are responsible for the free Catholic schools have frequently come out in favor of a special professional preparation which would supplement the regular secondary school teacher-training program.

A teacher is promoted to the rank of principal of a school on the basis of two criteria: first, pedagogical and administrative abilities, as demonstrated on the job; second, an examination for the principalship conducted by government authorities. As a rule, teachers aspiring to become principals of Catholic private schools must also take this type of examination.

Professors in German universities are of two types, professor ordinarius (full professor) and professor extraordinarius (something less than full professor, yet with professorial rank). All German universities are operated by the government, and professors are paid by, and responsible to, the Minister of Culture. The position of privat dozent is a university teaching position, but the person occupying this position must seek his own sources of income, as he is not paid a salary by the university, that is the government.

Academic freedom for teachers in Germany exists to a high level since all teachers receive a distinctively academic preprofessional preparation, which is not the case in many other countries. Notwithstanding, the teachers at private Catholic schools pledge themselves in writing to practice freedom of teaching in consonance with the moral and religious doctrines of the Church. Only very rarely does a case arise whereby the Church places a limitation on the freedom of learning and of teaching.

There are no Catholic universities in Germany. Consequently the teacher-training colleges are the only sectarian-oriented institutions of higher learning at the university level. Great significance is attached to the guarantee of freedom of learning and teaching at these *Pädagogische Hochschulen.*

Many German Catholic lay teachers are members of the Catholic teacher organizations, the Association of German Catholic Teachers (predominantly for male teachers, but also for female teachers in elementary schools, and the Association of German Catholic Women Teachers (for female teachers in all types of schools). There are other smaller organizations for Catholic teachers of religion and for teachers in Catholic vocational schools.

German Catholic teacher organizations are affiliated with the Federation of Catholic Educators, which is a member of the World Association of Catholic Teachers, the *Union Mondiale des Enseignants Catholiques* (UMEC). Catholic teachers in Catholic as well as in neutral and nondenominational schools are members of all the Catholic teacher organizations of the appropriate type.

Unfortunately there are no exact statistical data available on the number of Catholic teachers in Catholic schools who are members of non-Catholic teacher organizations. Nonetheless it may safely be assumed that at least 60 per cent of the Catholic teachers do not belong to Catholic teacher organizations. Unhappily, many Catholic teachers do not belong to any teacher organization at all.

The Parents
and the
Catholic School

The very basis and foundation of the Catholic school system in Germany have always been the right of the parents. Notwithstanding, a very fundamental change in the educational policy of German Catholicism vis-à-vis parental responsibility in Catholic schools has recently taken place. This change consists in the transformation from a purely juridico-political understanding of the right of parents to a primarily theologically and pedagogically motivated concept of parental authority. This important change, not often understood by some of the more superficial critics, has jettisoned pure legalism for a deeper educational and religious *raison d'être*.

Following the end of World War II, Catholics had to insist that the Nazi formulae for parental rights in education be scuttled, and that a purely juridico-political modernization of parental responsibility be initiated. The First Law for the Organization of the School System in North Rhine-Westphalia, promulgated on April 8, 1952, is still widely regarded by German Catholics as a model piece of legislation adapted to that era. This law, which was greatly influenced by the work of Christine Teusch, Bernhard Bergmann, and Josef Hofmann, is noteworthy because it introduced the concept of "educational community," that is the unity of school, family, community, and state. Thereby a reformative concept highly prized since the days of Peter Petersen was introduced into the educational enterprise. This concept was legalized and made mandatory for an entire *Land*. It is a moot point, however, whether or not the opportunities inherent in this law have thus far been utilized sufficiently for the actualization of parental responsibility in the school. Nevertheless, a legal precedent has been set for the assertion of the parents' primary responsibility for the entire education of the child, including his education in school. In this 1952 North Rhine-Westphalia law, it is specifically stated that "The educational path of the child is determined both by the wishes of the person in whom the right of education is vested, and by the talents, aptitudes and abilities of the child. . . . Together, parents, teachers, and pupils of a school form the school community."

German Catholics consider education of and within the family as a prime political issue. "The education for responsibility to State and Church and other social institutions begins in the family," in the words of Menziger in his article in *Arbeitstagung Saarbrücken*.

The actualization of parental rights and responsibilities presupposes that type of education of parents which at once acquaints them with education in its entirety, which gives them a realistic picture of the school system, and which enables them to evaluate properly their own pedagogical activities conducted within the family circle so as to improve this phase of their offspring's education. Seminars for parents and schools for mothers have become permanent institutions of Catholic adult education. Both are increasing steadily in importance and in standards. Today parental responsibility in education is no longer usurped by the clergy. In the words of Josef Grüb, "Parents have the prime task of actualizing their own responsibility. Christian parents have the duty to bring their own educative mission into conformity with the Christian concept of education." (Cf. *Grundsätze Katholischer Schulpolitik.*) These views correspond with those of Protestant experts. Thus, for example, Ernst Steinbach, a theologian from Tübingen, regards the school as "an original function of the home which, via the division of labor, attains independence." To Steinbach, education "opens the young people's eyes to their intellectual position, their stand before God, i.e. faith. Education is therefore essentially always religious in nature and formally oriented toward a certain creed." (See his *Zur Neugestaltung der deutschen* Schule.)

To the same degree that the primary authority of the parents in matters of school and education is emphasized, the authority of the state in education is deemphasized.

Most, if not all, German schools below the university level have an association of parents. In some cases parents have a definite voice in certain regulatory policies of the school. Thus, for example, the parents' association might take care that no more than two quizzes are given to the students per month or that all tests must be announced beforehand.

Responsible authorities in the German Catholic Church have recently been advised to refrain from stressing too highly the role played by those Catholic parents who consciously prefer the denominational school system. Whether this percentage is identical with that of the actual church-goers is unknown. (Cf. Bernhard Linke's article in *Schule und pluralistische Gesellschaft.*)

Although it has long been held that the educational potential of Catholic parents can be increased through the education of these parents, there is still a great gap between the ideal and the reality, between furtherance and fulfillment. (Cf. Gustav Siewert, *Elternhaus, Familie und Schule als Erziehungsgemeinschaft.*)

In the days immediately following World War II, there still remained the ideal of the old type of Catholic family whose educational concepts strongly mirrored patriarchal traits, the prototype of Linke's "active family." This concept viewed a large family not as a social burden but as a fulfillment of the meaning of marriage. But today the notion of marriage and the role of the family are portrayed much more dynamically and attractively. The introduction of parental rights into the educational sphere has also offered new impulses to the juridico-political and moral theological revision of the rights of parents, as Josef Mandl has noted. (In *Das Elternrecht nach der natürlichen und übernaturlichen Ordnung*.) The constitutional lawyer, like the culture-politician, cannot help but incorporate the factual pedagogical and ethical potential of the parents into what Wilhelm Geiger terms "legal considerations concerning the relationship between parents and school." (In *Festschrift für Anton Betz*.)

As far as the application of the rights of the parents in the school is concerned, Catholic experts are not suggesting that the parents "take over the school" or that they question the competence of the teacher, the school's pedagogical structure, or the state's role in educational matters. Catholic authorities are certainly concerned about making sure that the rights of parents are taken seriously. Such rights, as Geiger has noted, include the right to initiate and direct questions to the school and the right to be informed about the achievements and the structure of the school.

Catholics, Protestants, and all other groups in Germany are encouraged by Article 6.2 of the Constitution regarding the rights of parents. It is unfortunate, however, that while Catholic and Protestant points of view were being defined more clearly and compared with each other, heated arguments relating to the "arsenal of cultural, political, and fratricidal strife" as well as accusations of "political dogmatism" and "denominational one-sidedness" were hurled about. (On this final point, see Paul Fleig, *Elternrecht in evangelischer Sicht*; the most important study of the Protestant viewpoint is perhaps that of Stein, Joest, and Dombois, *Elternrecht*.)

Special Educational Problems Facing Catholic Schools in Germany

The most serious problem currently facing the German Catholic school enterprise is the fact that many Catholic parents are no longer convinced of the significance of a Catholic government school in its own right. Added to this, these parents also reject the parochial (private) Catholic schools in favor of non-Catholic nondenominational schools. Above all, many parents desire a Christian nondenominational school, that is a school for students from all Christian denominations. The crisis is aggravated by the fact that in many places—especially in rural areas—parents do not even have a choice between Catholic and nondenominational schools.

Sometimes the erroneous impression that the German Catholic Church wishes a kind of school monopoly is projected. But no monopolistic claim is advanced, at least theoretically, by the Catholic Church in Germany.

Over and above the foregoing, several other special major educational problems in the Catholic school system in Germany demand attention.

A first major problem is the elimination of the educational deficit among German Catholics. It was not until after 1945 that German Catholicism began to avail itself of certain specifically democratic, cultural, and educational nature opportunities, the right of equal access to educational facilities, and the support and promotion of the gifted, for example. (As Lutz has noted, relatively little open democracy in school matters existed in the Weimar era.) After 1945 equal access to educational opportunities and support of the gifted were encouraged by forward-looking elements within German Catholicism in order to overcome the age-old educational inferiority. To be sure, between 1910 and 1930 a few men like Karl Muth, Hermann Platz, Georg Schreiber, and others attempted to instill in the German Catholics a desire to attain equality in educational and cultural matters. But such efforts had no widespread effect. By 1945 there were numerous indications of "educational inferiority" of German Catholics. In the postwar era, the law granted Catholics, like all other groups in a democratic state, free access to all professions and, therefore, to prestige positions and areas of influence. Notwithstanding, the percentage of secondary school graduates who are Catholics, the number of Catholic students at the university level, the percentage of Catholics in positions of leadership—in the diplomatic service, in management, in business and industry, in education, and in the higher echelons of the military—is not commensurate with the percentage of Catholics in the total German population. Indeed, since 1960 German Catholics have been openly talking about the "Catholic educational deficit" as an established fact. Karl Erlinghagen, S.J., one of the chief students of this phenomenon, lists the following as some of its causes: a type of nineteenth- and twentieth-century politics which is hostile to the Church; the inferior social position of most Catholics, for whom it was impossible to attain leading positions in politics, in the universities, in business, and in cultural activities during the days of the Prussian ascendancy when "unity of throne and altar" was maintained in the Protestant sense of the term; finally, the ingrained Catholic distrust of inclinations toward the intellectual life, caused in no small part by its *Weltanschauung*, and the hostility of the universities toward the Catholic way of thinking during the nineteenth century and the early twentieth century.

Since 1960 Catholic educationists and other intellectuals have increasingly emphasized that it is not because of some factor inherent in Catholicism that Catholics are suspicious of culture and education. But this is countered by the argument that religions often have innate cultural factors; for example, the Calvinist doctrine of predestination of the elect (*Calvinistisches Sendungsbewusstsein*) instills a strong inner drive for higher education and indeed imparts an elitist thinking to all educational considerations. Be this as it may, it must be noted that even in a democratic society, legal and social structures are not necessarily equal in all respects. According to law, Catholics are entitled to pursue any kind and level of education and to rise to any position; yet there are unwritten laws within certain elite groups which serve as a barrier. Ingroup elitist milieux often wish to preserve themselves from infiltration by an outgroup. German Catholics believe that these unjust unwritten laws are inconsistent with the democratic ideal. Consequently prominent Catholics working with Catholic organizations have launched an educational and cultural offensive to overcome the educational deficit among German Catholics. Some measures in this direction include appeals to parents to send gifted children to institutions of higher learning; the advocacy of the so-called "second road" to education; the establishment of new Church-affiliated secondary schools; concern for increased opportunity for continuing education in rural areas; support for gifted students through foundations (*Stiftungen*). The *Cusanuswerk*, established in 1955, offers financial, moral, and intellectual assistance to exceptionally qualified students. Such promotion of talented young people presupposes that Catholic parents, particularly those from lower socioeconomic classes, will change their own attitudes toward education, culture, and the intellectual life. All too often are Catholic parents content for their children to remain in their own class; motivation toward betterment is frequently not as high as it should be. The educational alienation of some German Catholic parents means that children, including the academically gifted, are not sufficiently exposed to a family milieu encouraging educational aspiration. Consequently there is an increasing demand for "quiet facilities," for rooms (often at the parish center) in which children from such families can do their homework under supervision in an atmosphere conducive to learning. A 1964 workshop of the Central Committee at Münster declared that "German Catholicism must make every effort to create an 'atmosphere of challenge' in which educational assistance for the individual becomes the concern of everyone."

Even today educational quietism among the lower strata of the Catholic population maintains that eternal salvation is not determined by either education or success in life. These German Catholics reject the notion that education, as Franz X. Eggersdorfer emphasized in the 1920's, can be "a realization of salvation in the child" and therefore, indeed, is so concerned.

Catholic parent and family organizations ought to endeavor to make clear to parents that concern for a truly adequate education which affords optimal opportunity for growth of their children's talents is indeed an apostolic task. Catholics who are in positions of national, cultural, or educational leadership should interest themselves in the support and the promotion of gifted students. (See F. Pöggeler's article in the 1964 *Ordo Socialis*.)

There is considerable indication that "educational reserves" among the Catholic population of Germany are still more abundant than those among the Protestant population. Thus the intensive promotion by Catholic associations of institutions of the "second road" to education, as well as institutions concerned with vocational continuing education for adults is vital. For instance, the German Jocist movement is demanding with increasing urgency the establishment of a regular annual and paid "educational vacation." (Such an educational vacation was pushed through the Belgian legislature by the Belgian Jocists and Belgian Catholic trade unions.)

Finally, all efforts to overcome the Catholic educational deficit are intimately connected with whether or not German Catholics will succeed in achieving "equal access to educational opportunities." Thus Bishop Dr. Pohlschneider, an authority on matters of educational policy, stated publicly that at least in the realm of private (free) schools the opportunities are still not equal: "The Constitution and laws guarantee the right to establish free schools. But for years these institutions have been deliberately kept small and treated like legally inferior stepchildren, in that, contrary to public schools, they are denied necessary government assistance. . . . At times one even gets the impression that certain groups fear that under the conditions of equal opportunity the achievements of such educational institutions would surpass those of the public schools." This accusation, directed toward the legislatures and educational administrators of the various Länder, is perhaps the strongest concerned with democratic educational policy voiced by a Catholic authority since the end of World War II.

A second major problem concerns the participation of German Catholics in the reform of the German school system. It is a demonstrable fact that any person or group striving to influence cultural and educational policy in a social structure must engage in educational reform and planning. In recent years it has been asserted that Catholic educational policy in a democratic Germany is not sufficiently oriented toward planning and reform; further it is claimed that the whole Catholic educational policy is conservatively and/or reactionarily oriented. In the opinion of the present writer, such an allegation is far too sweeping and hence does not reflect an accurate assessment of Catholic efforts to renew the educational system creatively. Credit must be given to German Catholicism, due to its recognition of the "social question," for having entered into many secular spheres concerned with educational policy as early as the nineteenth century. The close connection between educational and social policy has been a characteristic trait of Catholic educational policy for a long time. From the late nineteenth century to the present, the great social encyclicals of the popes have become the touchstones of German Catholic educational policy, as Paul Fleig has conclusively demonstrated. (See his article in the January, 1962 Katholische Frauenbildung.) The educational programs of the German Jocist movement and of the German Kolping Foundation which appeared in 1965 are among the most important contributions to the educational policy of present day German Catholicism. Apropos of this, the 1964 Stuttgart Memorandum of the 80th German Catholic Congress, as well as the 1964 educational program of the Association of Catholic German Women Teachers must also be mentioned. The fact that German Catholicism has worked out several important educational programs raises the question of whether Catholicism should push through one compulsory program on the basis of the "uniformity" of its policy. How catholic would such a program be? No matter how much the programs mentioned agree in principle, each nevertheless emphasizes certain special objectives; thus, for instance, the Jocist program stresses a paid "educational vacation" together with the demand that the school evolve from a morning-session school to an all-day school

(*Ganztagsschule*), a proposal presently rejected by other Catholic associations and institutions. The program of the Association of Women Teachers understandably emphasizes modernization of the education for girls and women.

One should not form the wrong impression that the uniformity of Catholic educational policy suggestions is excessive. There was considerable debate over the Stuttgart Memorandum before a statement agreeable to all parties was reached. For example, the German Kolping Foundation severely criticized the original draft, objecting that "the particular situation of the education of girls and women, the requirements of education for old people and . . . the different stages and forms in professional and adult education" would not find "the attention which they deserve [in the Stuttgart Memorandum]." In the Kolping declaration, religion and art are emphatically treated as educational concerns, whereas business, technology, and politics are mentioned only in passing.

In surveying the different Catholic educational programs, one rarely encounters something that has not already been suggested in one form or another by non-Catholic groups. Indeed, one gets the impression that in Catholic proposals, certain existing educational demands are merely approved; Catholicism must encounter considerable difficulty in approving the existing demands. "A Declaration Concerning the Restructuring of the German School System" promulgated by the German bishops in 1960 contains, aside from a cautious assessment of the necessity for reform, an equally cautious admonition to be circumspect. The fact that the highest ecclesiastical authority in Germany shows more prudence toward reforms than do individual professional education associations is understandable and indeed justified; it is, however, unfortunate that those professional associations which are more qualified and more competent to advocate educational reform have developed scarcely any new ideas of their own. It seems that since 1924 German Catholicism has in educational policy been so preoccupied with the single dimension of safeguarding an education in conformity with denominational principles, that there was not enough energy left for other equally worthwhile educational platforms. In retrospect one can also see that too much energy was spent on the criticism directed at the Bremen Plan of the AGDL, as well as that directed at the Skeleton Plan offered by the German Committee for Educational Affairs. The Catholic Association of Teachers was virtually the only German Catholic group which endorsed the Skeleton Plan, particularly the proposal to extend the elementary school over two additional years. A good many German Catholics have thus far not realized that the seemingly successful tripartition of the school system into primary, intermediate, and secondary schools originated as a counterpart of the former partition into three social classes and was not a result of pedagogical considerations. Yet the tripartite division has become a pedagogical pseudo dogma.

The German Institute for Knowledge and Education, technically an interdenominational group but in practice dominated by Catholics, has published a counterproposal to the Skeleton Plan, mainly in the area of culturo-educational policy. However, this counterproposal has not received too much attention. Even the Overall Plan for the Reorganization of the German Educational System has been accused by qualified critics of failing to add any new policy dimension. Yet this plan, since it deals with the entire school system, will be viable only if it is greeted with great enthusiasm by experienced people.

The strengths of the new Catholic educational plans and programs lie in their recognition of sound pedagogical principles; their weaknesses are in their lack of concrete suggestions for reform. It is fortunate that German Catholicism acknowledges that educational reform cannot come solely from structural changes in the educational system. Catholics hold that the educational structure must be determined by the content, objectives, and ethos of education. Thus the educational program of the Association of Women Teachers furnishes a good example of a Content Plan, which in this respect represents the opposite of the mere Skeleton Plan. The richer the content, the easier congruent structure is created. It remains questionable whether reform should be a permanent motivation in the educational system. Catholic spokesmen such as Heinrich Peter have rightfully pointed to "fundamental limitations of an 'inner' school reform." (See his article in the January, 1961 issue of *Österreichische Pädagogische Warte*.) An important limitation for reform exists where the Catholic believes he has found the true kind of faith and of education also; obviously those who hold a relativist view of life are more frequently interested in change. Yet it is a fact that as far as school reform and Christian school policy are concerned, Catholic experts most of the time have little more to say than that we make ". . . the school reform subservient to us in those realms in which this has its justification . . ."; which means hardly more than a "baptism" of prefabricated suggestions for reform which did not originate among Catholic thinkers. (See Karl Anton Ederer in *Die katholische Schule*, 1957.)

Since the Catholic *Weltanschauung* is laid down and codified more rigorously than the plurality of Protestant views, Protestantism can remain more open and, in Uhsadel's phrase, "more independent" in this respect than Catholicism. Because of this fact, the clarion call for more flexibility is heard repeatedly also among Catholic educational experts (for example, Hermanns' speech). The call for more flexibility is even extended to a more liberal attitude toward the non-denominational school, above all in areas where these schools are also the regular schools for Catholic children and hence cannot be circumvented. A testimony of genuine flexibility in German Catholicism's present cultural policy is offered in its concern with a broader, more universal educational political horizon than a "purely German one"; "the world-wide uncertainty—perhaps in regard to the developing countries—is more keenly heeded by Catholics than by other German groups." (See Paul Fleig, *Die Weltweite der Problematik*.) Fleig rightly demands an "education toward an intellectual offensive," toward increased cultural activity among German Catholics. Until statements which demand priority in cultural and educational policy within the context of political subjects are taken seriously, there can be little genuine hope for true, pervasive structural reform in education. (Of interest here is that in this respect German Catholicism is joining forces with the Christian Democratic Party. Cf. Josef Hofmann, *Kulturpolitische Aufgaben in der Sicht der CDU*).

A third major problem facing German Catholic education is the reform of the educational system in rural areas. This represents an urgent need since a large number of German Catholics live in rural areas. In 1953 German Catholics established a completely new and effective educational institution called the Rural Seminar. By the beginning of 1967 there were nearly 1000 such institutions throughout the Federal Republic. The purpose of the Rural Seminar is to inform rural adults, especially the younger generation, about the changing situation in rural life. The Rural Seminar hopes to educate rural dwellers; consequently sociological and pedagogical topics have primary consideration. (See Franz Pöggeler's article, "Das Ländliche Seminar" in *Erwachsenenbildung*.)

Since the end of World War II, German Catholics have established more rural schools for continuing education than has any other group. The primary objective of rural seminars and of rural schools for continuing education is not so much the introduction of the urban educational system into the rural school, but rather to furnish pedagogical self-help to the rural population (not only the farmers). It is true that a congruence between the progressive urbanization of the rural school and advanced educational structures has thus far failed to materialize. That the German bishops are vitally interested in a modern rural school can be seen from the 1963 Statement of the German Bishops Concerning the Question of Modern Rural Schools. The statement proceeds fron the following presupposition: "The secularization of all realms of life is a characteristic trait of modern society. Rural areas have not been excluded from this trend. Confronted with this destructive feature of the modern age, the school has to see that the rural child is educated in such a way that he will attain a religiously based independence and a mastery of life." The bishops' statement is not directed against reasonable forms of merging small village schools. But it does demand that denominational programs be guaranteed when such consolidations occur. Thus the statement rejects an a priori schematic centralization which has not been adjusted to local needs. Occasionally the bishops' statement has been labelled reactionary. However, it must not be forgotten that German Catholics have advocated flexibility in rural school reform, with the goal of providing within the one overall structure different forms of rural schooling. For example, as early as the nineteenth century German Catholics urged shared-time programs whereby several schools in a village would retain their separate identities but function as one, overall, cooperative unit. In this shared-time program, an individual teacher would teach major subjects in his parent school, while teaching an elective at the same time in the neighboring school, just as colleagues from these neighboring schools would also teach their electives at several other schools. Certainly such a solution presupposes a high degree of mobility and adaptability. German Catholics appreciate the fact that the upper levels of elementary school can no longer be conducted in an optimal pedagogical manner in small schools. Consolidated schools are an educational imperative. Catholic experts are also agreed that the question of smaller or larger rural schools is chiefly a matter of the availability of teachers. Thus, for example, the Catholic Oldenburg Teachers' Association sees clearly that it is impossible to "halt" the "process of secularization among teachers. . . . The association realizes that as this secularization progresses . . . serious consequences will manifest themselves in regard to staffing small rural schools."

Many Catholic parents in rural areas are no longer willing to suffer from poor school structure and organization for the sake of retaining an all-Catholic school.

A fourth major problem is the general area of supplementing the normal Catholic school system with a Catholic adult education program. Since World War II German Catholics have invested their greatest educational energies in the field of adult education. The fact that this development has not received sufficient attention within the context of German cultural growth as a whole is suggestive of much of Germany's attitude toward Catholicism. German Catholicism had by 1945 a rich tradition of adult education. Much to their credit, German Catholics have not simply revived old forms and institutions, but have created a series of completely new institutions. These include Church-supported schools for continuing education, rural seminars, social seminars, social institutes, seminars for parents, foundations for family education, seminars on Catholic doctrine, centers for education, schools for mothers, adult education academies such as Munich's celebrated *Katholische Akademie in Bayern*, and so forth. The effect of these institutions is equal to that of nondenominational schools for continuing education; indeed, it clearly surpasses the comparable educational activity of Protestantism. (Protestantism, too, has created new structures of adult education, such as the adult academy, which serve as models for the Catholic academies, such as the Catholic Academy in Munich.)

These new Catholic institutions comprise only one half of Catholic adult education; the other half is represented by the educational efforts of associations which today are more vigorous than before National Socialism. The pedagogization of Catholic associations may be considered as a genuine achievement of reform, because it places an association in the mainstream of fostering those educational opportunities which are the hallmark of a democracy. (Cf. Heinz Budde's article in the 1958 *Arbeitstagung Saarbrücken* and Franz Pöggeler's article in *Erwachsenenbildung*.) Adult education has been treated extensively at all Catholic congresses and workshops of the Central Committee from 1948 to the present. Adult education fulfills an important function for the growth and mission of the Church in that the Church and the world therein find new points of contact, particularly in the areas of politics, social life, and business. (Cf. Bruno Dreher's article in *Katholikentag 1956 in Köln*.) With the broadening and deepening of adult education, especially in social and political affairs, German Catholicism has reached an openness toward politics and society which formerly scarcely existed. Political and social education, education in marriage and in the family life are the focal points in Catholic adult education.

Through its adult education programs, in cooperation with certain associations such as the Jocists and the Kolping Foundation, German Catholicism has also developed new structures in vocational education. Work-study programs and correspondence courses have been developed for the workers. Closely connected with this is the so-called "second road to education" for working people. The expansion of Catholic adult education, especially after 1950, was viewed by certain cultural and political groups as unreasonable competition for the government-operated schools of continuing education. Therefore, these groups recommended that the adult education provided by the Church be limited to religious education. Despite this opposition, Catholic adult education has not allowed itself to be restricted unduly to this narrow concept of religious education, because religious education is not only a "subject" but also a principle permeating all the different areas of education. (Cf. Josef Höffner's article in Unsere Seelsorge, March, 1963.) Catholic adult education today has entered into a relationship of equal partnership with schools of continuing education. Indeed, Catholics are encouraged to make use of schools of continuing education; German Catholics do not see competition between Church and state in the area of adult education as an evil, since competition is of the essence in a democratic society.

The organization representing the many associations and goals within Catholic adult education is the Bundesarbeitsgemeinschaft für Katholische Erwachsenenbildung (Federal Study Group for Catholic Adult Education), founded in 1957. This association has utilized the Institut für Erwachsenenbildung (Institute for Adult Education) in Münster, a section of the German Institute for Scientific Pedagogy, for purposes of theoretical foundation and the training of salaried and nonsalaried adult educators. From 1953 the Institute has conducted two-year Adult Education Courses for adult educators from Germany and neighboring countries. In this way the Institute functions as a center for intensive professional education of adult educators which is at present unique in form.

The strong engagement of German Catholicism with adult education has increased considerably the maturity of laymen in a broad stratum of the Catholic population, which in turn has strengthened the general interest of Catholics in shared public responsibility to the Church, to the state, and to society.

A fifth major problem for German Catholic schools is achieving a sense of identity and distinctiveness. The three principles underlying the purpose of Catholic schools, as outlined briefly in the second section of this essay, will serve as a sketch for the following treatment. The first principle, it will be recalled, is that of doctrinal conformity of education. In contemporary German Catholicism, a major portion of the educational activity is directed toward the actualization of this principle. Catholic education begins with the presumption that the Catholic Church as a spiritual and ecclesiastical community has both the right and the authority to create structures and institutions of its own for all levels of the educational system; furthermore, that the Catholic Church possesses the wealth of qualifications to endow its educational institutions with values and goals; and finally, that education is not neutral, but rather is deeply influenced by decisions emanating from its total world view. "By its very nature, education is dependent on a system of values," states the 1964 Stuttgart Memorandum on Educational Policy. According to this memorandum, "education of Catholic children is best achieved in a Catholic school, since it is in this type of school that the personal values of Catholic man can be fully realized." In German Catholic thought, education based on doctrinal conformity fulfills the freedom of faith and conscience (which should be felt in all education) as well as the *Elternrecht* and the principle of overall totality and unity of education. But "also for the purpose of promoting a pedagogical competition in the educational system" a spiritual plurality of educational institutions must be available to all children, in the words of the Stuttgart Memorandum. The school advisor of the German episcopate in his 1964 *Brief an Eltern* described the Catholic school as "that school which is one with the family in dogma and in life, in belief and in religious knowledge, in prayer and in Mass, in instruction and in education. In the Catholic school all teaching is, as a totality, conditioned by Faith; it is a school in which the center is the Lord Who is deeply concerned with the salvation of man. This is the school which conforms to our conscience." Such a view is based on the concept that the Catholic way of life—which, incidentally, extends beyond national borders and is based on the cosmopolitan community of Christianity—should turn the school into a place for genuine reflectiveness. The comprehensiveness of the total *Weltanschauung* should be effected by offering a Catholic educational system which comprises all knowledge. (Cf. Franz Pöggler's 1958 article in *Grundsätze katholischer Schulpolitik.*)

In the pronouncements of the Church in Germany since 1945 various arguments have been raised to substantiate the principle of doctrinal conformity. The "Catholic Principles" of the Fulda Episcopal Conference (1956) base the right to doctrinal conformity on the *Elternrecht;* a recurrent theme in the Stuttgart Memorandum is democratic basic rights, such as freedom of worship and conscience as well as freedom of competition in spiritual life. All this does not imply that Catholics seek a privileged position; rather it is to emphasize that each group in a democratic society is entitled to schools which allow the principles of that denominational group to be instilled in its children. The consequence of this is, of course, a pluralistic educational system, one based on the multiplicity of systems of belief and thought, as opposed to a simplistic nondenominational school system. In the years following World War II the school controversy centered principally around the juridical and political phases of doctrinal conformity; in recent years the axis has shifted toward stress on the theological and pedagogical aspects of Catholic schools. Simultaneously the realization has grown that the development of faith must be made available in various types of institutions. (Cf. Günter Schulz-Benesch, *Vom Stil katholischer Schule,* and Franz Pöggeler's 1955 article in *Schriften der katholischen Akademie, Stuttgart.*)

Since in modern Catholic interpretation a school can only be called Christian if it is a "cell in the corpus Christi mysticum," the Christian spirit of a school can only be pneumatic; as such it can be guaranteed only by the Church, and not by the state. It is for this reason that it is more appropriate to speak of a Catholic school rather than of a denominational school. The latter is a legal term not a theological one. The Catholic Church, however, regards each school, whether Christian or a-christian, as a reflection of some kind of *confessio.* With this argument, the Catholic Church repudiates the frequent attempts to call its schools one-sided or narrow-minded. (See the pertinent writings of Thaddäus Siron, O.F.M., Adolf Heusler, and Josef Haffner.)

The second broad principle underlying the Catholic school's search for identity is the principle of pluralism. The recurrent attacks on the principle of doctrinal conformity (a principle which is valid for all levels of education including university and adult education) have prompted certain groups in the German Catholic Church to center intensive attention once more on the problem of spiritual (rather than simply social) pluralism. German Catholics do indeed consider spiritual pluralism (that is the variety of religious and spiritual ideas) a heavy burden on the German educational system. Yet at the same time the elimination of spiritual pluralism would inevitably result in a deterioration of spiritual life and a resultant loss of freedom.

Pluralism is valued as a constituent principle of a democratic society. Much in the same way that a democracy must provide for a multiplicity of political parties, so also must it insure that a plurality of spiritual ideas has a right to existence. To be sure, the existence of such a spiritual plurality must be within the framework of the state and contributory to the common good. These constitute the limits of pluralism.

In recent years a misunderstanding of the concept of pluralism has arisen from the interpretation of certain ecumenical movements generated by Vatican Council II. Some German Catholics have transferred their desire for unification of the separated churches to the area of education; these persons maintain that in the educational sphere a reunification should be effected by abandoning the denominational school in favor of the nondenominational school (in the Christian sense). Here looms the danger of indifferentism. The spirit of ecumenism cannot be achieved by an indifferent and passive attitude. Pluralism—insofar as it is experienced as a burden on the supraconfessional community—"can only be overcome by the individual within himself, and provided he is able to live and act in accordance with a uniform philosophy of life based on knowledge and conviction." These are the words of the 1964 educational program of the Association of German Catholic Women Teachers. The Stuttgart Memorandum of 1964 deals with the problem of pluralism from the constitutional viewpoint: "The democratic order in a pluralistic society requires that, in the establishment of an educational system, the individual's right to his personal development is recognized; that any creed is respected and that freedom of conscience is guaranteed. Any forced uniformity and monopolization of the educational system will contravene these basic rights." This statement refutes the traditional concept of a "principal school," that is the notion which holds that only the government school promotes the best kind of *Weltanschauung* in the state. It is from the vantage point of spiritual pluralism that non-Catholics can best understand the Catholic view of doctrinal conformity. Only that school system which allows the parents to choose from among denominational, nondenominational, and a-denominational (no religious instruction at all) schools is tolerant and democratic in the pluralistic sense. Only that school system is democratic which forms its foundation on these "three columns." Since 1945 the attractiveness of the "three-column theory" has sharply increased as German Catholics have found their ideal school system exemplified in the Netherlands. Also since 1945 German Catholics have rejected the accusation that separate Catholic schools violate the principle of social togetherness through their ghettolike isolation. As early as 1948 the denominational school was described as rooted in the "community of the people" and as subject to this broad community. The concept of the "nondenominational school" was reversed insofar as it was proved that the community of men, among themselves and together with God, which results from the common faith, is the most intense type of communalization in human society. (Cf. the 1948 work of Oswald Opahle, Else Schmücker, and Josef Mertens.)

Catholics have frequently criticized the higher ecclesiastical authorities for inconsistent policies for the actualization of the principle of doctrinal conformity and the recognition of the problem of pluralism. Thus the hierarchy demand denominational schools for kindergarten, elementary school, teacher-training, extracurricular youth activities, and adult education; however, the hierarchy strangely does not demand denominational secondary schools. This criticism of the German hierarchy is well justified. It may be rather for reasons of suitability that a denominalization of secondary and vocational schools has not been urged by the hierarchy. Even the majority of the Catholics would not yet agree with the Church for sectarian secondary and vocational schools. In this connection it might be noted that Bishop Dr. Pohlschneider, educational adviser to the German hierarchy, proposed the "possible establishment of a German Catholic university," with obvious reference to such institutions of higher learning in other countries. The objections voiced to the bishop's proposal were doubtless directed more against the practicality of establishing such a university than against the theoretical validity of the proposal.

The third broad principle underlying the Catholic schools' search for identity is the principle of freedom of education. Since the end of World War II the German Catholic Church has relied more heavily on the principle of freedom in its pedagogical and cultural demands than before 1933. Here also the German Church looks to foreign countries for models—The Netherlands, France, Belgium, and the United States. Liberté de l'enseignement is a cornerstone of Catholicism's cultural engagement. In the countries named, freedom of education does not only imply the right of the Church to establish curricula or teaching programs in its institutions; rather, freedom of education relies on a foundation which is nonexistent in the German Federal Republic, that is separation of church and state. In countries with separation of church and state, the government-operated schools are neutral or even secularized. Denominational schools are excluded from the government-operated school system; instead, these schools are established as independent church schools which are supported by the state financially and ideologically, as in The Netherlands. "Free" in this sense is therefore synonymous with "independent."

After 1945 German Catholics were very much attracted by the type of freedom of schools existing in such countries as The Netherlands. This may cause German Catholics to raise the question of separation of church and state. Many supporters of freedom of education, however, hope to block this separation because they wish to retain government-operated denominational schools. To what, then, does the ever intensifying clamor by German Catholics for freedom of education refer?

The German episcopate views this demand as having particular reference to "freedom to organize the educational system according to a total world view." In a critique of new "school reform plans" (although not specifically mentioned here, the Bremen Plan is clearly implied), the 1960 Fulda episcopal conference strongly maintained that a reorganization of the educational system can only be acceptable if in the restructuring the total *Weltanschauung* can be retained. Utilizing the motto "tolerance for Christians also," the school advisor of the German episcopate stresses that "we can only speak of genuine freedom if the State solemnly respects the personality of its citizens, and if it offers them concrete opportunities to actualize their personal and their family life according to their religious convictions."

German Catholicism does not desire a privileged status when it requests "pedagogical and cultural freedom"; rather, it desires that all citizens have the opportunity of this freedom. Only those ignorant of the modern Catholic concept can maintain that "Catholic Church" and "freedom" are contradictions in terms.

Freedom of education cannot exist in Germany so long as the parents "in various German *Länder* are not granted the rights of man to which they are entitled under the General Declaration of the United Nations; namely that even today in various German *Länder,* Christian parents are denied that degree of free exercise of conscience with regard to the education of their children which they had before the National Socialists came into power." (*Wandelt euch. . . .*)

German Catholics have recognized since 1945 that the Church's influence in education might increase at a faster pace than at any other time since the Enlightenment. Indeed, the Church's educational system might actually come to full bloom. It was also realized that models of foreign school systems could not be imported directly into Germany without encountering serious difficulties. Unfortunately the "liberal" (in the favorable sense of the word) basis and thrust of Catholic school policy have, since 1945, met with great lack of understanding by various other groups concerned with education. According to Catholic opinion, even Protestant educational thought still maintains an excessive preference for a unified school system. To be sure, throughout the entire new era of democratic school policy from 1945 to the present, the efforts of German Catholicism to inaugurate a fresh understanding of cultural and pedagogical freedom has not been greeted with appreciation even by Catholic teachers and parents. Many persons suspect that the demands for more freedom for Catholic initiative are merely a cloak for the Church not only to secure new influence in school matters, but also to pave the way for wider Church control over German education.

Many Catholics are quite willing to see the drive for pedagogical freedom restricted to the area of private schools. However, the present writer, in opposition to this limited view, agrees with Robert Frohn, who in his report of the 1964 *Zentralkomitee* wrote, "The principle of freedom of conscience must not be limited to certain aspects of the educational system but must penetrate the whole complex."

Regrettably, it cannot be denied that since 1945 the Catholic Church has not fully utilized its new-found educational freedom; for example, it has failed to establish its own secondary schools. Perhaps the only areas in which the Church has capitalized on its educational opportunities are those of adult education and out-of-school youth activities. In order to show that a greater Church initiative would also be fruitful in other educational spheres, it might be well to review some proposals recently advocated by Catholic educationists. The core of educational activity, especially in the school, is inherently free of government influence because the fundamental pedagogical acts (devotion, encounter, service, avowal, decision, and so on) are subject to personal action and hence cannot be enforced, organized, or controlled by the state. It is neither the task nor the prerogative of the state to judge the pros and cons of a pedagogical method, or to develop scientific curricular schemata, or to generate religious life. Because the Catholicity of a school can be guaranteed only by the Church, the juridic structure of a school (that is a public, government-operated school or a free, independent school) is of secondary importance. The degree of Catholicity of a school is not affected by the state's assembling nominally Catholic teachers and pupils in a school. (See the article by Franz Pöggeler in the 1959 book by Arndt, Geiger, and Pöggeler.)

Some German Catholics of stature have asserted that the most consistent type of Catholic school is that which is not supported by the state or by the community, but solely by the Church. The type of school would be decided on by parents and teachers alike—even at the risk of a decrease in the number of Catholic schools. In this connection, proposals for Catholic pilot schools have been made by educationists such as Erlinghagen (1946) and Pöggeler (1960).

The Catholic Church is realistically aware that the *modus operandi* of government-operated school districts will prevent securing a desirable measure of pedagogical freedom for public government-operated schools in the foreseeable future. It is a known fact in Germany that the avant-gardist schools initiating educational reform have largely been private schools. The conscience of a democracy, however, is not soothed by cultivating pedagogical freedom merely in private schools; in the long run educational liberty should characterize not only secondary, but also regular elementary schools as free Church schools. This has as yet not been legally possible. (See Christine Teusch's article in Paul Westhoff's book on the 1957 *Tagung* at Köln.)

Church authorities find that obstacles to the establishment of more Catholic schools lie partly in the lack of necessary permanent fiscal support and partly also in the shortage of teachers who are experienced in exercising pedagogical freedom and initiative. A new breed of teacher must be found, one who fosters pedagogical experimentation, one who possesses the ability to liberate the students to an expansive freedom, even a freedom which takes the form of opposition so typical of youth. (See the article by Hubert Fischer in the *Westhoff* volume.)

One of the most frequent atavisms of German traditional anti-Catholicism is the suspicion of a possible Church-enforced conformity of faith and freedom of the mind; in the past and at present the anti-Catholic polemicists have made many efforts to substantiate this thesis. (See the important book by Bishop Dr. Wilhelm Kempf.) In a 1956 publication by outstanding Catholic scholars and educators quite a daring attempt was made at popularizing the new Catholic ethos of freedom in education. Unfortunately this attempt was not received with enthusiasm by Catholic teachers, to say nothing of the cultural policymakers. Nevertheless there are indications that in the near future the striving for cultural and pedagogical freedom will remain the *Leitmotiv* of German Catholic cultural policy.

Selected
Bibliography

Arndt, Adolf, Wilhelm Geiger, and Franz Pöggeler. *Schule und Staat*. Studien der Katholische Akademie in Bayern, München. Munich: Verlag Karl Zink, 1959.

Erlinghagen, Karl, S.J. *Die Schule in der pluralistischen Gesellschaft*. Freiburg-Basel-Vienna o.J: Verlag Herder, 1956.

Fleig, Paul, ed. *Freiheit in Erziehung*. Herausgegeben vom Bund katholischer Erzieher. Freiburg: Verlag Herder, 1956.

Grundgedanken zur Gestaltung der Schule. Herausgegeben vom Verband der katholischer Lehrerschaft Deutschlands. Cologne, 1956.

Grundsätze katholischer Schulpolitik. Herausgegeben vom Bund katholischer Erzieher. Freiburg: Verlag Herder, 1958.

Heuser, Adolf. *Die katholische Volksschule*. Bochum o.J: Verlag F. Kamp, n.d.

Katholische Grundsätze für Schule und Erziehung. Erarbeitet von der Fuldaer Bischofkonferenz (Deutscher Episkopat). Herausgegeben von der Bischöflichen Hauptstelle für Schule und Erziehung. Cologne, 1956.

Pöggeler, Franz, ed. *Das Wagnis der Schule*. Die katholische Schulerneuerungsbewegung. Freiburg-Basel-Vienna o.J.: Verlag Herder, n.d.

Pöggeler, Franz. *Katholische Erwachsenenbildung*. Munich: Verlag Kösel, 1964.

Sacher, Wilhelm. *Die katholische Schule*. Innsbruck-Vienna-Munich o.J.: Tyrolia Verlag, 1954.

Catholic Education
in the Netherlands

by Jos. J. Gielen
and W. J. G. M. Gielen

A Short History
of Dutch
Catholic Education

The Republic of the
Seven United Provinces of Holland, 1579–1795

Catholic schools were not officially permitted during this period. Freedom of education was unknown. Anyone who desired to found a school needed the permission of the municipal government. There was no national school system. Each of the seven provinces and the larger cities had its own educational regulations.

Teachers were required to be members of the Reformed Church, even in the Catholic districts (Brabant, Limburg). Tight control and censorship insured that anything in conflict with the Reformed Church was banned from schoolbooks. In the Catholic districts, too, no "papist" books, statues, or rosaries were permitted, and teaching was not allowed to be suspended on "papist" holydays. In general, however, the actual practice was somewhat milder than the written law.

The Batavian Republic
and the Annexation by France, 1795–1813

The revolution of 1795 brought about the separation of Church and state. Nonetheless, freedom of education was not among the many liberties granted by the new constitutional regulations of 1798. Indeed, the law of 1806 required that no schools could be established without the permission of the government. In the government schools no doctrinal teaching was allowed. The teacher was, however, "to instruct the children in all social and Christian virtues." Only those books could be used which were on the approved list drawn up by the Secretary of the Interior. This list of books breathed the spirit of the Aufklärung and of an enlightened Protestantism. Private schools also were forced to use this list and could deviate from it only under certain conditions, by permission of the school inspector, for example.

School inspectors were responsible for the supervision of the teaching in both government and private schools, and there was virtually nothing which could be done without their approval. These inspectors doubtless did much to raise the standard of elementary education. Almost all of them were followers of the *Aufklärung* and thus remote from the world of belief and thought of Catholics and orthodox Protestants. Their meshing of school inspection and *Aufklärung* was a principal cause of the school controversy which ensued.

The School Controversy, 1813–1917

The Act of 1806 and its accompanying regulations were in keeping with the aims and policies of the "enlightened despot," William I, who came into power toward the end of 1813. He used these as a means to weld the Protestant North and the Catholic South (Belgium) into a spiritually homogeneous whole, living according to the ideas of the Enlightenment and freed from the fetters of the clergy. No school inspector was appointed who had not proven himself to be a follower of Enlightenment and rationalism. It goes without saying that the school inspector saw to it that candidates who adhered to orthodox doctrine failed in the interview which preceded the examination for teacher. No book which smelled of the musty air of clerical obscurantism was to be read in the schools. Permission for establishing private schools was granted only if the applicant had shown clearly that he was willing to go the same "enlightened" way as the government.

In Belgium the attacks of the king on the religious orders which governed the schools, together with the abolition of the seminaries, led to Catholic-liberal cooperation (Belgian secession, 1830).

About 1825 the Catholics in the northern part of the kingdom began to rebel against the king. The Catholics of that era still thought largely in terms of a cooperation between church and state, as before the French Revolution. Separation of Church and state was considered a revolutionary principle. Consequently Catholics at first did not seek the solution to their difficulties in founding their own schools, but rather in the reformation of the government school. Thus, for example, they proposed that if possible the government schools be divided into separate units for Catholics, Protestants, and Jews. Only when these attempts failed did Catholics seriously consider erecting their own private schools, a development which occurred in the early 1840's.

In 1848 freedom of education was formally incorporated in the constitution. Despite this liberal advance, a large number of Catholics remained supporters of the government schools. In 1878, however, when a new law threatened, in all kinds of devious ways, to suppress the private schools, Catholics rallied and vigorously supported their educational institutions.

It was the state policy of compulsory absolutism, together with a spirit of clerical liberalism, which alienated the Catholics from the government schools and caused them to found their own private schools. Correlative to this, Catholics began to realize the necessity of a close bond between school, Church, and family.

In 1889 the first Christian coalition government succeeded in securing a small subsidy for the private school for the first time in Dutch history. At that time many supporters of the private school were still fearful that a state subsidy and the conditions attached to it might hamper the freedom of teaching. However, the growing influence of the Christian political parties, as well as a more lenient attitude of the leftist groups toward the private school, settled this fear. In 1917 an amendment was added to the constitution stating that any private general elementary education meeting the legal requirements would be subsidized by the government at the same rate as government education. This became known as "financial equalization." The de Visser Act of 1920 spelled out the details of this clause at greater length. The Dutch bishops founded the Roman Catholic Central Bureau of Education, located in The Hague, with a view to effective cooperation in effecting the provisions of this complex act.

Secondary education, on the other hand, was regulated by an 1863 law which had provided for the possibility of state subsidy for private schools. Notwithstanding, Catholic secondary education did not flower until much later, the first school being founded in 1904. Catholic interest in establishing their own secondary schools in the early 1900's was given impetus by the conflict between the natural sciences and religion, a conflict which often caused schools to suspect both the study of the sciences and the preparatory training for it.

The Modern Period, 1917–Present

After the de Visser Act had become effective, private schools soon excelled the government schools. The economic crisis of the 1930's, however, had a very bad effect on the entire educational system, including the salaries of teachers and the number of pupils per class. Freedom of teaching was threatened during the years 1940–1945, when the German occupation demanded that teachers be loyal to the Nazi regime. This was strongly opposed by the Catholic schools under the leadership of the bishops. Toward the end of the war all schools were forced to close because of wartime chaos.

After the liberation vigorous attempts were made to restore the various kinds of schools. There were proposals for a revision of the entire Dutch educational system. These proposals led to new legislation, but the time was not yet ripe for a fundamental revision of pedagogics and didactics. Practical educational innovations after 1945 were directed by the three pedagogical divisions—government, Protestant, and Catholic.

Since 1920 financial equalization has been extended to all fields of education. The Catholic University of Nijmegen, founded in 1923, received its first state subsidy in 1947. By 1970 this will total 8.5 per cent. Nursery schools, training colleges, and secondary education currently enjoy 100 per cent state subsidization.

Developments since 1945 have shown increasing interference by the government in Catholic schools. With this the question has arisen whether freedom of education is perhaps at stake. A law has already been passed which opens some possibilities for experiment. Recently Catholics have begun to debate the advisability of maintaining private, Catholic, nongovernment schools.

The Aim of Catholic Education

An 1868 statement by the Dutch bishops declared that the aim of the Catholic school is to make religion a pervasive force in the entire school experience. Until 1965, however, no one had made a serious effort to answer the question of how such integration was to be achieved. The reasons for this are as follows: first, until 1920 Catholics were reluctant to go on for advanced education, fearing the quite common antireligious slant of university education; second, at the founding of the Catholic University of Nijmegen in 1923 didactics were completely neglected and only taken up seriously about 1955; third, the school controversy had as its express purpose the foundation and maintenance of private schools, especially as a defense against the anti-Christian influences of the government schools.

Until very recently a school was thought Catholic "of itself" if the teachers were Catholic, if it had a Catholic atmosphere, and if Catholic teaching methods and Catholic books were used.

The aim to offer a "protective milieu" necessitated by the circumstances was certainly attained in the past, but this goal has since become meaningless. Besides, excellent practitioners have always made a good Catholic *school*, although to accomplish this one was almost completely dependent on non-Catholic scholarly assistance (except that from Germany—Otto Willman, X. Eggersdörffer, among others, and from Belgium—the University of Louvain, for example).

Subsequent to 1945 the Catholic Center of Pedagogics has helped to solve the problem of the actual aim of a Catholic school. Yet The Netherlands is still very far from the realization of the stated aim of Catholic schools.

The Relationship between Catholic and Government Schools

Government Legislation Which Has Affected Catholic Schools

In 1848 freedom of education was included in the constitution "except for supervision by the government." Over and above this, as far as elementary and secondary education are concerned, freedom of education is granted to all schools "except for the examination of the proficiency and morality of the teacher, both to be decided by law." Catholics have never protested against these state limitations of freedom because education is an important factor in the commonweal entrusted to the care of the government. For the same reason Catholics also accepted the following constitutional rule: "education is the object of the continuous concern of the government."

"Supervision" and "concern," however, as well as the subsidy stipulations, have led the private school to model itself after the government school. This may have, and indeed in some cases has had, detrimental results. For example, the law binds all elementary education (and therefore private education) to the list of compulsory subjects named in Article 2, paragraph 1, of the Elementary Education Act. At the root of this article lies the rationalistic idea that knowledge can be divided into separate subjects. Consequently this rationalistic idea is also the standard for Catholic education. Another instance is Article 11 of the Secondary Education Act, which prescribes instruction in two modern languages for the first year, one of which must be French. It would have been better not to bind the (private) schools to this government preference for French.

Supervision and concern are carried out by means of the government school inspection. Among the tasks of the inspectors are to see to it that the law is observed and "to bring education to a fuller bloom." The way in which this is sometimes interpreted and put into practice has given rise to speculation as to whether there does not linger in the inspection of Dutch education the eighteenth-century idea that education *to its fullest extent* is fundamentally the business of the government. For instance, it has been proven that the legal obligation to draw up a schema for the activities in nursery school and to hand this over to the inspector gives the latter the opportunity to interfere with the pedagogic and didactic aspects of the private school. (Cf. Pelosi, *Vrij Onderwijs*, p. 156 ff.)

Comparison of Catholic Schools with Government Schools

In political debates on education great care is taken to insure that legislation gives the same opportunity for development to both government and private schools. Added to the inclination to make precise rules, even in small details, such equality causes the private school to make considerable sacrifices of freedom in order to enjoy state financial subsidy.

There is no basic difference in the standards of the government and private schools. Teachers in Catholic schools pass their examinations under supervision of a government delegate and do their work according to nearly the same legal regulations and with the same financial possibilities as their colleagues in the government schools. The stipulations of the Compulsory Education Act and those governing the admission to schools for secondary and university education apply in equal measure to both types of education. Although these regulations are not unfair, the fact remains that the private school has seen its autonomy decrease with the increase of its rights.

The Present Form of Catholic Schools in The Netherlands

The present school system for The Netherlands is embodied in the constitution and acts, and applies to government and private schools.

It is therefore impossible to talk of a "Catholic school system" in The Netherlands. "Freedom of direction" and "organization" are guaranteed; nonetheless, in addition to government inspection, the Catholic schools are subject to an episcopal inspection, and have their own Central Bureau, their own organization of school boards and teachers, and their own Center of Pedagogics.

Nursery schools are governed by the provisions of the Act of December 8, 1955. There are government and private nursery schools, both financed in exactly the same way. Education on the basis of a play-and-work plan is given to children who are at least four years of age. For each group of forty children, one teacher may be employed. Supervision is exercised by a head inspectress, by a few other inspectresses, and by one inspector; government schools can, in addition, call upon a municipal inspection through the Court of Mayor and Aldermen.

Elementary education has its own separate organization. The Elementary Education Act of 1920 signalled the end of an important and bitter phase of the school controversy. The Act itself begins with a few general regulations, including among other things, a list of compulsory and facultative subjects, control of the morality of teachers, admission of pupils, and the kinds of elementary education insofar as it is completely or partly financed by public funds: (a) standard elementary education, given in schools with six consecutive grades; (b) advanced standard elementary education, continuing for two years beyond the six years of standard education; this level is intended for children who do not apply for secondary education but who are still of compulsory school age when leaving the sixth grade of the standard elementary school; (c) continued education, also lasting for two years, for those who have passed the compulsory school age limit (both advanced standard elementary education and continued education are comparatively rare); (d) advanced elementary education, comprising at least three but usually four years of education linking up with the sixth grade of the standard elementary education; (e) special elementary education, given in schools for children who are mentally or physically retarded, or who cannot follow ordinary education regularly and fruitfully for some social reason, or whose behavior makes it necessary for them to receive a special education.

When the Secondary Education Act (see below) takes effect, the schools described under (c) and (d) will also find their exact place therein under the headings of elementary and secondary general education (LAVO and MAVO).

The chief supervision rests with the minister of education, who is aided by head inspectors and inspectors. Local school supervision is exercised by the Court of Mayor and Aldermen; the city council can employ a staff of inspectors if required.

Secondary education in The Netherlands falls under the jurisdiction of the Secondary Education Act, which has come to be known as the "Mammoth Act" or Cals Act (after the minister who passed it). This act does not go into effect until 1968.

Secondary education is subdivided into four types: (a) preparatory academic education; (b) general secondary education; (c) technical training; and (d) other forms of secondary education.

Preparatory academic education consists in preparation for education at a university or at an institute of technology. The length of a student's stay in this type of secondary school is normally six years. There are three basic kinds of preparatory academic secondary education—*gymnasium, atheneum,* and *lyceum.* The *gymnasium* offers the traditional classical education. In the "A" branch the primary emphasis is placed on the classical languages, whereas in the "B" branch the principal stress is on mathematics and the natural sciences. The *atheneum* replaces the *hogere burgerschool* (a nonclassical secondary school) insofar as it prepares for studies at a university or an institute of technology. Here also there is a branch "A," which stresses economic and social subjects, and a branch "B," which emphasizes mathematics and the natural sciences. The *lyceum,* which has an undifferentiated first year, is a combination of the *gymnasium* and the *atheneum.*

General secondary education (AVO) is subdivided into advanced, intermediate, and elementary secondary education (HAVO, MAVO, LAVO). The HAVO (advanced secondary education) aims at broadening the student's general education, as well as preparing him for those careers for which no education at a university or institute of technology is required. At the same time it is intended to be a basis for higher professional training. In the HAVO the old *hogere burgerschool* of 1863 can be recognized in its original form, that is as a preparation for public functions and definitely not as a preparation for the university or for the institute of technology. The HAVO education is offered at schools with a five-year course. In addition to this, it is possible for a student to follow up with three years of education at a preparatory academic school, or with four years of intermediate secondary education, or with two years of preparation for a teacher-training college with an "HAVO top." It should be noted that included among others under HAVO are the secondary schools for girls, which until 1968 were governed by the Secondary Education Act of 1863. The MAVO (intermediate secondary education) is given at schools with a four-year course. These schools may also have a branch with a three-year course. (See also above under elementary education.) The LAVO (elementary secondary education) is given in the first (and sometimes also in the second) year of schools devoted to elementary technical training. (See also above under elementary education.)

Technical training is given at the following types of educational institutions: schools for technical training; domestic science schools (for girls); schools of agriculture; trade schools; schools of economics and business administration; teacher-training colleges (nursery, elementary, and secondary school teachers); schools of social pedagogics (youth work, adult education, social planning, personnel management, public health and sports); and art schools. In the first five of these, and in the seventh also, there are three separate levels, advanced, intermediate, and elementary technical training. Elementary technical training consumes three or four years, whereas intermediate and advanced training take a maximum of four years. Teacher-training colleges have a first and a second course (the first is a two-year course, the second a one-year course), preceded by a two-year preparatory course. (See also HAVO.)

The various types of secondary schools could be united into a comprehensive school. The first year of day schools for preparatory academic and advanced and intermediate secondary education is an undifferentiated one. In the *gymnasium*, Latin could easily be added. This is the so-called "bridge year." Until the new Secondary Education Act goes into effect, the Secondary Education Act of 1863, the Domestic Science Act of 1919, the Teacher-Training Act of 1952, and other legal regulations will remain in force.

Other forms of secondary education include training facilities for young people beyond the compulsory school age.

The following types of education do not come under the Mammouth Act: the apprentice system (courses related to practical experience on the basis of an agreement between employer and legal representative of the apprentice), special secondary education, military education, and so forth. For these there are or will be special legal regulations.

Supervision of secondary education resides in the Minister of Education, who is assisted by the Inspector General of Education, head inspectors, inspectors, assistant inspectors, and advisors. For agricultural education, however, supervision is the province of the

Minister of Agriculture, aided by a director, head inspectors, and inspectors.

University education is an entity unto itself. The Act of 1960 distinguishes between universities and institutes. A university has at least three faculties which must always include the medical faculty or the faculty of mathematics and science. There is one central inter-faculty which must always include philosophy.

Besides the old State Universities of Leyden, Groningen, and Utrecht, there are several other types including: the Institutes of Technology of Delft (1905), Eindhoven (1959), and Enschede (1964); the Municipal University of Amsterdam (1876); the Catholic University at Nijmegen (1923); the Dutch Reformed University at Amsterdam (1887); the Catholic Institute of Economics at Tilburg (1927); and the private nondenominational Institute of Economics at Rotterdam (1913). The State Institute of Agriculture at Wageningen (1917) falls under a separate law.

The Catholic University of Nijmegen dates back to 1923. It comprises the central interfaculty of philosophy, the faculties of theology, law, medicine, mathematics and science, arts, social sciences (psychology, sociology, pedagogics), and the interfaculty of geography and prehistory. The Institute of Economics at Tilburg has also a faculty of law and a faculty of social sciences.

A compulsory education law was passed later in The Netherlands (1900) than in other countries, primarily as a result of the school controversy. When private schools were still few, compulsory education would have forced parents to send their children to government schools.

Compulsory education starts as soon as the child has reached the age of seven and ends either at the close of the school year in which he will have completed at least eight years of attendance or reaches the age of fifteen. The requirement of compulsory education can also be met by receiving private tutoring at home. This occurs very seldom.

Cases of unauthorized nonattendance at school are reported by the headmaster to the school inspectors. They are then investigated by the local committee for the prevention of nonattendance after which, warranted by the inspectors, the judge passes sentence.

Control Structure of the Catholic School System

As of January 1964, 1736 of the 2850 Catholic elementary schools were administered by a parochial church or public assistance council,

418 by a religious institute, 480 by a foundation, and 216 by an organization. Administration by an organization is more common in secondary education and technical training. The large religious institutes, foundations, and organizations have their own administrative staffs; for the remainder, many headmasters of elementary schools are still charged with administrative, financial, and other responsibilities.

The aim of these administrative bodies is the promotion of the interests of the administrators and teachers in the particular field of education covered by the organization. The Catholic organizations enumerated are governed by the *Nederlandse Katholieke Schoolraad* (Catholic Education Committee of the Netherlands). This committee, which is composed of the organizations mentioned, is the highest authority in Catholic education. The aim of the committee is to promote Catholic education in the Netherlands.

At the base of the episcopacy's adoption of the statutes amended in November 1965 is its recognition of the personal responsibility of each individual Catholic. If the episcopacy should find that the Education Committee is not sufficiently concerned with the quantitative and qualitative level of Catholic education, it has the right and the duty to compensate for these shortcomings by founding schools itself, or by promoting the foundation of schools, or by otherwise issuing specific educational mandates.

Catholics in The Netherlands presently enjoy a reputation throughout the world as highly progressive and forward-looking in almost every respect. The entire question of the evolution from clerical control to lay control of Dutch Catholic education clearly represents a concrete illustration of this fact. The Catholic Education Committee was founded in 1910 as a committee of clergy. But by 1959, on the initiative of the episcopacy, the bishops gave a share of their control over Dutch Catholic schools to laymen. This was effected by allowing part of the membership of the Catholic Education Committee to be appointed on the recommendation of the Catholic Parents' Committee and of the Committee of Contact (an organization composed of Catholic teachers' unions). In June 1966 a major reform of the twenty-two-member Catholic Education Committee took place, whereby three of its members were representatives of the Catholic Parents' Committee, sixteen were delegates of the Catholic Parents Committee, and only three were nominated by the Dutch bishops. Thus the primary responsibility and control of Catholic education in The Netherlands has been transferred from the episcopacy and clergy to Catholic laymen, with the bishops' role being

self-restricted to the direct pastoral ministry. In transferring the episcopacy's principal authority over Dutch Catholic education to laymen, Cardinal Alfrink said in an inspiring address before the Catholic
Education Committee: "Today your bishops lay the full responsibility
for the well-being of the Catholic schools on your shoulders; on you,
parents; on you, teachers; on you, school boards; who together constitute our faithful, over whom we have been appointed as helpers
and whom we wish to serve with our pastoral care." Consequently
control of Dutch Catholic schools has been transferred to lay people,
with the bishops as their helpers, as the American National Catholic
Welfare Conference news service so aptly put it.

Some Statistics on Catholic Schools

According to the census taken in 1960, 40.4 per cent of the population was Catholic, 37.6 per cent Protestant-Christian, 3.6 per cent
a non-Christian religion, and 18.4 per cent had no religion at all.

The following table presents pertinent comparative data on government and Catholic schools at all educational levels.

No data for either government or Catholic schools are available
for the following crucial categories: median student enrollment at all
school levels; median pupil class size at all school levels; median school
size of schools in rooms at all school levels. Nor are there data indicating the percentage of Catholic students at each level of the government school system.

For elementary schools the law calls for a minimum of 1040 clock
hours per year to be spent in school. There are no regulations deline-
ating the precise distribution of these hours over the course of the
week. However, custom and practical reasons have led to the following: four full school days of two sessions each (9:00 A.M. to 12:15
or 12:30 P.M.; 1:30 P.M. or 2:00 P.M. to 4:00 P.M.) and two half
school days (Wednesday and Saturday mornings from 9:00 A.M. to
12:30 or 1:00 P.M.). In 1962 the free weekend was adopted as standard practice in business and industry; since then the free weekend is
becoming increasingly popular in elementary schools (but not in the
higher school levels, except in the universities). With the introduction of the free weekend, attempts by the schools to fulfill the legal
requirements commonly occur in one of two ways: either by making
Wednesday a full school day or by a combination which extends both
the afternoon session of every full school day and the Wednesday
morning session as well. Each class period customarily lasts thirty to

Statistical Summary, Catholic and Government Schools*

	1963			1920, or 1925, or 1930*		
	Government schools	Catholic schools	Other schools	Government schools	Catholic schools	Other schools
Total schools nursery	1,055	1,797	2,048	238 (a)	809 (a)	1,515 (a)
Total schools elementary	2,917	3,782	3,816	3,591(inc)(b)	2,431(inc)	2,203(inc)(b)
standard elementary	2,464	2,863	2,451	3,325 (b)	2,175 (b)	1,939 (b)
continued elementary	346	461	445	266 (b)	256 (b)	264 (b)
domestic science	107	458	920	n.d.	n.d.	n.d.
Total schools secondary	167	154	99	117 (c)	27 (c)	27 (c)
gymnasia	31	46	9	34 (c)	11 (c)	6 (c)
hogere burgerscholen	75	45	31	70 (c)	11 (c)	21 (c)
girls secondary	61	63	61	13 (c)	5 (x)(c)	—
Total universities	21,699 (y)	9,878 (y)	319 (y)	—	190	
Total students nursery	95,274	196,745	142,989	36,154 (a)	83,168 (a)	41,728 (a)
Total students elementary	448,805(inc)	890,972	498,432(inc)	473,524(inc)(b)	439,261(inc)(b)	323,997(inc)(b)
standard elementary	367,468	618,626	409,307	446,397 (b)	422,833 (b)	313,298 (b)
continued elementary	81,337	105,797	89,125	27,127 (b)	16,428 (b)	10,699 (b)
domestic science	n.d.	166,549	n.d.	n.d.	n.d.	n.d.
Total students secondary	36,314	45,546	19,598	18,900	2,676	3,302
gymnasia	6,717	12,450	693	3,465 (c)	939 (c)	674 (c)
hogere burgerscholen	22,721	18,682	11,159	13,616 (c)	1,423 (c)	2,628 (c)
girls secondary	6,876	14,414	7,746	1,819 (c)	314 (x)(c)	—
Total universities	n.d.	n.d.	n.d.	n.d.	n.d.	n.d.

	1923	1933	1943	1953	1963	1966
Total enrollment Catholic University of Nijmegen	190	560	725	1,475	4,575	6,000

*(a) 1925 figures
(b) 1930 figures
(c) 1920 figures
n.d. no data available, or data for this chart did not exist at the time indicated

inc. incomplete data
(x) total of all nongovernmental schools, Catholic, Protestant and non-denominational
(y) 1958–1959 figures

forty-five minutes. There are three vacation periods in the course of the year: five weeks in the summer, ten days at Christmas, and ten days at Easter. There is also a short two- or three-day holiday at Pentecost. In the near future all vacation periods will be lengthened slightly; the summer vacation period will then start at the beginning of July instead of at the end of July.

For secondary schools there is no law regulating the total number of hours which must be spent in school. However, there are indirect regulations, since it is necessary to comply with the directives issued by the Minister of Education with respect to the curriculum. These directives stipulate the number of hours per week to be devoted to each subject. This varies from school to school, according to the type. The total number of hours per week is about twenty-six to twenty-eight for the lower grades, and thirty-two to thirty-four for upper grades. The directive prescribes the minimum; every school may exceed the minimum but this is possible to a very limited extent only. The new act, operative in 1968, divides the obligatory class hours into a number which must be spent studying required subjects (a number noticeably lower than the pre-1968 figure) and a number which must be devoted to elective subjects. The summer vacation period lasts six to seven weeks; Christmas vacations, ten to fourteen days; Easter vacations, ten to fourteen days; and a brief two to five day holiday at Whitsuntide. Recently there has been a trend to consolidate the two school sessions on Mondays, Tuesdays, Thursdays, and Fridays into one long session extending from 8:30 A.M. to 2:00 or 2:30 P.M., with two short recess periods of ten and fifteen minutes, respectively. Each class period lasts forty-five to fifty minutes (fifty to sixty minutes in the technical training schools).

Officially, university studies for the *candidaats* degree take two to four years, with two to four years for the *doctoraal* degree, depending on the area of doctoral concentration (for example, law two plus two, education three plus two, classics four plus two).

University lectures are forty-five minutes long. Officially, the summer vacation period lasts from the second Saturday in July to the third Monday in September; Christmas vacation from the Saturday immediately preceding Christmas to the third Tuesday following that Saturday; the Easter vacation from Spy Wednesday until ten days thereafter. In reality lectures are only given for twenty-six to twenty-eight weeks, and hence the university academic year lasts only that length of time. For many years this half-calendar year was merely a tradition; now, however, it has become a necessity because of the overburdening of many of the professors and their staffs, which has resulted from the fantastically rapid growth of university education. In 1957, 26,700 students were enrolled in the university; by 1963 the number had jumped to 43,000. Indeed, predictions of the number of students who will be enrolled in a given future year have always been exceeded by the actual enrollment figures.

After World War II efforts were made both to repair quickly the school buildings which had been partially destroyed, and to erect new schools at a pace fast enough to keep abreast of the burgeoning enrollment. In most instances temporary schools were set up for this purpose, sometimes of the wooden prefabricated kind used in Scandinavia. There was also a frightening shortage of residential housing. Consequently construction of new and up-to-date school plants received relatively little attention. Since the late 1950's, however, increased attention has been given to school construction and architecture, albeit only on a small scale. Assistance in this came from the Information Center for School Construction in Rotterdam, which studied the new opportunities and the latest advances in school architecture to be in the best position properly to implement these advances when the time proved ripe. Such implementation became possible, on a limited scale at least, with the increasing annual amount of money made available for school construction: in 1960, $60 million; in 1964, $100 million. In 1960, 551 schools were built, with 3045 classrooms and 109 gymnasiums, and 717 classrooms and 13 gymnasiums were modernized; in 1964, 637 new schools were erected, 158 new gymnasiums were built, and 635 classrooms and seventeen gymnasiums were modernized.

Legal regulations governing school construction cover the size of the classrooms (three cubic meters per pupil), the amount of lighting from the windows, playgrounds, and athletic fields, the location of the school (no obstruction within 200 meters, safety with regard to traffic, and so on), offices for the principal and staff, toilets and cloakrooms, ventilation, heating, acoustics, and artificial lighting.

There are two main types of new school buildings: the corridor-type school and the hall-type school (in 1957 the respective costs of these two types were $7500 and $8000 per classroom). The former type arranges for classrooms and offices to be built off the corridors (mostly long); the latter type creates more free space. New trends in school architecture, happy to say, are more inspired by pedagogical principles than was true in previous times. For example, the traditional benches are often replaced by tables and chairs; in addition to the regular classrooms, there are special rooms for such creative sub-jcets such as crafts, drawing, and painting, and secondary schools may add an auditorium for assemblies of the whole school. Two per cent of the total construction costs may be spent on aesthetic decoration such as sculpture, paintings, stained glass windows and the like.

Financial Support of
Catholic Schools
in The Netherlands

The government bears the financial burden of almost all Dutch education. The amount of money it gives to the government schools is the basis for determining the extent of the state subsidy for private schools. Thus a financial equalization with regard to public funds is obtained for both government and private education.

The Elementary Education Act of 1920, in accordance with the new constitutional provisions of 1917, provided for financial equalization of both government and private general elementary education, that is standard elementary education. For a private school to be eligible for subsidy, it must be on a par with that of the comparable government school. In appraising the caliber of the private school, the freedom of private education with regard to choice of teaching materials and employment of teachers must be assiduously respected. Further, the constitution decrees that in *all* subsidized private education at every level, from nursery schools through the university, freedom of control must be observed.

The Elementary Education Act of 1920 makes the following specific stipulations. An incorporated body must formally request the city council to compensate for the expenses incurred with the foundation of a private school. The application must be accompanied by a statement that upon its opening the school will enroll at least the minimum number of pupils required by law. This enrollment figure varies with the number of inhabitants of the municipality and with the type of elementary education (standard, advanced, or continued) to be given in the school building. The statement must be signed by the parents of the children who will attend the new school. In addition a bond in the amount of 15 per cent of the founding costs must be deposited in the municipal treasury. A description of the building, the number of classrooms, for instance, must also accompany the application.

If the application complies with the legal requirements the city council *must* act on it favorably. Thus whenever the legal requirements are satisfied, the subsidy is insured automatically. In subsequent expansion or rebuilding, the city council has the right to decide whether by approving the application "the normal demands to be made on the giving of elementary education would be exceeded."

The cost of maintaining a school building is paid for by the government, provided the school fulfills a number of conditions pertaining to the administration of the school, the curriculum, the time schedule, the minimum number of teachers, the administration of attendance at school, the salaries and the legal position of the teachers, the school building, the number of pupils attending the school, and the filling of vacancies.

Subsidization for the material cost of operation is calculated on a per pupil basis determined annually by the city council for government education. The subsidy never exceeds the actual expenses incurred.

Apart from the various types of subsidy mentioned in the preceding paragraphs, there remain additional costs which the municipality must bear, the salaries of special subject teachers and transfer costs, for example.

The government also pays the salaries of teachers. The number of teachers is determined on the basis of a teacher-pupil ratio fixed by law. Municipalities are forbidden to allocate any money to private elementary schools except under those stipulations covered in the law. However, this restriction does not apply to special elementary education for retarded children, since there are still no legal regulations governing this category of school. Subsidies for special elementary education are based on the Royal Decree of October 28, 1949. If specified conditions are fulfilled, these special schools are entitled to a state subsidy consisting of the compensation for the salaries of the principal and of the statutory teachers. Moreover, if the municipality owns such a school, the regulations for compensation for operating costs are the same as in the case of standard elementary education. On the other hand, if the municipality does not own such a school, the city council then sets a reasonable sum.

Financial equalization also obtains for nursery schools, albeit the constitution demands this only in connection with elementary education. In contrast to elementary education, the government pays not only the salaries but also the founding and the operating costs of nursery school buildings. To become eligible for state subsidy nursery schools must meet the same requirements that apply to elementary education. The bond is higher—20 per cent of the founding costs—since nursery schools enroll pupils who are still under the compulsory school age. If a municipality allocates more money to its nursery schools than is being compensated for by the government, then the municipality must pay the difference to private education.

The new Secondary Education Act (Cals Act) also provides for government subsidization for private schools at this level. The plan of support is described as follows. The Minister of Education draws up annually a Plan of Schools for those secondary schools which are eligible for compensation from public funds in the next three calendar years. The minister takes as his point of departure those requests for admission to this plan which have been sent to him by or on behalf of city councils and school boards. It is possible to submit a so-called division plan, for example, for all Catholic secondary schools.

In any case, if an examination reveals that the final class of a given school will be attended by at least the number of pupils required by law, such a school will be accepted as part of the minister's Plan of Schools. This applies to preparatory academic education (VWO: *gymnasium, atheneum, lyceum*), to general secondary education (HAVO: advanced, intermediate, elementary), to elementary technical training, elementary domestic science education, and to elementary and secondary agricultural training. The minister has not yet deemed the time ripe to fix the number of pupils in schools other than those listed. However, he does have the power to incorporate them into the plan, a power for which he is accountable to the parliament. It is always possible to appeal ministerial decisions on education to the Crown.

Private schools can be erected and maintained on a private budget without resorting to the Plan of Schools procedure. This is a result of freedom of education. Of course this possibility is not open to government schools, because they must be maintained exclusively by public funds.

The calculation of the subsidy is not uniform for all schools. One example will suffice to illustrate this point. With the minister's approval, the compensation for the founding costs of a private school for preparatory academic or advanced general secondary education includes the interest and redemption of loans contracted to cover these expenses. Operating costs and salaries are subsidized on the basis of the government's expenditure for its own schools. If a municipality spends more on its schools than the government compensation, it must pay the difference to the private schools within its territory.

The Academic Education Act gives "equal opportunity for development" to government and private universities and institutes. Private universities and institutes receive annually a state subsidy of 98 per cent. In addition, the government contributes to the expenses which students incur over and beyond attendance at the university. The amount of the subsidy must not be in excess of "what, according to the prevalent opinion in this country, is necessary for the equipment and maintenance of a university or institute of economics." There can be no private institutes of technology or agriculture unless, in the opinion of the minister, such institutes fit into the complex of provisions for research and academic training.

The regulations for total financial compensation of the staff of subsidized private schools are the same as for government employees: salaries, pensions, fringe benefits, health insurance, extra emoluments, and travel expenses. Financial compensation for all teachers, government and private, comes under the civil law. All costs are subsidized equally in both government and private schools.

According to the provisions of the Act of 1955, there is no tuition for all government and publicly maintained private schools in the following categories: standard elementary education, advanced standard elementary education, special elementary education, the first and second year of continued elementary education, preparatory academic and general secondary education ("advanced education" after 1968), elementary domestic science education, and the first year of elementary agriculture and gardening schools. Tuition fees for the remaining advanced education are charged on the basis of the income tax assessment. Academic education tuition fees per academic year amount to f. 200. ($60). After four years of study the tuition is free.

The Curriculum

Curricula in Catholic schools are basically tied in with those which the law prescribes for government schools. In all schools, government and Catholic, extracurricular activities insofar as all pupils participate in them are rare: athletic clubs, field trips, debating clubs, "academies" which organize conferences, occasional annual sports festivals, and so on are the exception rather than the rule. In 1954, however, a School Music Society was organized but even before that there were regular school concerts. From 1954 to 1965 there were 2240 concerts held in 199 towns and villages.

The law binds all schools to a subject-centered curriculum. Curricular innovation is rather rare except for the addition of such subjects as sociology. The curriculum, designed according to legal statutes on education, is tightly structured and must be followed rigorously.

The syllabus is composed by experts in subject areas with some assistance from teachers who contribute the "experience dimension."

The professor at a university is completely free to make his own syllabus. Thus his is the decision on the choice and extent of the subject, as well as on the time he wishes to spend lecturing on it or investigating it. The government regulations pertaining to this, as laid down in the Academic Statutes, are at once very general and very brief; consequently each professor may interpret the Academic Statutes as he pleases. Nonetheless, university professors adhere to the rule that the first years of study (up to the *candidaats* degree) are in the main an introduction to the different sciences and therefore provide a general education; specialization only begins afterward and leads to the *doctoraal* degree. But even here the government does not issue detailed syllabi, and the professor may and does deviate to a great extent from the regulations.

Education in nursery schools is given according to a play-and-work plan which, among other things, contains games and physical education, work with materials designed to further development, modeling, drawing, musical education, story-telling, and the learning of nursery rhymes.

The curriculum of schools for standard elementary education comprises the following subjects: reading, writing, arithmetic, Dutch language, national history (including Dutch government), geography, traffic, nature study and hygiene, singing, drawing, physical education (and for girls, in addition, plain needlework). To these subjects are sometimes added handicrafts and Friesian language. The curriculum must provide for a minimum of 1040 hours per school year. In the first three grades it covers chiefly reading, writing, arithmetic, and the Dutch language.

Advanced standard elementary education comprises the same compulsory subjects as listed above, plus general history, handicrafts for boys, plain and art needlework and domestic science for girls. Elective subjects include mathematics, commercial subjects, agriculture and gardening, and the Friesian language (and handicrafts for girls).

Continued elementary education (ULO) comprises the required subjects of standard elementary education. Apart from these, instruction is given in at least three of the following subjects: French, German, English, mathematics, and business education. In addition, course work in the following fields can be given: general history, handicrafts, agriculture and gardening, art needlework, domestic science, Friesian, Spanish, and Esperanto. There is a final examination drawn up by the three MULO organizations and supervised by them, partly through a foundation.

The MULO diploma entitles the graduate to enter many lower social administrative functions. There are two types of diploma, the "A" and the "B," the latter indicating a concentration in mathematics and science. Some of the graduates continue their education either at an advanced technical school (including teacher training institutes) or at a secondary school. After 1968 MULO will be known as MAVO (intermediate general secondary education) and will be subject to the general reorganization of all secondary education.

Subsequent to 1968 the curriculum of a *gymnasium* will comprise the following subjects: Dutch, Latin, Greek, French, German, English (language and literature), history and institutions, geography, sociology, mathematics, physics, chemistry, biology, music, drawing, handicrafts, and physical education. The inclusion of Greek language and literature was the subject of heated parliamentary debates. Sociology is a new subject. At the *atheneum* the same subjects are taught, with the exception of Greek and Latin. A new subject, economics and law, has been introduced into the curriculum.

The curriculum for the *gymnasium* and related secondary schools is, however, less important than the time schedules and examinations. The examinations are principally school examinations, with but a small number of state examinations. The operative time schedules are strict. After 1968 the Cals Act will admit a few changes, a beneficial development which permits a little latitude in a very rigid curricular system.

The curriculum of the advanced general secondary education (HAVO) includes the same subjects as the *atheneum*. The subject economics and law is divided here into the separate subjects of economics, business administration, and law. These subjects are not mandatory in those schools whose curriculum emphasizes literary and cultural subjects.

The HAVO does not prepare the student for the university. Indeed, there is considerable doubt as to the future existence of the independent HAVO school. Education at this type of school attempts to provide a preparation for tasks and functions in which more highly educated persons are employed, yet for which no university education is required. Therefore the curriculum in an HAVO school can make greater provision for individual differences in interests and ability by taking into account the vocational interests of its students and the social milieu in which they wish to participate when they enter the world of work.

Intermediate general secondary education (MAVO) will replace the present ULO and will have the same curriculum as HAVO. However, instead of economics, business administration, and law, only commercial subjects will be taught. The difference between preparatory academic training (VWO) and HAVO lies in the standard applied and in the speed and the method with which the subject matter is taught. MAVO is considered primarily as a basis for later technical training; consequently the curriculum attempts to provide for individual differences in interests and abilities of the students.

Of parenthetical interest is the fact that many pupils either do not finish school or do pass their final examinations only after repeated attempts. Two principal reasons may be adduced for this unfortunate phenomenon. First, the curriculum is overloaded. Second, there is a lack of horizontal articulation, that is the opportunity of changing from one type of school to another without loss of time. To solve this problem the Cals Act has introduced the bridge year. Under this plan education in the first year of day schools for VWO, HAVO, and MAVO includes the same subjects, of which the following are compulsory: Dutch and two modern languages, one of which must be French. In the *gymnasium*, Latin can be added to these. During this bridge year the pupil has time to adapt himself to the atmosphere of secondary education, especially to the rigorously enforced departmental system of separate teachers for the different subjects.

The curriculum in elementary general secondary education (LAVO) is composed of the Dutch language, history, and geography, sociology, mathematics, nature study, music, drawing, handicrafts, and physical education. Sociology is not a required first-year subject in day schools. LAVO is given in the first year, or in the first and second years of schools for elementary technical training, or in independent schools with a two-year course.

Especially through its incorporation into elementary technical training, LAVO will be more directed toward the technical training which will follow it. For those pupils who still of compulsory school age have not yet made a vocational choice or who do not wish an advanced education, the independent LAVO school might well continue to fulfil an important function.

An Order in Council will determine more closely which elective subjects may be incorporated into the curriculum of schools for preparatory academic and general secondary education. The number of electives a student may take is limited. There is always an opportunity to teach religion at private schools.

For elementary, intermediate, and advanced technical training a distinction is made between general subjects and preprofessional courses. In elementary technical training, the general subjects embrace the Dutch language, history, geography, sociology, mathematics, nature study, music, drawing, handicrafts, and physical education. Intermediate and advanced technical curricula always include the Dutch language and physical education.

The legal regulations for technical training are not very detailed in order not to hamper the development of this type of education, which is much newer than AVO (general secondary education). Only in the preparation of nursery school teachers and in teacher-training colleges is there a legally prescribed curriculum. A teacher-training college has a first and a second course. The first course takes two years, and the second lasts one year. Both of these courses are preceded by a preparatory course which is part of the HAVO curriculum. For an independent preparatory course in which there are legal possibilities, the law prescribes a curriculum which coincides with that of HAVO but without economics, business administration, and law. Such a curriculum, therefore, is the noneconomically oriented "differentiation" of HAVO.

Education in the first course comprises: (a) the teaching process and methodology (called pedagogics) and its auxiliary sciences—educational psychology and child psychology; (b) general didactics and introduction to the didactics of the subjects of basic education (basic education is the new term for elementary education); (c) the Dutch language, history, geography, physics, biology, arithmetic, writing, traffic, music, drawing, handicrafts, and physical education, in connection with the didactics of these subjects; (d) the Dutch language and literature, and knowledge of cultural and social life; (e) music, drawing, handicrafts, and physical education.

Instruction in the second course (which lasts one year) provides for study in greater depth of the subjects of the first course mentioned under (a) and (d). The second course curriculum also affords special study of certain subjects in the field of didactics chosen by the student with the approval of the director. It complies with the regulations laid down in a government decree enacted after consultation with the teachers' council. (The teachers' council is an advisory body to the government.) Physical education also comprises a vital part of the curriculum of the second course.

The curriculum is not sufficiently related to life and to life problems. The bookish nature of the curriculum stems from the so-called "didactic intellectualism" or "materialism" which places much more emphasis on the quantity of learning than on its basic value. Consequently neither the pupil nor the teacher is the chief thing; rather, highest status is that of the subject matter, which typically is not taken from real life but from the textbooks. The textbooks, in turn, are based on larger, more scholarly works. Since World War II, however, there has been an increasing trend toward incorporating newspaper reports and commentaries, television and radio documentaries, and introductions to current events given by the teachers themselves. The subject matter so assembled is partly gathered by the pupils and is criticized and evaluated in all-class discussions.

Instruction

The principal methods of teaching in all types of Dutch schools are: explaining, commenting, narrating, illustrating, hearing lessons, and using textbooks. All of these pedagogical procedures are performed by the teacher. There are in addition many exercises for the pupils—written exercises, tests, and final examinations.

Audiovisual devices such as television, radio, and motion pictures are just beginning to be introduced. There are three educational radio broadcasting organizations. The first of these is the KRO educational broadcast (Catholic), which is available for use in 2300 schools, about 750 of which make active use of it. The NCRV educational broadcast (Protestant) is available to 1500 schools. The Dutch educational broadcast (governmental) is available to an estimated 1000 schools. Educational television is only now emerging from its experimental stage. The school broadcasting program is 95 minutes long and is aimed at different age groups, ranging from the highest grades of elementary schools to the highest grades of secondary schools.

Discussions, role-playing, panel discussions, and other sophisticated teaching methodologies are rare; indeed, until a short time ago they were not used at all. In all probability the sum total of all these newer teaching processes amounts to about 10 per cent of the total teaching time. There are virtually no lessons which feature teacher-pupil planning.

However, there are in The Netherlands 250 Dalton schools (of which ninety-five are Catholic), fifty-eight Montessori schools (of which thirteen are Catholic), and about ten "free schools" (in the spirit of Steiner). Among the 4900 nursery schools, of which 1797 are Catholic, 86 per cent (88 per cent of the Catholic schools) make use of Froebel materials, 4 per cent (5 per cent of the Catholic schools) use Montessori materials, and 5 per cent (5 per cent of the Catholic schools) use mixed materials.

Motivation for learning in school arises chiefly out of a social utilitarian base. In elementary schools the prime motivation to learn arises from a desire to gain admission into schools at a higher level. In secondary education the prime motivation is to receive a diploma which will open the way to matriculation at a university or institute, or will help the successful graduate to obtain a position in society. In general, a process of entrance into society via the successful performance in school is operative. The type of social sphere to which one eventually gains entry is greatly conditioned by the type of school which the student attends. The process of group activities in class depends on the type of school. Group activity is most prevalent in the MULO and least in the *gymnasium*, in HBS (advanced general secondary education), and in MMS (secondary schools for girls).

Homework forms an important part of Dutch education. However, pupils are not taught sufficiently how to study by themselves. To remedy this situation, the Cals Act has made provision for study hours so that the students can receive the benefits of supervised study.

Because of the highly utilitarian nature of motivation, competition among students rather than cooperation tends to predominate. To curb this overemphasis, however, many superior teachers attempt to moderate and blunt this highly competitive thrust. Cooperation has been effected in individual schools by some student group work but even this is not widespread. Nonetheless, conscious, scientifically oriented intrinsic motivation to learn is still not characteristic of Dutch Catholic or government school teachers.

A periodic evaluation is made of what the students learn in class. Every lesson typically includes some sort of informal teacher evaluation of the students' learning. At regular intervals the teacher tests the students in a more formal manner. At the end of a trimester or of a whole school year there are major examinations. Evaluation is usually expressed in ciphers from one to ten. The results are determined principally by the tests given at the end of the trimester or school year. With the exception of reading tests, standardized evaluation instruments are a rarity. Most of the examinations are teacher-constructed.

Parents are informed of the results of their children's evaluation at least three times a year through special school reports. But there is considerable dissatisfaction with this policy. On parents' afternoons and evenings, as also during consultation hours, parents have the opportunity to request information or opinions on the reports. Of course the pupils themselves exchange opinions about the results, but only among themselves.

Supervision of instruction in every type of school, including Catholic schools, rests with special government inspectors. In government schools, these inspectors have a supervisory, an advisory, and sometimes a decision-making function (for example, suggestions for the nomination of teachers). They have to evaluate the time schedules and the curricula and can make changes in these, but only in accordance with the law and with the Royal Decrees. For private schools, the government inspectors have the duty solely of seeing whether the subsidy conditions are fulfilled. Among these conditions is the control of time schedules and curricula, which they are, however, not permitted to alter. Because of their professional organizations, teachers are in such a strong position that the inspectors can take action only against those who exhibit woefully inadequate teaching skill or who are guilty of moral turpitude. Even here strict constitutional regulations carefully delimit the type of censure by the inspectors. Consequently teachers are seldom officially censured by the inspectors.

It should be reiterated that everything in Dutch education is based on the constitution and the Royal Decrees, sometimes even to the smallest details. Within such a tight system there is very little room for personal initiative. In secondary education this situation will fortunately be ameliorated somewhat by the Cals Act.

The inspectors see to it that the syllabus is followed rigorously and that there is no deviation from the curricula and examination regulations. At examinations they are aided or represented by expert outside government examiners. Other types of advice, control, and evaluation seldom occur.

The Program of
Religious Education

The precise nature and function of religious education in Dutch Catholic schools have been going through an evolution for some time.

Religious education in Catholic elementary schools traditionally has meant three hours of religious instruction per week (including bible and liturgy); in secondary schools there are two hours for the lowest grades and one hour for the higher grades. Religion has always been treated too much as a subject like all others, prescribed by the syllabus and schedule and taught as a subject. Thus it has been characterized by tests as well as major examinations and checking of homework. The results of religious teaching have been measured in exact marks. All too often Catholic schools have been regular schools with religious education tacked on, given from 3 to 10 per cent of school time. Religion has always been taught by priests or has been under their supervision, with the help of either the catechism or of handbooks. This state of affairs quite naturally led to the question of whether religious education is governed by the same didactic laws as secular subjects or whether it is in the first place and more than anything else a matter of "witnessing." Until 1960 the former trend prevailed, after that time emphasis on the latter came to the fore due to the influence of Vatican II. The same pedagogical methods and techniques employed in teaching secular subjects were commonly used until 1960. In 1965 the catechism was abolished as a pedagogical base, and the following program of religious education was instituted. In the elementary school, first and second grades, two half-hour periods per week are devoted to religious instruction. In the third and fourth grades one half-hour period and one three-quarter hour period is the rule. In the first to the fourth grades religion is taught by the regular lay teacher. In the fifth and sixth grades one half-hour period is taught by the priest, one half-hour by the teacher (telling and reading stories from the bible), and one full hour is devoted to pure catechesis.

In the secondary school two hours per class per week are devoted to religious instruction. The teaching method from the first to the fourth grades (MAVO), the fifth grade (HAVO), and the sixth grade (VWO) is required to take gradually the form of a dialogue; from the third grade on (fifteen-year-olds) it must progress to the level of pure "conversation."

The free time thus made available by the new schedule can be used for regular conferences of teachers and priests, for the celebration of the Eucharist with a single class, for occasional catechesis, and so forth.

The content of the religious education program can best follow the cycle of the Church year, and it must spring from the following concepts. First, religious instruction is to be considered only as a means to provide guidance, orientation, and commitment in religious matters; it may no longer be considered as a subject in the typical school sense. Second, religious knowledge has a different character and moves on a different plane from secular knowledge, to which it is nevertheless related as a necessary means to gain insight into human life and the modern world. Third, its didactics are therefore also governed by the general canons and processes of teaching, but its particular structure and its particular breadth force the teacher to interpret it differently, to apply it differently, and to incorporate it into forms of dialogue which aim at personal commitment and common religious experience. All didactic intellectualism must be rejected because reason, despite its importance, must not be allowed to dominate in a program designed to affect the will.

Forward-looking specialists in religious education agree that the school's program of religious education ought not to become "schoolish." By the use of sophisticated teaching methodologies, it must stimulate the emergence within the classroom situation of actual problems which are of concern to young people. Infantilization of behavior and of subject matter should be avoided. The "new theology," modern biblical exegesis, and the liturgical renewal offer great possibilities for giving meaning and reality to the holy mystery in the life of the individual. Such a vitalized religious education program demands a greater scrupulousness in the use of the teaching processes and personal encounter, as well as a remarkable personal commitment among the teachers. While Dutch educationists generally agree on these points, the work of developing such a program is still in the initial stages.

The pervasion of all education with the spirit of Catholic religious experience is the foremost problem which confronts Catholic education in The Netherlands. The old way of doing things has shown too few beneficial results and has since become inadequate in almost every respect. The integration of religion into the entire educational program has typically been of secondary importance. Priests have never been prepared professionally for this kind of work, and even now their training in these matters is very meager indeed. The outmoded concept that to be a good teacher it is sufficient to have a good knowledge of one's subject also governs priestly formation in the seminaries. The fact that one tries to fill this serious gap exclusively with psychology and sociology shows how deeply this outmoded and erroneous concept is rooted. Religious instruction given by the professionally prepared classroom teacher is therefore, as a rule, much more effective, and this type of religious instruction is becoming increasingly prevalent.

Religious instruction is supervised by priests who are supervised by the episcopal school inspector. School mass, confession, and retreats (all with obligatory participation) are becoming obsolete, a step which is considered forward. There is virtually no research in this entire field of religious education, and the little that is being done is meager in scope, as well as unscientific. In many instances the church council is also the school board, and the parish priest president of both. This situation has stimulated far-reaching services to the parish, especially with respect to activities outside the classroom—directing choirs and youth organizations, for example—but it is disappearing.

In view of the legal stipulation that the professional preparation of teachers must be of equal quality for both Catholic and government schools, there is no discernible difference in quality between Catholic and government or Protestant school teachers. Further, it is not possible to state that Catholic teachers at Catholic schools are better Catholics than the Catholics who teach at government schools.

Student Personnel and Guidance Services

As a general rule, most of what might be termed "personnel and guidance services" depends upon personal initiative. The principal exception to this consists in a few services which have been instituted by the councils of large municipalities or by groups of small municipalities. Among the services of large municipalities are remedial teaching, visiting teachers, and the further care for former pupils of special elementary schools. The last-mentioned is also performed by groups of small municipalities. Municipalities take care of the school health service also. Moreover, there are vocational guidance services, together with centers, which offer advice on the choice of school. Child guidance centers exist. In brief, there are two authorities which take care of guidance services, the municipal government and organized private initiative. The government often provides financial support, but it does not itself lend assistance.

Some personnel services are available in the schools—school doctor, dental service, remedial and psychological services, for example— while other services are offered at independent centers especially established for this purpose. All personnel services employ specialists: medical doctors, psychologists, and a few remedial teaching specialists. Group guidance and counseling are still in their infancy. The occasional large-scale investigations have been mainly in the field of teaching results, as for example in the province of North Brabant, for which special tests were constructed. In the Catholic child guidance centers there are typically a priest, a psychologist, a psychiatrist, a pediatrician, a social worker, and sometimes a remedial teaching specialist.

The Netherlands has seventy-seven child guidance centers of which thirty-four are Catholic. Moreover, it has 2004 infant welfare centers which are chiefly visited by parents for consultation about the physical health of their children. The school health service employs 370 full-time physicians, twelve psychologists, 281 school nurses, and 139 assistants who take care of 2,278,000 pupils (as of the beginning of 1964). Of the 967 municipalities, 189 do not participate in the school dental service. This service offers three different types of programs: sending the pupil to a dentist (thirty-five services), providing dentistry in the school (118 services), and a mixture of these (six services).

There are regular checks on the nutrition of school children. In many instances the school provides milk, for which a small charge may be made. The study of dietetics has been introduced into the curriculum of the teacher-training colleges.

The contact center Bedrijfsleven-Onderwijs (Industry-Education) has taken the initiative of appointing youth employment officers. These officers give vocational guidance in the schools and also supply information regarding the many possible places of employment in trade and industry. By 1966 there were approximately 400 of these officers.

There is still insufficient coordination in the whole area of personnel and guidance services, largely because these services have been introduced from the outside and often without consultation with the school. This difficulty is compounded by disagreement about the competence of the various experts.

The Staff of the
Catholic Schools

Statistically, Catholic education comprises by far the greatest percentage of the schools in The Netherlands. Since 1965 religious instruction in Catholic schools has been given chiefly by laymen rather than by priests. The teachers hold a separate diploma in religion for this purpose; indeed, practically all teachers hold this diploma. In the early 1960's there was a strong movement to give laymen further education in religious instruction to enable them to replace the priests. In general this is looked upon as an important step forward. A concomitant of this development is the decline in the number of priest-teachers in Catholic schools. This is partially related to the decrease in the number of vocations, notably among the sisters and the brothers.

The professional preparation of teachers for secondary schools (general secondary education, *gymnasium*, and so on—the so-called VHMO) up to 1952 had not been pedagogically and didactically oriented. Rather, such preparation centered exclusively on training in the science related to the subject to be taught. The underlying thought was that knowledge of the science is sufficient to make a good teacher. In 1952 a modest start was made to provide didactic training through an introduction to pedagogics, didactics, and adolescent psychology. Moreover, teacher candidates are now being introduced to the didactics of their special subject; during their training they must spend a short time (forty to eighty hours) at a secondary school. Efforts to expand this system have been unsuccessful so far.

The staff of the nursery schools and of the elementary schools consists of a principal and a corps of teachers. The number of teachers per school is dependent on the number of pupils enrolled; the proportion is regulated by law and must be observed by the Catholic schools. Regardless of size, each school has one principal. To cope with the numerous administrative duties which consume a great deal of time, large schools attempt to obtain an administrative assistant.

Secondary schools have as their head building officer either a director (directress) or a rector (rectress). If the secondary school is very large, the chief administrative officer is assisted by a subdirector(s) or co-rector(s) or co-rectress(es). The number of teachers in these schools depends on the aggregate teaching hours and subjects. Whereas in nursery schools and in elementary schools teaching is always a full-time job (except for teachers of special subjects such as gymnastics, needlework, and so forth), the functions of teachers in secondary schools vary greatly. Twenty-six teaching hours per week is considered a normal load. In some instances, however, the load reaches thirty-four hours; in others it may fall to five hours. In instances such as the last, the teachers often work part-time at other schools in order to earn their living.

Men still predominate in the teaching profession; nonetheless a slow feminization of teaching staffs is noticeable in The Netherlands.

Legal sanctions may be applied if a teacher disturbs the peace or commits an immoral offense. At Catholic schools such sanctions may also be invoked if it becomes apparent that a teacher is neglecting or deviating from religious belief or the moral code. These sanctions consist of temporary suspension and/or dismissal. At the university, academic freedom is a matter of course.

In keeping with the philosophical division of all public activities, there are three organizations in the educational field for each type of school, with only a few exceptions. There are three professional organizations for nursery school teachers, three for each of the two types of elementary school teachers, and three for each of the secondary school teachers. All of these professional associations work very closely with the government, as do the three Pedagogic Centers mentioned earlier.

The Parents
and the
Catholic School

Contact between parents and the school is extensive. It is very animated in Protestant schools, best organized in government schools, and more or less neglected in Catholic schools. The explanation for the disparity in school-home relations lies in the absolute confidence of Catholic parents in the church councils (principally in the parish priest) and in the clerical and lay teachers, a confidence which makes them view these individuals as acting in *loco parentis*.

Parent-school contact is essentially personal and occurs almost exclusively in situations involving learning difficulties, behavior problems, or choice of school. Organized contact is brought about by parents' afternoons and evenings, by invitations to parents to attend classes, by school newspapers, and since 1952 by parents' committees. The composition of these committees and their functions are governed by an episcopal set of rules. These regulations accord parents the right to serve as an advisory body in all activities both inside and outside the classroom as well as to function as a grievance committee. The representatives of these committees elect a Diocesan Parents' Committee in each of the seven dioceses of The Netherlands. Representatives meet annually to elect the members of the National Catholic Parents Committee.

There has been little change in the statistics since 1963. At that time they were as follows: 1762 Catholic nursery schools had 168 Parents Committees; 2857 Catholic elementary schools had 1283; 225 Catholic advanced standard elementary schools (LAVO and LEA) had 37; 455 Catholic schools for continued elementary education had 69; 256 Catholic special elementary schools had 36; and 175 Catholic secondary schools (HAVO and *athenea*) had 70. It is readily apparent that out of a total of 5800 Catholic schools, less than 1700 have a parents' committee. Many committees have been organized not through the initiative of the parents but by the school board or the headmaster; quite a number of them are asleep. The national hierarchy via diocesan to National Parent Committee is inefficient due to lack of financial resources. Dutch Catholic educationists are therefore searching for other avenues to stimulate the interest of parents in what is supposedly *their* (the parents') school.

Special Educational Problems Facing Catholic Schools in The Netherlands

The problems which face the Catholic schools in The Netherlands today are essentially the same as those which face every kind of school in the modern world. The origin of the concept that the real aim of the Dutch Catholic school is to offer a protective and sheltered milieu is a result of the school controversy and the debates surrounding it. To create this protective and sheltered milieu it was considered necessary to have Catholic teachers, a Catholic atmosphere, Catholic subjects, and Catholic teaching methods. However, the school as school at that time had a different function from what it currently is supposed to have. From a social point of view, the school had to deal with the static society of that time. In the present dynamic society, only the first of the four needs mentioned above still remains a necessary condition. Even so, all four factors taken together are by no means real guarantees that the desired Catholic character of the school will certainly result. As a protective milieu the Catholic school has become useless to children of the modern open and pluralistic society. It is conceivable that a Catholic atmosphere too strongly emphasized might alienate the pupils from their Church. In no case would it suffice nowadays to teach Catholic subject matter exclusively. Such a stance would make the pupils defenseless against the many non-Catholic elements in the modern world with which they inevitably come in contact, such as radio, cinema, television, the press, and social intercourse with non-Catholics. To be sure, such contact is not infrequently a humanizing factor. Ecumenical activities have become a necessary ingredient of life, and in consequence an imperative for true education also.

The fact that all Dutch schools need reform and renewal demands a revision of the principles of education. The existing principles of Dutch education are very much rooted in the rationalism of the Enlightenment and as such have dangerous consequences for modern educational practice. Thus, along with a decided lack of integration in the subjects taught, there is also a naive belief that knowledge can be measured exactly. Further, there are a liberal ideal of knowledge, an overloading of the curriculum, a series of overly detailed examinations, and a worship of diplomas. All of these remnants of the Enlightenment tend to produce didactic intellectualism and materialism which, although moderated in the course of time, have not yet disappeared. These outmoded educational principles are anti-social and anti-intellectual in the sense of not being directed toward an understanding of the world and society. Indeed, such principles have even become anti-human in that they do not correspond with the rights of human beings, which pupils surely are. This means that these educational principles are detrimental to the Catholic character of a school. Consequently these erroneous principles pose a serious problem for the average teacher and an insurmountable problem for the weak teacher. The gifted teacher alone is still capable of giving the school a Catholic character, and this despite its actual didactics.

Hence the striving for a new type of Catholic school to a large extent coincides with the efforts toward educational renewal of the Protestants and the government. The unique Catholic character of a school must be seen in its Catholic-inspired teaching, that is to say, where such a Catholic dimension is possible without being obtrusive. In modern mathematics, intuition and vision (and the inspiration resulting therefrom) are regarded as sources of creative thinking. In a school tinged with rationalism these qualities cannot be given their proper place. Nonetheless the use of analytic reason cannot be banned from the school. On the contrary, the only objection to reason is the exclusiveness which it had attained in the schools. In other words it is not reason which has to be fostered at school, but rather the intelligent human being. This is to say that the school must produce the intellectual aspect of the pedagogic phenomenon. In this context intellect must be understood in the sense of St. Thomas Aquinas, not only strict reason as such, but also common sense, comprehension, insight, sense of . . . , and so forth. Reason, too, must be understood in its original meaning, that is method, acting according to logic, reasoning, intellectual capacity, insight, motivation, principles, systematic theory, opinion, point of view, argumentation. Out of this wide range of meanings, the Enlightenment isolated but one, namely analytic reasoning according to strict logical principles.

Returning to the original meaning of intellect and reason, the aim of the Catholic school would be "to give insight into and an overall picture of the world of the pupil and, as far as possible, of the adult world." Education would thus become Catholic through the Catholic-inspired insight into life and the universe. It is the task of Catholic didactics to find out the ways in which this is hampered and how it can be promoted. The essence of a Catholic school, then, is first and foremost to be a good school, with a free and open approach to actual life and the modern world from a modern Catholic point of view. This perforce demands that the teacher be a Roman Catholic. However, even this prime condition is not a reasonable guarantee that a Catholic school will develop of itself. A Catholic school will result only: (1) if Catholicism is continually kept alive in the school; (2) if education is freed of the obstructive influences mentioned, namely didactic intellectualism and materialism; (3) if Catholic teachers are trained to be on the alert for those fruitful moments when teaching presents the opportunity to help lay the foundation of and/or to enlighten the pupil's own vision in an ecumenical sense. Whether the primary condition of Catholic teachers in Catholic schools will lead to the desired results depends to a great extent on practical didactics and the help they receive from scholarships. The creation of a Catholic milieu, however, can have dangerous consequences for the Catholic character of the school if such an environment causes religious practices and religious knowledge to become schoolish. In a Catholic school atmosphere there is a real risk that the pupils will look upon the Catholicism they receive solely as a school matter, to be forgotten or at best to be continued in postschool years in a rather uncommitted fashion.

The task of reforming and renewing Dutch Catholic education is made very difficult by the fact that all schools in The Netherlands are still subject to the influence of the old rationalistic, liberal ideal of knowledge. Compounding this is the fact that all Dutch schools have been exposed to an overemphasis on socialization and that during the last decades attention has been focused almost exclusively on psychology to the neglect of sociology, fundamental anthropology, and particularly to the disregard of sound pedagogical processes and methodologies. Furthermore, the fact that Dutch Catholic scholars have ignored the study of pedagogics and didactics has led to a situation in which these sciences are studied almost solely by non-Catholics, whose interpretation has become the standard way in which Catholic school teachers exercise the pedagogical and didactical aspects of their teaching.

Fortunately there are progressive developments which augur well for the future of Dutch Catholic education. Experienced and capable Catholic teachers have the opportunity to create a truly Catholic school. But regrettably, as in every other profession, such teachers are in the minority. Up to World War II a Catholic school milieu was useful, although to a diminishing degree, because Catholics did not in fact have equal rights before the law and because society at that time was not in the same dynamic state of development toward openness and pluralism as it is today. With the new *Zeitgeist* some mature Catholics are beginning to meet the challenge. From a scholarly point of view Professor Hoogveld of the Catholic University of Nijmegen has skillfully promoted philosophical pedagogics. Helpful pedagogical advice has come in a limited way from Germany and Flanders. Finally, well-honed suggestions were given by such experts as J. J. Verbeeten and Father S. Rombouts.

After World War II the development of Dutch Catholic education was accelerated by the following factors. First, there was an increasing desire to reform the teacher-training colleges. This stemmed from a growing awareness not only in educational circles but also from outside the schools that many social activities have, apart from their psychological and sociological aspects, a pedagogical aspect (guardianship, children's care, child guidance centers, foster homes, national health services, juvenile courts). Thus a broader basis of interest has been given to pedagogics as practiced by Catholics.

Second, there has been an enormous increase of interest in the science of pedagogics and didactics in educational circles. In 1964–65 this interest made possible a considerable expansion in the staff of the pedagogics institute at the Catholic University. This institute has since become the largest in The Netherlands. The number of students increased 525 per cent from 1956 to 1965, there being 369 students of pedagogics enrolled in the 1965–66 academic year.

Third, the invaluable service provided by the Catholic Center of Pedagogics (subdivided into a number of bureaus representing the various branches of education—elementary, secondary, technical, and agricultural) has helped Catholicism to recognize the new needs of education. It also has given advice and practical assistance in the schools themselves.

Fourth, the Cals Act offers concrete opportunities for a grand new start in contemporary secondary education. As a result of this act, there are not only opportunities for reducing the barriers to the operation of a Catholic vision in Catholic schools, but also countless possibilities for moving forward in a positive direction.

Fifth, the aftermath of the school controversy, still noticeable up until 1960 (but less since 1945), no longer impedes an open and virtually complete cooperation with government and Protestant schools.

Primarily, the actual problem, then, is precisely how to make teachers at Catholic schools theologically committed and didactically capable guides for their pupils with regard to modern life and the modern world as seen from the point of view of the new theology. This question must be answered if the Catholic school in The Netherlands is to survive. Indeed the very necessity and even the desirability of the Catholic schools in The Netherlands is being questioned in Dutch Catholic Cicles. There is much less assurance of the attachment of present-day Catholic parents to the Catholic school as "their" school than was true a quarter of a century ago. If the Catholic character of the schools does not manifest itself more strongly in the teaching, then surely their survival is in grave doubt. Parents rightfully demand a good school. If, however, the distinct character of Catholic education as described in this section is effected, then everything which justly disputes the continued existence of the Catholic dimension in Catholic schools tends to disappear. The question, for example, of whether the crafts are a Catholic subject will no longer require an answer because it will have become irrelevant. Nor does one still have to be concerned with the currently unacceptable demand to teach principally so-called Catholic subject matter, since in the opinion of the present writer all subject matter can in practice be taught from a Catholic point of view, with an infusion of the Catholic dimension. Further, teaching itself can be improved greatly through the unity which the Catholic vision gives to the subject matter and to the acquired knowledge, namely because both of these are rooted in a Catholic world picture which is at once living and personal. This picture itself can receive more light from so-called secular subjects which can broaden the intellectual horizon and give it a firmer structure. In other words, this new teaching methodology has a strong humanizing influence and is therefore better suited for permeation with a Catholic vision.

Another stumbling block in the creation of a truly Catholic school is the civil law. The law governing schools is much too detailed. Even the Cals Act, which is a fortunate exception to the rule, suffers somewhat from this defect. The Catholic Center of Pedagogics, as well as the other two centers, are unable to do much about the matter because they are overworked and are in dire need of important expansion. Without a considerably greater subsidy from the government the three national centers simply cannot spread their wings. The Roman Catholic Bureau of Education in The Hague also needs a sizeable government subsidy to be able to fulfil its vital coordinating function. Greater legal liberty, together with increased opportunities for the science of pedagogics and didactics, would enable Dutch Catholic educationists to make more valid scholarly experiments and to do more research than is currently being undertaken.

In any event, Dutch Catholic educationists do have a few professional organizations at their disposal. Further, they are beginning to grasp the actual problem. Foreigners will perhaps find the Dutch system ideal for private (Catholic and Protestant) education. From a financial point of view it is indeed ideal, but in the past the internal organization was not in proportion to the external possibilities. Some have realized this axial point. Among these, honorable mention must be given to Professor Buytendijk, who as early as 1921 appeared to comprehend the problem. He rejected the individualistic "proud" school, "the school with only religion"; instead he wished to replace this type of school with the social and humble school inspired by religion. It took forty years for the vision of Professor Buytendijk to penetrate to the frontal awareness and concern of Catholic educationists.

Conclusion

Inasmuch as the structure of Dutch education differs significantly from that of other countries, for the sake of clarity it might be well to conclude this essay with a summary of the most salient points.

Practically all school costs are paid by the government. From a material point of view, freedom of education can be realized without difficulty. One drawback here, however, is that parents no longer have to make financial sacrifices for "their" school.

The precious good mentioned above was gained from the school controversy which lasted eighty years, demanding complete attention and all-out efforts. Consequently too little research and too few changes in education itself were made. With the victory in 1917 came a false feeling of having reached everything, and people failed to understand that in 1917 and in 1920 it was only the *possibility* of a Catholic school which had been created. In the long run this failure to actualize the possibilities had serious consequences. For more than forty years the government showed an insufficient interest in scientific researches in the field of education. Indeed the question was raised: "Why should a Catholic school exist?" The former Catholic Minister of Education, Mr. Bot, declared rightly that education (including Catholic education) would have to undergo an "internal revolution."

The realization that an educational revolution is necessary is in itself a breakthrough. There are three organizations that will wage this educational reform: the Central Bureau of Education (which is limited in scope to administrative and legal support); the Catholic Center of Pedagogics (which is responsible for promoting regeneration *in* the schools); and the Institute of Pedagogics at the Catholic University of Nijmegen (which deals in basic research).

Freedom of all education—in government and in private schools —is too limited in The Netherlands, because of the overdetailed school legislation and a plethora of decrees anent its execution.

The democratization of education is making too little progress. In 1935, 6 per cent of the lower socioeconomic classes received an academic education; by 1954–55 it had advanced to only 7 per cent and by 1961–62 to a mere 9 per cent. For the middle class this rate amounted to 46 per cent and 45 percent for the last two years, respectively, and in the upper classes to 47 per cent and 46 per cent.

The fundamental reasons for the unduly slow development toward a real regeneration of Dutch government and private schools lie in the preservation of the obsolete foundations of education and the corollary rationalistic approach to the problems, together with the Dutch tendency to perfectionism. Superimposed on these, and perhaps most crucial of all, is the deep distrust between advocates and opponents of private education. Fortunately, during the long administration of Minister Cals a great deal of this distrust disappeared. This augurs well for a thorough reformation and modernization of Dutch education which should lead to a new, up-to-date educational system, suited to Dutch culture and society and to modern man.

Selected
Bibliography

Aarts, J. *Schoolrecht, Schoolstrijd, Schoolwet in Nederland,* 2 vols. "Opvoedkundige Brochurenreeks," 62 and 65. Tilburg-Antwerp, 1931–1932. (An historical survey of the school controversy.)

Crijns, J. M., et al. *De Mammoetwet. Voornaamste aspecten in verband met de schoolpraktijk.* Roosendaal, n.d. (Some important aspects of the Secondary Education Act.)

Gielen, Prof. Dr. Jos-J. "Naar een nieuwe katholieke school," *Pedagogische Cahiers,* 1. 's Hertogenbosch, 1966. (Toward a new Catholic school.)

Hentzen, Dr. Cassianus, O.F.M. *De Politieke Geschiedenis van het Lager Onderwijs in Nederland. De Financiële Gelijkstelling,* 5 vols. The Hague, 1925–40. (Political history of the financial equalization.)

Idenburg, Dr. Ph. J. *Schets van het Nederlandse Schoolwezen,* 2nd ed. Groningen, 1964. (A general and up-to-date survey of the Dutch school system.)

Matthijssen, M. A. J. M. *Katholiek Middelbaar Onderwijs en Intellectuele Emancipatie.* Assen, 1958. (The role of Catholic secondary schools in the intellectual emancipation of Catholics in The Netherlands.)

Pelosi, E. *Vrij Onderwijs. Maatschappelijke organen voor het onderwijs, met name voor het vrije onderwijs.* Tilburg, 1960. (A public law organization for the free schools.)

Of the many periodicals the following may be helpful:
Het Schoolbestuur (edited by the R. C. Central Bureau of Education)
Opvoeding, Onderwijs en Gezondheidszorg
Jeugd, School en Beroep

Catholic Education in Italy

by Vincenzo Sinistrero

A Short History
of Italian
Catholic Education

The history of Catholic schools in Italy coincides with the history of the Church itself. These schools, including universities, were founded by the Church, at first transmitting the treasures of Latinity, and in modern times extending their scope to popular education. The present-day situation, however, developed with the establishment of the modern state in Europe.

As early as the eighteenth century, the regional Italian states (excluding obviously the Papal States where the schools were rigorously Catholic) began to subject the Church schools to the power of an Illuministic absolutism. These regional Italian states drew inspiration from the policies of the Bourbon courts, from the Austrian Hapsburgs, and from the Protestant sovereigns who also applied the principle of *cujus regio ejus religio* to the schools.

When the Napoleonic storm had passed, the regional states tightened their control over the schools, thus strengthening the monopoly which they exercised with the Church. The states made this move in order to re-establish the former regimes.

A typical example of what happened was the policy put into effect by the kingdom of Piedmont. During the years 1729, 1733, 1771, and 1772, first Vittorio Amedeo II and later Carlo Emanuele III drew up *Costituzioni* for the schools. In 1822 these constitutions were given new force by Carlo Felici, who reinforced the clerical monopoly in the schools. School directors had to be clerics, and teachers and pupils were required to observe all the practices of worship as well as being obliged to lead a religious and moral way of life. If they were remiss in the latter, they were suspended or expelled from the school.

The same power of vigilance and of religious and moral censorship over the schools, especially over the primary schools, was granted to the ecclesiastical authorities in the kingdom of Naples and in Sicily, a condition which lasted until the year 1860.

The revolution which rocked Europe in 1848, from Paris to Vienna to Italy and which brought Piedmont into war against Austria, also invaded the schools. By virtue of the Boncompagni Law of October 4, 1848 (No. 818), the government supplanted the Church and the clergy in power over the schools. All schools whether public or private came under the jurisdiction of the Ministry for Public Instruction (Articles 1, 3, 33) even in matters of ecclesiastical discipline and religious instruction.

On November 13, 1859 the Casati Law (No. 3725) was promulgated. This law was in the spirit of the 1848 revolution and was intended to strengthen the autonomy and the laicization of the state. Thus this law corresponded to the national movements elsewhere in Europe (and in Piedmont itself) toward national unification against the separatist forces of the regional states (which included the Pontifical States allied with Austria). It was later extended to the whole of the new kingdom of Italy with the Coppino Law of July 15, 1877.

With the framing of these laws, the supplanting of the Church by the state in the schools became definitive. The government schools alone thus became recognized as legally valid with respect to studies and examinations as well as for fiscal support from public revenue.

The nongovernment schools could still exist but at their own expense and only as *scuole paterne*, under the direct responsibility of parents, or as *scuole private*, private schools. All pupils attending nongovernment schools were obliged to take examinations in the government schools if they wished to have legally recognized academic qualifications (Articles 246–253). A form of *scuola pareggiata* or standardized school was, however, recognized. If such schools adhered to the state regulations regarding teachers, pupils and studies, they could obtain legel recognition of their course of studies and examinations.

The Casati Law, which centralized all power over the Italian schools in the Ministry of Public Instruction, established the rule of bureaucracy over the schools. The entire structure became rooted in the twin axes of the eight-year *ginnasio-liceo* (general secondary school), thus imposing the authoritarian Napoleonic system which has remained in force until the present day. The reform project which began in 1962 is still within the same basic framework that had been in effect since 1859.

The war conducted by the new state to make the new school system prevail was relentless, and contributed much to the struggle against the Papal States. With the occupation of Rome on September 20, 1870, the final rupture was effected between the new state and the Catholic population, a fissure which has caused so much harm to both sides.

The Gentile reform proposed for the schools by the Law of May 6, 1923 (No. 1054) kept intact the norms established by the Casati Law. However, it introduced an *esame di Stato*, or state examination, at the end of the upper secondary school course for admission to the universities with programs. This 1923 law also established examining commissions appointed by the government to judge all pupils whether from government or nongovernment schools (Articles 88–94).

The Lateran Treaty and Pacts of February 11, 1929 between the Church and the Italian government in Article 35 of the Concordat sanctioned the state examination to insure "the effective equality of conditions for candidates of government institutes and candidates from *scuole di instruzione media* (upper secondary school) maintained by ecclesiastical or religious bodies." Article 36 extended the teaching of Catholic doctrine in the government schools from the primary to the secondary level. Expenses would be met by the government, and parents retained the right to withdraw their children from schools of this kind.

In keeping with the spirit of the 1929 Concordat a new law was passed on January 19, 1942 (No. 86). This law, which is still in force, gave to *scuole legalmente riconosciute o parificate* (approved schools) the same legal rights for studies and examinations as those of the government schools (Article 6). It also granted schools maintained by public or ecclesiastical bodies the privilege of *pareggiamento* or standardization (Article 8), comparable to that granted by the Casati Law.

After the fall of Fascism and the monarchy following World War II, a new republican constitution came into force on January 1, 1948. It introduced revolutionary and basic changes into the politico-juridical principles arising from the Casati Law. Under the Casati Law Italian schools had been almost exclusively modelled on the classical Napleonic elitist standard of education. The new law introduced into education twentieth-century democracy calling for a school system open to everyone. Thus education was conceived as an opportunity for the development and growth of every boy and girl. The constitution therefore recognizes in its "fundamental principles" (Articles 1–12) and in "The Rights and Duties of Citizens" (Articles 13–54) the sovereign rights of each individual within the social structures in which he operates—as a student, as a member of a family, the Church, the school, the teaching profession, or the government.

The following constitutional regulations have special application with respect to education.

Parents have the duty and right to maintain, instruct and educate their children (Article 30).

The Republic will assist by economic measures and other means in the promotion of the family in the fulfillment of its functions, paying special attention to large families; it will protect mothers, children, and youth, supplying the resources necessary to this end (Article 31).

Lower education lasting for at least eight years is both compulsory and free of charge. Capable and deserving students, even if deprived of financial means, have the right to attain the highest levels in their studies (Article 34).

Corporations and private individuals have the right to establish schools and institutes of education, without any onus on the state. The law in establishing the rights and obligations of nongovernment schools which demand equality must give them full liberty and in scholastic matters must treat their pupils in the same way as pupils in the government schools. A state examination is required for admission to or graduation from the various levels and grades of school and for the lawful practice of a profession (Article 33).

By these norms the constitution sanctions the right of the family to its choice of school and to economic aid from the government for education and the right to free schooling during the compulsory level of education, that is from six to fourteen years of age. Further, the constitution guarantees the right of the nongovernment school both to exist freely and to have an "equality in full liberty" with the government schools, at least in the sense that studies and academic qualifications have legal value equal to that of the government schools.

Regarding the acceptance of financial aid, the phrasing of Article 33, which recognizes the liberty of the schools without any onus on the state, has thus far been interpreted in two ways: (1) that the government cannot provide subsidies for nongovernment schools; (2) that the government should not but can provide subsidies for nongovernment schools. In practice the government has thus far neither granted financial aid to families (Article 31 of the constitution) nor for the compulsory area of schooling (Article 34), with the exception of certain grants providing for the education of economically underprivileged students. No government aid can be envisaged as long as the present lineup of political parties in the national parliament continues to exist.

The historical curve which began in the eighteenth century with the domination of the schools by the Church swung in the opposite direction in the following century with the transfer of the monopoly to the state. The present century witnessed not only the recognition of the rights of the state, but also the rights of the family, the Church, and the schools, which were granted not only freedom but a certain equality with the government schools as well.

The Purpose of Catholic Schools in Italy

With the revival of democracy after World War II and the maturation of the Constitution of the Republic giving rise to many and diverse types of free associations, the Catholic school system began its own organization. The Church did this through the establishment in 1947 of the Federation of Institutes Dependent on Ecclesiastical Authority (FIDAE). The Federation coordinated the kindergarten, the primary, and the secondary schools, all of which are virtually exclusively conducted by religious institutes of men or women. Other schools in these categories include diocesan and parochial schools.

The *Statuto* officially approved by the Sacred Congregation of Seminaries and Universities on December 22, 1963 determines the nature of the Federation as follows.

[The Federation] promotes the growth and the perfection of the federated institutes and protects their interests; it contributes to the assertion of the dignity and the rights of schools of Catholic inspiration (Article 3).

To achieve these ends the Federation: provides for the pedagogical and didactical improvement of the federated institutes by means of research, conventions, publications, and other forms of activity; it assists the religious institutes in their relations with the authorities and with external dependents; it collaborates with other associations of Catholic inspiration—especially associations of teachers—in the formation of a Christian conscience trained to deal with problems of education and of the schools; it deals with all questions relating to schools and their improvement, making timely recommendations to the proper authorities regarding the means to be adopted; it establishes and maintains relations with similar national associations and with those of other countries; it publishes the official bulletin, *Docete* (Article 4). The Federation is assisted in its work by a delegate of the Sacred Congregation of Seminaries and Universities (Article 6).

Central authorities comprise: the general assembly, the general presidency, the central Council and Board. Regional authorities consist of: the regional assembly, the regional presidency, the regional Council and Board;

the diocesan delegate, and the authorities established for a particular need (Article 7).

Female [religious] institutes, through their own representatives who participate in the general assembly, will have the right to the same type of vote as do representatives of male [religious] institutes (Article 18). Each [religious] institute contributes to the operating expenses of the Federation through a fixed annual sum and through another sum that is proportionate to the number and category of its students (Article 19).

So far, this has been the only source of revenue available to the Federation.

The statutory aims of the Federation are reaffirmed, updated, and applied periodically by *messaggi* (messages) sent by the Sacred Congregation of Seminaries and Universities to the Assembly of the Federation. These are supplemented by allocutions of the Holy Father, which he gives to the Assembly during the annual audience on the occasion of the General Assembly.

Today, moreover, the Catholic schools recognize their educative and apostolic goals in the Declaration on Christian Education of Vatican Council II promulgated on October 28, 1965.

The Relationship of Catholic Schools to Government Schools

Government Legislation Which Has Affected Catholic Schools

Catholic schools obviously come under the juridical discipline which applies equally to all nongovernment schools. In contemporary Italy six juridical types of school exist or, more precisely, have a legal right to exist. The first type of school is the *scuola paterna*, which is founded by the initiative of individual parents or groups of parents (Articles 251–253 of the Casati Law and Articles 29–31 of the constitution).

The second category is the *scuola privata* (private school), so named because neither the studies completed in these schools nor the academic qualifications granted by them have the same legal value as those of the government schools. Those who conduct these schools may be private or public bodies.

The third classification of schools is described as *dipendente dall'* *Autorità Ecclesiastica* (dependent on ecclesiastical authority). The government recognizes in Article 7 of the constitution that the Church has "independent and sovereign" existence. Further, the Concordat stipulates that the Church has special power with regard to marriage (Article 34), conducting of schools (Article 35), and providing religious instruction in the schools (Article 36). Finally, the government has established the right of *Enti* (corporations) as well as private persons to open schools and institutes of education (Article 33). Because of these three major legal provisions, it seems justifiable to place in a third major category of schools those educational institutions which are subject to ecclesiastical authority and which are open to all students of both sexes that it decides to accept. Thus it is apparent that these schools in certain respects form a different category from those operated by private persons. The present law appears to confirm this classification. Law No. 86 of January 19, 1942 contains a clause dealing expressly with "special arrangements regarding schools which depend on 'ecclesiastical authority.' " The law provides, *inter alia*, that doctors of sacred theology and of other ecclesiastical disciplines, canon law and in *utroque jure* (canon and civil law), for example, are admitted to state examinations so that they might teach certain sciences in schools conducted by ecclesiastical authority. Students attending special educational institutions which prepare for the priesthood or for the religious life may sit for legally recognized examinations in FIDAE schools rather than in the government schools (Article 31–32).

A fourth category of schools, one given special juridical status by virtue of Article 39 of the Concordat, is that *per la formazione e la cultura degli ecclesiastici* (schools for the training and culture of clerics, for example, seminaries), insofar as they are exempt from any form of "interference from school authorities."

A fifth type of school is *la scuola statale* or government school system. This class of school must be understood not as the exercise of a function which is proper to or derives from the government as such, but rather as the actual operation of a public service from public funds for the benefit of the public in general. Properly understood within the framework of the constitution, this fifth category is a service which complements but does not substitute for the other types of schools.

The sixth main classification of schools includes those which are granted a certain *parità* or equality with the government schools.

The law envisages three distinct forms: schools whose standards (*pareggiata*) are comparable to the government schools and which adopt the full government system including public competitive examinations for the selection of teachers. These schools thus obtain legal status for their studies and academic qualifications, without however receiving any government grants. They may be said to sacrifice freedom for conformity (Casati Law and the Law of January 19, 1942, No. 86).

Schools called *scuola parificata* are those in which the teachers must be equipped with government *abilitazione* (authorization) in the science which they teach. Students must be matriculated for the class which they attend. Moreover the government program and calendar must be followed in order that studies and academic qualifications receive legal recognition. They receive no government grant (Law of January 19, 1942, No. 86, Articles 1 and 6).

The *scuola paritaria* are schools which have the benefit of full freedom and for which there may be independent teaching regulations; notwithstanding, they enjoy legal validity in the same way as the *scuola pareggiata* or the *scuola parificata* (Constitution, Article 33). The latter form is not yet allowed as the government has not to date promulgated a law which would put into effect Article 33 of the constitution (which has been in force since 1948) neither for the *scuola paritaria* nor for the new conditions of the *paterna* and *privata*. The long delay arises from the platforms of the various political parties, the right-wingers (Fascistophiles, Monarchists, and Liberals) as well as the left-wingers (Socialists and Communists). Both sides are opposed to nongovernment schools and handicap the Christian Democratic Party, which as of 1966 had only a plurality in Parliament (less than 51 per cent).

The Present Form
of Catholic
Schools in Italy

The Organizational Level

The *scuola materna* is for children from three to six years of age. Until 1966 virtually all these schools were private; indeed only eight were government schools. Seventy per cent of these nursery kindergarten children are cared for by religious sisters who have a diploma from the *scuola magistrale*. The kindergartens educate the children in collaboration with the parents.

Beginning in 1966–67 a government *scuola materna* system is being launched with revenue established by the Law of July 24, 1962 (No. 1073), which will become effective following the law under discussion in parliament in April 1966. These schools will make heavy inroads into the Catholic private kindergarten enrollment.

Compulsory education is of eight years' duration, from ages six to fourteen. The child spends his first five school years, from six to eleven, in the *scuola elementare*; the next three years, eleven to fourteen, in the *scuola media* (intermediate comprehensive school). (See chart, letters b and c.)

The *scuola elementare* is divided into two cycles of two and three years, respectively, each concluding with regular examinations. The elementary *licenza* (diploma) permits the graduate to advance to the *scuola media*.

In the government elementary schools the majority of the teachers of both sexes are practicing Catholics. A primary reason for this is that about 30 per cent of the women teachers during the last twenty years have attended teacher-training schools (*Istituti Magistrali*) which are conducted by religious sisters.

The *scuola media* is the only school level which has been the product of genuine educational reform in Italy in recent years. The *scuola media* was established by the Law of December 31, 1962 (No. 1859) and replaced all previous schools and programs for students aged eleven to fourteen. The *media* is a comprehensive school which completes the period of compulsory education, terminating with the *licenza media*, a diploma from the intermediate school which permits the graduate to advance to the next higher school level. (See chart, letters d and t.)

Following the intermediate comprehensive school (*scuola media*) there is the higher secondary schools system. At this level schooling is aimed not only at furthering the student's personality development and giving him a general liberal education, but also in providing him with a professional or preprofessional orientation. It is this final aspect, preprofessional orientation, which forms the point of departure for three separate scholastic tracks, each geared to a different type of career. Track I is university preparatory education, in which graduation from the higher secondary school is not terminal but rather preliminary to matriculation in the university. (See chart, letters a' and t'.) This track is of the longest duration and is aimed at equipping students for the highest learned and scientific positions in Italy. Track II extends over an intermediate term, usually from ages fifteen to nineteen. There are three basic classifications of higher secondary schools in Track II: the teacher-training secondary schools preparing young women to teach in nursery schools and kindergartens (see chart, letters f and g); technical institute secondary schools preparing persons to enter divers technical professions (see chart, letters h-n); secondary schools for the arts training students for careers in the artistic professions (see chart, letters r-u). Track III is of brief duration. Schools in this category are the higher vocational secondary schools. They prepare their students to enter certain kinds of executive positions (see chart, letters o-r).

The secondary school system for pupils aged fifteen to nineteen is therefore divided into four *ordini*, or groups: schools giving general formation called humanistic (letters d-g on chart); or giving technical formation (letters h-n on chart); professional (letters o-q on chart); or artistic (letters r-u on chart).

In the first group of higher secondary schools, the humanities, there are the following: the *liceo-classico* (letter d on chart); the school of the traditional Greco-Roman humanism (letters a'-t' on chart) which qualifies graduates to enroll in all the faculties of the university except in the Faculty of Teaching (*Facultà di Magistero*); the *liceo-scientifico* (letter a' on chart), which includes Latin but stresses mathematics and science, and whose graduates may enroll in all faculties of the university except in the Faculty of Letters and Philosophy (*Facultà di Lettere e Filosofia*; the *Istituto Magistrale* (letter f on chart), which includes Latin and whose thrust is the preparation of elementary school teachers; the *scuola magistrale* (letter g on chart), which prepares women teachers for the nursery schools and kindergartens (*scuola materna*).

The second classification of higher education schools, the technical group of schools, provides the training of the so-called *tecnici intermedi*, an intermediate group of technicians in industry. This class of technicians falls between the managerial group and those technicians who possess university degrees, on the one hand, and those technicians with only the short period of training, on the other. These intermediate technicians are trained for production or services in the following areas: agriculture, industry, surveying, accountancy, marine technology, certain activities performed also by women, such as dietetics and community guidance. However, there are still other areas under the purview of this general classification of higher technical secondary schools since technical institutes (*istituti tecnici*) can be organized for other fields of activity, such as those already operative for tourism and those for company secretaries.

The third broad category of higher secondary schools includes those belonging to the professional group and which prepare for the practice of largely manual activities in the various areas of production —artisan, agricultural, commercial, hotels and tourism, marine activities, dressmaking, and so forth (letters o, p, q on chart).

Higher secondary schools of the fourth type are the art schools. Following an administrative tradition, these schools all belong to a special system headed by a General Department of the Ministry for Public Instruction. They provide for the following periods of training: brief, for artistic craftsmen (*artigianato artistico*, letters r and s on chart); intermediate, for teaching art or applied art in the lower middle school (*media inferiore*, letter s on chart); and long, destined for a higher theoretical and practical training (*formazione superiore teorica e practica*, letters t and u on chart).

The government is presenting to parliament new plans for laws introducing innovations necessitated by the reorganization of the *scuola media* into the upper secondary system. These innovations are required for pedagogical, didactical and social reasons. A *Liceo linguistico* (linguistic lyceum) is being added to the existing *licei* for the teaching of modern languages. The *Istituto Magistrale* (teacher-training school) will be upgraded to the status of a five-year *Liceo Magistrale*; the *scuola magistrale* will last for four years. All the five-year courses in both the *licei* and the *istituti* will be operated on a double cycle, that is a two-year cycle followed by a three-year cycle so that the biennium of the fourteen- to sixteen-year group can be organized as a comprehensive school with studies including disciplines which are common to all and which are particular to each. The purpose of this cycle system is to facilitate the horizontal articulation of students from one school to another. From the four *licei*—classical, linguistic, scientific, teacher-training—students have access to all university faculties. Students from the technical institutes can likewise pass to the corresponding faculty.

In addition to those schools and courses which provide professional training and which depend on the Ministry for Public Instruction there are also *Corsi di addestramento professionale* (CAP), training courses for the professions. These CAP's are under the Ministry of Labor. About 500,000 students annually attend these courses. Indeed, over 50 per cent of these students belong to CAP's organized by Catholic institutes or schools (see *Associazioni Cristiane Lavoratori Italiani*, ACLI).

Higher secondary education terminates at the age of eighteen to nineteen with an *esame di Stato* (state examination) prescribed by Article 33 of the constitution. The content and format of the examination are based on examination programs and on government examining committees. All students in government and nongovernment schools present themselves before these committees, as do *privatisti* (those who have not attended any school having legal status for studies). These state examinations qualify for admission to the university, so that the university cannot impose any entrance examination of its own on candidates. Successful outcome on the state examination is also required for license to practice the profession corresponding to each school.

There are in Italy forty-four government and private universities, only two of which are Catholic and *pareggiate*, that is equivalent to the government institutions. These two are the Catholic University of the Sacred Heart in Milan, and the Maria Assunta Teacher-Training Institute in Rome.

The Catholic University of Milan was founded in 1921 by Agostino Gemelli, an atheist physician who became a convert and entered the Franciscan Brothers. The university was rebuilt in 1943 after it was destroyed during World War II. Today it ranks as one of the finest Italian universities, with a library of over one million volumes. Apart from the high level of the teaching staff and the high caliber of the students it accepts, a primary reason for the success of the Catholic University of Milan is the legal formula of *pareggiamento* by which faculty and students must possess the same qualifications as those in government universities. This imposes heavy burdens, but it permits the exchange of faculty members and students with government universities. Such an exchange fosters the renewal of the academic body and prevents the Catholic University from becoming a Catholic ghetto cut off from the rest of the academic world.

The Catholic University of Milan is presently composed of several regional centers. At Milan itself there are five Faculties: Law, Political Science, Economics and Commerce, Letters and Philosophy, and Education. There is also the Institute of Statistics, as well as various Upper Schools of Specialization for graduates. At Piacenza there is a Faculty of Agriculture; at Rome, Faculties of Medicine and Surgery with twenty-one University Institutes and eleven clinics. At Castelnuovo Fogliani there is the Apostolic Institute of the Sacred Heart for female religious. Regular courses are given here for degrees with legal value in the following disciplines: letters, pedagogy, philosophy, mathematics and physics. At Bergamo there is the Upper School of Journalism and Audio-visual Media. At Passo della Mendola, a mountain tourist spot, there is the Mary Immaculate Cultural Center for summer courses and study conventions. At Milan, Piacenza, and Rome there are seven large convents for students and alumni who are continuing their studies; the University Press, *Vita e Pensiero*, publishes a dozen scientific reviews and thousands of books.

The *Maria Assunta Istituto Universitario Pareggiato di Magistero* in Rome was founded on the joint initiative of the Rome vicariat, the Sacred Congregation of Seminaries, and the Congregation of Religious. It was juridically erected and accorded *pareggiamento* status, like the Catholic University of Milan, by Decree 1760 of October 26, 1939. It is intended for female religious who follow courses for degrees in letters, pedagogy, languages, and foreign literature, and for a diploma for supervision in elementary schools.

The *Università Internazionale degli Studi Sociali* (International University for Social Studies) founded in 1944 with the name Pro Deo University had up to 1966 not yet received the *pareggiata*, although it is equipped with an excellent teaching staff and a large student body of Italians and foreigners. Pro Deo University is organized as follows: a Faculty of Political Science, which provides courses leading to degrees in political science and in economics and commerce; an Institute of Sociology; a School for Specialization in the Science and Technique of Administration; an Upper Institute for Foreign Languages, with a School for Interpreters; an Institute for the Science and Technique of Public Opinion, with courses in journalism, cinematography, radio, and television.

There are some thirty Catholic *Scuole di Servizio Sociale* (Social Service Schools) at the university level. These schools admit students of both sexes who have completed their higher secondary studies. They grant a diploma of *Assistente Sociale*. Several thousand graduates have entered public and private social service agencies. The level of scientific training in the schools of social service varies from school to school. All suffer from the juridical rigidity attendant upon graduation from a school of higher education which is not of formally recognized university stature. Consequently not even the most competent graduates of these *scuole* have been able to obtain legal recognition of their diplomas. This seriously weakens the student's professional opportunities because a nonuniversity diploma does not permit graduates to obtain positions in public administration at the level commensurate with their academic competence.

Concerning compulsory school attendance, the constitution (Article 34) states: "Lower instruction, imparted for at least eight years, is compulsory and gratis." Eight years of compulsory education is the rule followed by the nineteen countries belonging to the Council of Europe. Actual attendance, however, increases yearly toward a nine-year or a ten-year course. In England since 1947, compulsory education lasts from ages five to fifteen years, and in France it lasts from ages six to sixteen. In Italy where the law does not permit employment of youths under fifteen years of age, there is a tendency to keep children in school longer than the six- to fourteen-year compulsory period. (See Conseil de l'Europe, Strasbourg, *Rapport du Secrétariat*, 1965, pp. 138–143.)

Control Structure of the Catholic School System

While awaiting new legislation on nongovernment *privata* or *paritaria* schools, which would implement the freedom and equality granted by the constitution, every nongovernment school is bound by Article 1 of the Law of January 19, 1942 (No. 86) to conform to the regulations pertaining to government schools.

The Ministry of Public Instruction in Rome is in charge of all government schools. It also exercises official vigilance and control over nongovernment schools by means of thirteen general departments. One of these departments, for example, is the general department for nongovernment middle education. The kindergartens (*scuola materna*) and the primary schools come under the General Department for Elementary Education.

In each of the ninety-two Italian provinces there is a superintendent's office of studies (*Provveditorato agli Studi*) which controls and inspects all schools, excluding universities. It is a local arm of the Ministry of Public Instruction.

Within the Ministry there is a Higher Council of Public Instruction (*Consiglio Superiore della Pubblica Istruzione*). This Council has only consultative power over the Ministry. The Council itself is divided into three sections: the university section, the secondary school section, and the elementary section including the Kindergarten (*scuola materna*). The Council is composed of members elected by the schools and by others appointed by the Ministry.

Italian Educational System (1967)

school | a | b | c | 1 | 2 | 3 | 4 | 5 | 1 | 2 | 3 | 1 | 2 | 3 | 4 | 5 | 1 | 2 | 3 | 4 | 5 | 6 |

age   3   4   5   6   7   8   9   10   11   12   13   14   15   16   17   18   19   20   21   22   23   24   25

UNIVERSITY FACULTIES

d. Classical Liceo   a'. Letters and Philosophy
1 — 2 — 3 — 4 — 5 —   1 — 2 — 3 — 4 —
e. Scientific Liceo   b'. Law
1 — 2 — 3 — 4 — 5 —   1 — 2 — 3 — 4 —
f. Teacher Training   c'. Pedagogy
   School
1 — 2 — 3 — 4 — 1 —   2 — 3 — 4 —
g. Teacher Training   d'. Political Science
   for Kindergarten
1 — 2 — 3 —   1 — 2 — 3 — 4 —
h. Agricultural Voc.   e'. Economics and Business
   Inst.
1 — 2 — 3 — 4 — 5 —   1 — 2 — 3 — 4 —
i. Surveyors Voc. Inst.   f'. Natural Sciences and
                        Mathematics
1 — 2 — 3 — 4 — 5 —   1 — 2 — 3 — 4 —
l. Industrial Tech.   g'. Medicine
   Inst.
1 — 2 — 3 — 4 — 5 —   1 — 2 — 3 — 4 — 5 — 6 —
m. Marine Tech. Inst.   h'. Veterinary Science
1 — 2 — 3 — 4 — 5 —   1 — 2 — 3 — 4 —

b, c. Compulsory education

a. Nursery   b. Elementary   c. Interme-
   school   school   diate
   and   school
   kinder-   1 — 2 + 1 — 2 — 3 + 1 — 2 — 3   n. Girls Tech. Inst.   i'. Engineering
   garten   1st   2nd   1 — 2 — 3 — 4 — 5 —   1 — 2 — 3 — 4 — 5 —
a — b — c   cycle   cycle   o. Voc. H. S. for Girls   l'. Architecture
                                        1 — 2 — 3 + 1 — 2 —   1 — 2 — 3 — 4 — 5 —
                                        p. Voc. Training Inst.   m'. Nautical Institute
                                        (new type)
                                        1 — 2 — 3 + 1 + 1 —   1 — 2 — 3 — 4 —
                                        q. Trade School   n'. Industrial Chemistry
                                        1 — 2 —   1 — 2 — 3 — 4 — 5 —
                                        r. School of Applied   o'. Pharmacy
                                        Arts
                                        1 — 2 —   1 — 2 — 3 — 4 —
                                        s. Inst. for Applied   p'. Agriculture
                                        Arts
                                        1 — 2 — 3 + 1 — 2 —   1 — 2 — 3 — 4 —
                                        t. Art H. S.   q'. Fine Arts Academy
                                        1 — 2 — 3 — 4 — 1 —   2 — 3 — 4 —
                                                     r'. Statistics
                                                     1 — 2 — 3 — 4 —
                          u. Conservatory and Music Liceo   s'. Oriental Institute
                          1 + 1 — 2 — 3 + 1 — 2 — 3 — 4 — 5 —   1 — 2 — 3 — 4 —
                                                     t'. Institute of Physical Educ.
                                                     1 — 2 — 3 —

age   3   4   5   6   7   8   9   10   11   12   13   14   15   16   17   18   19   20   21   22   23   24   25

school | a | b | c | 1 | 2 | 3 | 4 | 5 | 6 | 7 | 8 | 9 | 10 | 11 | 12 | 13 | 14 | 15 | 16 | 17 | 18 | 19 |

In reading this entire essay, one must recall that there are detailed and comprehensive legal statutes governing all Italian schools, statutes to which both government and nongovernment educational institutions must scrupulously adhere.

Control over Catholic schools is on two levles, the government and the Church level. On the government level, the central power is in the Ministry of Public Instruction; provincial authority is vested in the superintendent's office of studies (*Provveditorato agli Studi*); local authority is vested in the principal in charge of the individual schools.

The Ministry of Public Instruction exercises executive power over nongovernment schools through the General Department (*Direzione Generale*) for primary education. Nursery schools also are subject to this department. There is a special General Department for Middle Education in nongovernment schools (*Direzione Generale della Istruzione media non statale*), deriving its principal powers from the Law of January 19, 1942 (No. 86). This statute regulates the establishment of new private schools and makes decisions on requests for legal recognition or of *pareggiamento*. The Director General is represented by a government inspector (*Commissario Governativo*) at all final examinations in those schools which possess legally recognized courses of studies and diplomas. The office of the Director General also checks on schools by means of unannounced visits by inspectors, and decides cases of suspension from office, closure, or other punitive measures. The Superintendent's Office of Studies shares in the ordinary and extraordinary powers of control over the schools and in the execution of ministerial dispositions in their regard.

The school principal (called the president or the manager of the school) is responsible to the law, as well as to the school authorities, teachers, pupils, and their parents for the professional administrative and didactical functioning of the school.

It must be borne in mind that government control of all schools in Italy is meticulous. The government controls the functioning of the school down to the last and finest detail.

The Church's authority over schools is exercised in two ways: first, by the hierarchy through both its Central School Office and through the local ordinary; second, by the major superiors of the religious institutes which conduct the schools.

The Central School Office for Italy is based at the Sacred Congregation for Seminaries and Universities. The Office was set up in 1932 by Pius XI in a letter of the Secretariat of State dated April 23,

1933 (No. 987). This was confirmed by another letter of August 23, 1934 (No. 2685/34), and the Office was given the name *Ufficio Centrale per gli Istituti Cattolici d'Italia*. The Office's jurisdiction extends to all schools and teaching institutes maintained by ecclesiastical bodies in Italy. All levels, types, and grades are included: nursery or kindergarten (*scuola materna*); elementary; upper and lower secondary; boarding schools; and educational institutes. Letter 9219 of the Vatican's Secretariat of State of October 26, 1960 extended the jurisdiction of the Central School Office to all social service schools and institutes. This includes para-university or lower level schools which are subject to Church bodies and also works or organizations of Catholic inspiration. The Office, moreover, supervises all religious instruction given in those schools subject to Church authority. The Sacred Congregation of the Council, however, has special jurisdiction in the area of religious programs and textbooks. Finally, the Central School Office has control over all teaching and educational institutions operated by canonically designated moral bodies, pious works, associations and corporations, as well as those maintained by individuals but which are entrusted to official Church bodies according to Article 29 of the Concordat.

Of the principal functions exercised by the Central School Office, the following are worthy of special mention. It supervises the religious, moral, didactical, disciplinary, and administrative operations of the schools. It gives directives to school people in collaboration with lawful religious and ecclesiastical superiors. It arranges inspections or visits to verify compliance with all the various school regulations. It gives its official *nihil obstat* for opening new schools and for recognizing their legality. (This is done by issuing a required document which must be presented to the central school authorities by ecclesiastical or religious bodies to permit the opening of schools or to grant them official recognition.) It gives its official *nihil obstat* for the recognition of ecclesiastical academic titles (doctorates or licentiates) so that holders of these titles may be able to enroll in the government universities or to teach in secondary schools (in accordance with Article 31 of the Law of January 19, 1942, No. 86). Finally, the Central School Office receives official notice from individual school authorities prior to the suspension, revocation, or closure of educational institutions subject to Church authority, according to Article 29 of the same law.

The Central School Office has promoted and set up in every diocese a special diocesan school bureau the function of which is to work out with schools the provisions required for the opening and recognition of Church schools and to see that these stipulations are properly implemented. The Bureau also checks to ensure that the schools under its care are functioning properly.

The Central School Office has also established the National Federation of Institutes Depending on Ecclesiastical Authorities (FIDAE), giving it its own statutes formally approved by the Sacred Congregation of Seminaries and Universities. Thus FIDAE is given a specific sphere of action, a sphere in which it is assisted by a delegate of the same Sacred Congregation. The Central School Office establishes norms guiding the relationship between individual lay teachers and FIDAE. The Office also controls the updating of the dependent institutes vis-à-vis the Christian needs of times and circumstances, establishing special goals for these schools to fit them for reforms in their regulations or their basic organizational framework. The Central Office seeks to expand the Church's school apostolate at all levels, coordinating and perfecting the various apostolic educational activities of the Church. It also defends the lawful interests of educational institutes maintained by Church authorities, promotes the growth of the individual institutes, provides assistance for their many needs, and seeks to assure their capacity to meet the exigencies of the modern world.

The Central School Office is assisted by a *Consulta Tecnica*, a body of educational experts who are asked to give considered opinions on important topics dealing with education in general and with schools in particular. The Central School Office also acts as technical adviser on questions dealing with relations between the Holy See and the civil school authorities.

The local Ordinary, of course, carries out the educative functions enjoined on him by canon law and cooperates with the Central School Office.

It is worth noting that historically the Central School Office as a branch of the Sacred Congregation of Seminaries and Universities was established in 1932 when the Fascists ruled Italy. At that time there was a desperate need of support for Catholic educational institutes and to carry out the many dispositions laid down in the Concordat of February 11, 1929. In 1953 the Italian Episcopal Conference (CEI) established a Committee for Cultural Activities (*Commissione per le Attività Culturali*). This Committee, which still flourishes, is assisted by the Committee of Educational, Cultural, and School Experts (COECS), which is made up of clerical and lay experts highly qualified in education and culture.

Nonetheless, the Central School Office retains its own powers until such time as the National Episcopal Conference of Italy carves out for itself its own spheres of jurisdiction over Catholic schools. With the emphasis placed by Vatican II on the power of national episcopal conferences, this development should not be long in coming.

According to the official Yearbook of 1955 (pp. 207–239), groups which operate schools depending on Church authorities are primarily those ecclesiastical bodies which are juridically recognized in accordance with Article 29 of the Concordat. These comprise the Holy See, dioceses, prelatures, abbacies, parishes, ecclesiastical foundations, male teaching religious institutes (about eighty), and female teaching religious institutes (about 180). Obviously each Catholic school is controlled primarily by that Church body which operates it; that is, a school operated by the Jesuits is principally controlled by the Jesuits. However, each school principal is subject both to the superior (superioress) of his (her) institute and to government educational authorities.

Following the first International Congress of the States of Perfection held in Rome in 1950, federations of religious men and religious women were established in Italy. The zones of influence and cooperation of these federations of separate religious institutes extend naturally to the educational field. The National Committee of Major Superiors (CISM, with about 200 members) was formally approved by the Sacred Congregation of Religious on November 30, 1960. The Union of Italian Major Superiors (USMI), which allies 388 congregations of sisters with 156,000 members, was established as a juridic entity by state Presidential Decree of June 9, 1964, No. 622. The latter controls various federations, including the Italian Federation of Religious Women Educators (*Federazione Italiana Religiose Educatrici*, FIRE) and the Italian Federation of Religious Women Social Assistants (*Federazione Italiana Religiose Assistenti Sociali*, FIRAS). The obvious need for and usefulness of coordinative organizations such as these, as well as that of the Federation of Institutes Depending on Ecclesiastical Authority (FIDAE), makes it all the more surprising that it was only in recent years that such apparent and natural organizational structures were established.

In general, vigilant control of Italian Catholic schools have been the subject of diligent and exact supervision of the legally qualified civil and ecclesiastical authorities. However, it is regrettable that this vigilance is concerned chiefly with juridical regularity and adherence to minute legal details. The type of supervision which promotes the upgrading and perfection of didactical and pedagogical processes is almost nonexistent, a sorry situation directly due to the almost total lack of qualified educational specialists equipped with the latest and most professional scientific and experimental training.

Some Statistics on Catholic Schools

The following table presents pertinent comparative data on government schools, Catholic schools, and laicist private schools at all educational levels.

Statistical Summary, Catholic and Government Schools*

	1963			1948		
	Government schools	Catholic schools	Private secular schools	Government schools	Catholic schools	Private secular schools
Total schools						
nursery-kindergartens	5,885	4,398	8,378	2,466	4,826	4,400
Total schools elementary	38,174	2,211	697	34,439	2,017	650
Total schools lower secondary	5,135	922	228	2,104	833	744
Total schools upper secondary	1,846	845	392	1,248	662	529
Total universities	n.d.	2	n.d.	n.d.	n.d.	n.d.
Total students						
nursery-kindergartens						
Total students elementary	4,042,073	272,112	62,611	4,534,776	254,376	58,376
Total students lower secondary	1,553,032	111,904	19,996	437,359	82,107	51,482
Total students upper secondary	857,661	94,080	57,797	279,508	48,568	42,292
Total students university	211,797	11,995	16,442	156,323	4,612	7,066
Median school enrollment						
elementary	106	123	90	n.d.	n.d.	n.d.
Median school enrollment						
lower secondary	302	121	88	n.d.	n.d.	n.d.
Median school enrollment						
upper secondary	465	111	147	n.d.	n.d.	n.d.
Median pupil class size						
elementary	16	25	19	n.d.	n.d.	n.d.
Median pupil class size						
lower secondary	23	27	21	n.d.	n.d.	n.d.
Median pupil class size						
upper secondary	21	22	22	n.d.	n.d.	n.d.

* All the statistics given in this study are official and come from the publications of the Central Statistics Institute (*Istituto Centrale di Statistica*), which is a dependency of the Board of the Council of Ministers. Tables were drawn up by an expert in school statistics from the same Institute.

The years 1948–49 and 1963–64 were chosen for comparison. Data previous to 1948 cannot be compared with those of the present for reasons connected with the development of the nongovernment schools. The latter achieved equality with the government schools with the Decree of June 3, 1938, No. 928, and later with the Law of January 19, 1942, No. 86. Moreover, the war of 1940–45 notably changed the relations between government and Catholic schools as it increased considerably the number of pupils attending the latter. About 1948 the situation took a decisive turn in the relationship between the two types of school.

The number of illiterates—a heritage from the nineetenth century and the result of the failure of the school legislation of the Liberal and Fascist governments, as well as two World Wars—according to the 1951 census stood at 12.9 per cent of the population over six years and 6.8 per cent of those between six and fourteen years of age. By the 1961 census the percentage had fallen to 8.3 per cent for the first group and 2.3 per cent for the second. The figure for the six to fourteen year group is nearly the lowest in the world.

The class schedule prescribes from four to six periods of sixty minutes each, six days per week for the secondary schools. The school day starts at 8 A.M. and ends at 2 P.M. There is a fifteen-minute break at mid-morning. The elementary school program lasts for four hours each morning.

The school year is divided into trimesters. The first of these runs from October 1 to December 23; the second, from January 2 to March 20; and the third, from March 21 to June 15. The elementary school program continues until the end of June, and as a rule nursery schools and kindergartens follow the elementary school calendar.

Vacations extend from December 23 to January 1; from Holy Thursday to Easter Monday. The long summer vacation extends from the end of the third trimester to October 1. Four additional holidays are granted annually on days fixed by the local or area Directors of Education (*Provveditori agli Studi*). Catholic schools follow the same class schedules, academic calendar, and vacation periods as the government schools.

School architecture in Italy is generally modern, sober, and relatively functional. Special areas are set aside for cultural, didactical, and remedial work, and athletic or recreational purposes. Plans for the standardization of school construction are being considered. The use of prefabricated parts for classrooms and even for entire schools is increasing.

Catholic school plants follow the same lines as do their government counterparts. However, as a whole, Catholic school plants are generally on a higher level than those of government schools. The reason underlying this is that, unlike government schools, Catholic schools can limit student enrollment and thus insure a good pupil to building ratio. Moreover, Catholic school authorities do not undertake new construction projects unless the requisite financial means are at hand. Finally, Catholic school officials search for the most modern architectural solutions to construction problems; in this they are spurred on by government supervision which is fairly strict in the whole area of school construction. It may be noted in passing that the government provides subsidies for the construction of nursery schools.

School architecture and construction are detailed and regulated in a series of government documents outlining the so-called "School Development Plan" for the five-year academic period 1965–70. The "Guidelines for the Multiyear School Development Plan for the Period following June 30, 1965" presented by Minister Luigi Gui anticipates the following pupil increase for the periods 1964–65, 1969–70, and 1974–75, respectively, in both government and nongovernment schools: for primary schools, from 4,417,000 to 4,714,000 to 5,315,000; for intermediate schools, from 1,775,000 to 2,078,000 to 2,319,000; for upper secondary schools, from 1,165,000 to 1,701,000 to 2,126,000; and for universities, from 256,000 to 373,000 to 519,000.

Taking into account the resources of the Italian economy, it has been reliably estimated that the sum of 21,340 billion Lire will be required for the construction of 3,086,000 school places in the primary, intermediate, and upper secondary government schools, basing the calculations on the needs of each of the three school levels respectively as being twenty-two, twenty-five, and twenty-seven students per classroom, and requiring a ground area of respectively fifteen, sixteen, and twenty square meters per pupil place. Law project No. 1552 presented by the Italian government to the Senate on January 21, 1966 re school construction for the calendar years 1966–70 reduces the figure to 12,100 billion Lire for 1,620,000 school places.

Financial Support
of Catholic
Schools in Italy

The government provides free education in those years covered by the compulsory school attendance law only for pupils attending government schools. Consequently despite the clear provisions of Article 34 of the Constitution, there is no government financial assistance to private schools, with a few exceptions noted below.

The financial burden of Catholic schools can be accurately estimated by the annual cost per pupil in government schools as far as operating expenses only are concerned. The operating costs of primary schools alone for the years 1955, 1960, and 1963 rose to the following figures for each of these years, respectively: 38,900 Lire to 61,200 Lire to 117,000 Lire (approximately $61 to $99 to $188). For lower secondary schools, the growth figures rose from 71,500 Lire ($115) to 84,932 Lire ($137) to 176,000 Lire ($285). For upper secondary schools, the cost increased from 96,400 Lire ($155) to 137,200 Lire ($221) to 226,000 Lire $365. These figures do not include an extra sum totaling 20 per cent of the quoted costs and paid by local bodies. Neither do these figures include the costs of school construction.

Catholic schools, with the exceptions noted below, are financed chiefly through student tuition and indirectly through the contributed services of the religious teachers, together with the generous sacrifice of lay teachers, whose salaries range from 25 to 50 per cent less than their counterparts in government schools.

The government allots extremely modest financial aid to private nursery schools and kindergartens (*scuola materna*). The fiscal subsidy has risen from an average of 1000 Lire ($1.60) per pupil per year in 1955, to 2000 Lire ($3.20) in 1965. Until very recently almost all nursery schools and kindergartens were privately operated. Now the government is launching a public nursery and kindergarten system which will be entirely tuition free. Many Catholics are of the opinion that this government system of *scuola materna* is an attempt by the laicist political parties to make serious inroads on the power and influence of Catholic nursery schools and kindergartens.

Certain types of equalized primary schools (*parificate*) receive financial subsidies from the government equivalent to 25–50–75–100 per cent of the salaries of teachers in these schools. However, to qualify for these subsidies, the schools must provide free education for all the pupils as well as give the complete repertoire of social welfare benefits to the entire teaching staff. Schools which specialize in vocational education (CAP), mentioned earlier in this essay, receive a government subsidy from the Ministry of Labor totaling 100 per cent of their operating costs.

Government universities are totally financed by public monies. However, since they are autonomous, self-governing bodies, they may also receive grants and endowments from individuals or public bodies for particular institutes, special programs, or for capital expenditures.

No state fiscal aid is provided for nongovernment universities. Nonetheless, these institutions may be given special grants by the government for such purposes as scientific research. But it must be noted that students at nongovernment universities receive the same grants-in-aid from the state as do students in government universities.

In addition to subsidizing certain types of Catholic schools to some degree, the government also gives financial assistance to students in Catholic and in government schools at all levels. To be sure, financially needy students are given sufficient fiscal support so that their lack of means does not impede their education. Special attention is given to students from working-class families. Moreover, students from government, standardized, or equalized schools (*scuole parificate o pareggiate*)—the latter include all the Catholic schools—enjoy equal government subsidies. From 1966–70 these grants for elementary schools will have risen to 162,000 million Lire ($259,-200,000). This includes such items as schoolbooks, meals, uniforms, transportation, after-school study, scholarships, places in boarding schools, sanitary and psychopedagogical assistance, vocational guidance, and so forth. For university students during this same 1966–70 period, 108,000 million Lire ($172,800,000) have been set aside for ordinary student subsidies, over and above annual allowances and scholarships for graduates (Proposed Law of January 21, 1966, No. 1543, before the Italian Senate). This means that for those enrolled in elementary and secondary schools, there is an average of 23,000 Lire ($37.28) allocated for the five years, 1966–70, or 4660 Lire annually ($7.46) per capita. For the universities the average sum is 562,256 Lire ($899.61) or 112,451 Lire ($179.92), annually.

Salaries, fringe benefits, and legal contractual arrangements for teachers in Catholic schools are governed by the cooperative contract of May 11, 1964 signed by both the Association of Administrators of Institutes Dependent on Ecclesiastical Authority (*Associazione Gestori Istituti Dipendenti dall'Autorità Ecclesiastica*) (AGIDAE) and by the Italian Trade Union for Nongovernment Schools (*Sindacato Italiano Scuola non Statale*) (SISNS), which is a branch of the Italian Confederation of Workers' Trade Unions (*Confederazione Italiana Sindacati Lavoratori*) (CISL). Consequently all school personnel in Catholic schools enjoy not only the freedom and dignity involved in academic freedom, but also some kind of equitable salary scale and fringe benefits such as pensions and health insurance. Unhappily, salaries are determined by the amount of tuition paid by the students of a particular school; thus teachers in schools catering to poorer families receive less than do their counterparts who teach in schools whose student body comes from the middle or upper socio-economic classes.

The Curriculum

Syllabi for all schools are drawn up by the government. The principal architect of school syllabi is the Ministry of Public Instruction, in cooperation with the various National Teaching Centers, the Upper Council of Public Instruction, and selected experts. Catholics wield a fair share of influence in drawing up the syllabi.

The curriculum for the kindergartens includes: religious education; training in the moral and social life; physical, intellectual, and linguistic education; freehand drawing; choral singing; games and work. These teaching programs were established by Decree of June 11, 1958, No. 584.

The following subjects are prescribed for the elementary schools: religion; moral, civil, physical education; history; geography; natural science; arithmetic; geometry; Italian; drawing and writing; singing; manual and practical activities (Decree of June 14, 1955, No. 503).

The curriculum in the intermediate comprehensive school (*scuola media*) is the same for all students: religion; Italian; history and civics; geography; mathematics; natural sciences; one foreign language; art; physical education. Elective subjects include during the second and third years the *esercitazioni tecniche o di lavoro*, a sort of prevocational training, and in the third year, Latin.

In addition to the prescribed curriculum there is a *doposcuola*, a form of supervised after-school study complementing the regular program. It is optional and free of charge. There are also remedial classes (*aggiornamento*) to help the slow students, and also adjustment classes (*differenziali*) for the maladjusted and the retarded.

The upper general secondary schools of the humanistic (*liceo*), technical (*tecnico*), or artistic (*arte*) types have a common group of subjects: religion; civics; Italian; one foreign language; history; geography; mathematics; science; and physical education. In addition, each broad category of upper general secondary schools offers its own specialties, as for example, Latin, Greek, and pedagogy in the upper secondary school of the humanities and the matter proper to each type of technical institute or art school.

The curriculum in the vocational schools is divided into two parts. The first part provides a general orientation to the liberal arts, whereas the second part offers a combination of vocational theory and practice. Normally, half the time is devoted to theory, and the other half stresses the practical aspects.

The universities comprise the traditional faculties where the student begins immediately to specialize in the discipline of his choice.

In nursery schools and kindergartens the curriculum is definitely centered around student needs and personal development. Such curricula as the Montessori system and other types of student-centered curriculum designs are much in vogue. In the lower secondary schools there is still some curricular emphasis on student needs and human growth. However, by the time the intermediate and the higher forms of secondary education are reached, the curriculum degenerates into the traditional, tightly subject-centered type. The Core curriculum, that dynamic American educational invention, is virtually unknown in Italian secondary education.

There have been some curricular innovations in the Italian school system. Most notable is the intermediate secondary school system (*scuola media*). Without a doubt, the *scuola media* represents the first attempt of the Italian educational system to provide secondary education for all youths according to the latest advances. It is patterned after the system and principles of the United States' secondary schools. Curricular innovations, though not as sweeping, have been introduced into the nursery schools and kindergartens (*scuola materna*), as well as into the elementary schools (*scuola elementare*). As a result of the establishment of the innovational *scuola media* system, some new curricular revisions were introduced into the upper secondary schools, beginning with the 1966 academic year.

Various educational groups as well as pedagogical Specialists in individual subjects propose curricular innovations. They also undertake some experimentation in this vital area. One of the crowning achievements of their activities was the establishment of the innovational *scuola media*. Among the first to take the initiative in the examination of, experimentation in, and setting up of the *scuola media* were Catholic members of the Italian Catholic Union of Intermediate Teachers (*Unione Cattolica Italiana Insegnanti Medi*, UCIIM). The *scuola media* represents an innovational attempt which involved a drastic revolution in the ossified and static school system. Other Catholics in the forefront of this curricula reformation were those belonging to the National Teaching Center for Secondary Schools (*Centro*

Didattico Nazionale Scuola Secondaria), to the Intermediate Schools National Trade Union (*Sindacato Nazionale Scuola Media*, SNSM), the majority of whose members are practicing Catholics, and also persons from the Catholic school system.

On the basis of the general overall government-imposed syllabus, teachers in each school (including Catholic schools) every year initiate a special revised curricular plan tailored to the needs of their particular schools. Such tailoring is extremely minimal since the government syllabus is at once minutely detailed and legally binding. The chief curricular individualization consists in arranging the school's educational activities and units of study, dividing both into one year's work of three trimesters. At the end of the school year the teachers make a final report on the year's work.

Official government directives and instructions stipulate that real life must form both the basis and the goal of the curriculum and indeed of the entire teaching process in all primary and intermediate schools. These directives are adhered to by at least 75 per cent of all the schools.

The text of the teaching programs for primary schools (Decree of June 14, 1955, No. 503) explicitly insists on the living concretization of theoretical instruction:

The consciousness of the basic characteristics of the child's make-up obliges the educational system to follow the already existing contours of what the child has previously learned, understood, and experienced from his family, from his natural and social environment, and from the educational institutions which he has already attended. Consequently the teacher must never overlook the child's attachment to and participation in his own particular milieu, in both the variety of manifestations and the moral and religious inspiration which animates that milieu.

The out-of-school environment with its many and varied life episodes, together with the social experience of daily living together in school, provides the teacher with the best opportunities for discussing matters relating to the pupils' sphere of interests in order to be better able to understand their inclinations and capacities and to orientate their conduct according to moral norms and good citizenship. In order to arouse an early awareness of the guiding principles of right conduct, the teacher will take care to lead the pupil gradually to reflect on the acts of individual living in the world of the school, the family, and society.

Above all, it is the pupil's own milieu with its numerous opportunities for historical and scientific interest which offers him a wider and accurate knowledge of the world.

The teaching of mathematics must likewise be kept in the closest contact with both the practical life and the interests of the child. Care must be taken to insure its concreteness and its meshing with day-to-day reality, related to even the most ordinary cases of family and commercial book-keeping.

The same principles as are laid down in the above decree underlie the curricula and the teaching instructions for the intermediate schools (Decree of April 24, 1963). And the same inductive method of beginning with specific factual data and proceeding to the initial generalization of broader concepts is officially prescribed for each of the intellectual disciplines.

Vocational education for the fifteen to seventeen age group follows the same didactical directives as those for the primary and intermediate schools.

In the upper secondary schools, however, the pedagogical method in force is the lecture. By its nature this method tends to preclude the relation of knowledge to life. Notwithstanding, there is a trend—admittedly only among a fairly small number of teachers—toward making the upper secondary school curriculum less bookish and more related to life.

Catholic primary, intermediate, and upper secondary schools follow their government counterparts at each level to the manner and degree in which they relate their curricula to life and life problems.

The growing trend in Italian government schools toward the rejection of bookishness, of grammaticalism, and of the imparting of abstract rules in favor of a greater orientation toward the concrete is being furthered by the increasing use of activity type programs, of group work, of research, of dramatization of historical and scientific facts, and so forth.

Instruction

As with the curriculum, the government wields tight control over the principles and procedures of instruction in both government and private schools. The methodological slant which the government wishes to pervade the teaching process is outlined in the introduction (premesse) placed at the beginning of the official government syllabus for each level of schooling. Since the government exercises punctilious control over all Italian schools, Catholic schools are bound to follow these instructional premesse.

For nursery schools and kindergartens, the *avvertenze*, or instructions of the previously mentioned Decree No. 584, note that the child "presents special characteristics shown in the prevalence of affectivity, of impulse and emotions over reasoning, of a lively need to explore and discover environment and concrete objects, of a vivid imagination, of an acute need for movement and activity as expressed in the form of games." With these *avvertenze* in mind, the instructional thrust of the school is focused on the child's processes of human development. Consequently the methods of teaching are based on the pedagogical and didactical procedures imposed by the unitary aspects of the life, activity, and education of the child. Such developmentally oriented teaching procedures can effectively promote the natural exercise of all the child's activities, facilitating his growth as an individual to attain life's highest values.

The *premesse* of Decree 503 governing elementary schools stipulate the following as the basic rationale for teaching procedures to be employed at this level. The instructional process must

. . . start with the child's concrete world, taking into account the entire intuitional, imaginative, and affective sweep of this world. It must strive to arouse in the pupil a desire to learn. It should help to develop gradually in him the attitudes of observation, reflection, and expression. It should be constantly preoccupied with furthering the pupil's formative process in every way. The teaching procedures should concretize the essential aim of the elementary school, which is not so much to impart a given corpus of ideas, but rather to communicate to the child the joy and taste for learning, so that he can act on his own initiative and retain these habits in his postschool years and indeed for the rest of his life. These key demands of the instructional process will receive greater and more immediate importance if they are recognized in two particularly crucial questions in contemporary education: its globality, and the problem of relating the schoolwork to the environment of the pupil. Thus the teaching process should revolve around prudently utilizing those procedures of action which spur the child on to seek diligently and understand profoundly what he learns.

The Decree of April 24, 1963 of the Ministry of Public Instruction, which issued the curricula for the new comprehensive secondary school (*scuola media*), sets forth *inter alia* the following considerations for the teaching process at this level.

Without losing its own essentially formative character, the new lower secondary school performs at the same time a pivotal role of guidance.

The study of the individual subjects will call for the greatest possible use of inductive processes, beginning with the life experiences of the pupil, his moral and affective world, the observance of facts and phenomena. Thus he can advance progressively to still more organic and intelligent organization of the knowledge acquired. The common, human, social formation of each pupil becomes the dominant motive of the joint or single action of all directors or teachers in every concretely opportune way so that the school can be transformed into a real community equally stimulating for all. Together with the accent on community, other elements indispensable to the individualization of the teaching process flow from legal statues, from the experience of the teachers themselves, and from the science of pedagogy. Chief among these types of teaching processes are enrichment courses, advanced courses, group or committee work, and in general, the procedures geared to tailoring the curriculum to fit the individual, incommunicable, and often diverse qualities of each pupil.

The thrust of the instructional process in the upper general secondary schools is the unitary formation of the student's personality through the liberal arts. In those schools which prepare the student for a profession, the instructional procedures are geared to vocational theory and practice understood both as source and extension of the human personality.

Kindergartens and nursery schools tend to be in the lead among Italian Catholic schools in the utilization of the most advanced pedagogical procedures. Indeed, some entirely new total methodologies were pioneered by Italian child educationists and are employed in quite a few schools. Outstanding among these are the totally new approaches of Maria Montessori (died 1952) and of the Agazzi sisters, Carolina (died 1945) and Rosa (died 1951).

Elementary schools utilize telling, acting-out and discussion methods. Some modern pedagogical techniques are utilized in the new *scuola media*. In the upper secondary schools and in the university the traditional lecture still holds sway as the almost exclusive pedagogical tool. The exception to this is seminar classes, where discussion is fostered. Audiovisual aids are quite widespread in schools at all levels. However, advanced pedagogical procedures such as role-playing, panels, symposia, and committee work are a rarity. Field trips are occasionally used.

Daily homework is customarily assigned to the students, even over feast days and civil holidays. But public opinion has curbed the amount of homework. Most assignments are of the traditional variety. Conduct assignments and other types of modern homework are not common.

Motivation is pretty much of the traditional type. Each teacher practices his or her own brand of motivation. In general, however, the quality is not high considering the results of research investigations of motivational psychologists and educationists. Fear of failing a course and thus being deprived of advancing to a suitable place in society in postschool years remains the dominant motivation. Nevertheless, in pilot schools and in experimental schools, teachers apply the most advanced motivational processes in their instruction.

In the preprimary, primary, and intermediate schools cooperation and inventiveness are gradually replacing competition and overdocility. Nevertheless, in the intermediate schools cooperatively oriented pedagogical procedures are encountering considerable faculty opposition. This is clear from the fact that nearly half of the intermediate classes are more or less firmly anchored to the outmoded individualism and competitiveness of former times.

On the upper secondary level, the evidence seems to confirm the general impression that the curriculum, teaching methods, basic philosophy, and the very structure of this educational level are fundamentally impregnated with the same individualism and, moreover, are opposed and even hostile to any form of cooperative or group-oriented learning experiences.

Progress is being made in the area of group-oriented and other cooperative teaching methodologies both by certain avant-garde groups of teachers and by pilot programs initiated by the National Teaching Centers for the Lyceums and Technical Institutes.

It will be a long time, however, before the efforts of these pedagogical pioneers will have substantially affected the majority of schools or of teachers. One basic reason for this is that the practice of educational competitiveness and individualism has become too deeply rooted in Italian culture. Moreover, the fact that government schools share in the self-sufficiency of the state tends to reinforce the cultural individualism among the faculty and to make the school's educational thrust subject to the modifying influence of family or pupils. Further, even in professional teachers' associations, the government school teachers are much more concerned with trade union interests involving higher salary and career advancement than with the improvement of the teaching processes and the curricula in the schools.

There are two principal practices for evaluating student learning. The first is the use of the traditional marking system, with all the drawbacks inherent in this outmoded practice. The marking system is the prevalent practice in the upper secondary schools (which employ a decimal index) and the universities (where thirty is the index). The second and more progressive practice of student learning evaluation is utilized in the elementary schools and particularly in the lower secondary schools (*scuola media*). This advanced evaluation method is that of the descriptive profile (*profilo*) of the student. This profile is worked out by the school's teaching council on the basis of observation and of written, oral, and practical tests. This collective profile is then recorded on the pupil's cumulative record card (*libretto scholastico*) which follows him in his progress from grade to grade. As a general rule, almost all examinations given in government and Catholic schools are teacher-constructed, with all the weaknesses inherent in such instruments. Even the government-administered final examinations are not standardized in the strict professional sense of the term. Nonetheless, pilot classes and experimental schools are working toward standardized tests.

Certain university centers have launched useful experimental research studies in student evaluation. But up to now the only center that has undertaken systematic psychopedagogical research and rating of tests for primary and lower secondary schools—using teams of internationally trained researchers together with a large body of professors and teachers from government and Catholic schools alike—has been the Institute for Education (*Istituto Superiore di Pedagogia,* ISP) of the Pontifical Salesian University (*Pontificio Ateneo Salesiano*). The Salesian Institute of Education utilizes among other things an electronic computer complex (Olivetti, ELEA, 60001S, linked with the American General Electric Corporation). Results of the school's evaluation of pupil progress is communicated to parents at the end of each trimester, and under certain circumstances more often. The policy of informing parents at parent-teacher meetings about the criteria on which these evaluations have been based is becoming more widespread. Notwithstanding, there is no genuine parent-teacher discussion of the school's evaluation at these meetings. Needless to say, pupils play no role in evaluating themselves as far as the official reports are concerned.

Supervision of instruction in Catholic schools is, as noted earlier, a function of government inspectors. Their role appears, at least to some, more one of making sure that each detail of the official regulations is complied with than of actually serving as a force to improve the teaching. Each principal of a Catholic school also plays his part in supervising the teaching in his school.

As is the situation in many other parts of the world, the instructional processes and standards in Italian schools are heavily determined by the testmakers, in this case the momentous government-administered final examinations. These examinations are particularly crucial at the end of each major school division, for example, the end of lower secondary school, the end of university studies.

The Program of Religious Education

The comprehensive and detailed government regulations which govern every nook and cranny of the educational program of government and Catholic schools apply also in the area of religious instruction. Being "equalized" (*parificate*) with the government schools, Catholic school curricula at each level are uniform in this area of religious instruction as governed by the norms of Article 36 of the 1929 Concordat and by the Law of June 5, 1930, No. 824.

Religious instruction through the completion of secondary school is compulsory by law. However, parents retain the right to withdraw their children from religious instruction classes.

In nursery schools and kindergartens religious instruction must be given for two hours a week. In the elementary schools it is given for ninety minutes per week in the first and second years, and for two hours in the third, fourth, and fifth years. One hour is prescribed weekly for the secondary schools.

Unless a student is enrolled in the Theology Faculty at the university, formal religious instruction in class ceases at the conclusion of secondary school. Consequently what religious education a university student receives is from nonofficial groups of various sorts. Chief among these is the student section of Catholic Action, that papally approved and exquisitely unique lay apostolic organization which brings the influence of militant Catholicism to bear on university youth.

Other Catholic influences in university education include the *Comitato Docenti Universitari*, CDU (Committee of University Teachers) and the *Federazione Universitaria Cattolica Italiana*, FUCI (The Italian Catholic Federation of University Students of both sexes). Organizations for intellectuals and professional people include the *Movimento Laureati di Azione Cattolica* (Movement of University Graduates of Catholic Action) and the *Unioni Professionali Cattoliche* (Unions of Catholic Professional people)—artists,

chemists, lawyers, businessmen, doctors, technicians, Catholic publishers, nurses, and so forth.

In the national lineup of Catholic forces, the Catholic Action
associations are controlled directly by the hierarchy. The professional
unions are governed by organs democratically elected by free and
secret ballot. Through their colleagues belonging to the corresponding non-Catholic democratic trade unions they have an influence
proportionate to their numbers.

Many modern teaching procedures are utilized in the religious
education program. Audiovisual aids have proved a special boon here.
National research centers attempt continuously to upgrade the religious education program. Further, religion textbooks are being constantly updated in accordance with the best domestic and foreign
empirical and theoretical research on religious instruction. Typical of
Catholic forces at work improving catechetical instruction are the
National Center for Catechetical Activities (CENAC) and the Catechetical Institute attached to the Higher Institute of Education at
the Salesian Pontifical University.

Permission to teach religion is reserved to the local bishop, who
in turn permits school authorities to designate teachers with his
approval. If the mistress of the nursery school kindergarten or the
elementary school teacher is not deemed suitable, other persons are
provided. Typically in nursery schools, kindergartens, and elementary schools, the regular classroom teacher also serves as the religion
teacher. On the other hand, in the third, fourth, and fifth grades of
elementary school, a priest is given an additional twenty half-hour
classes yearly. In the middle schools the religion teacher may be the
priest or a religious or a layman.

Usually religion teachers are either professionally prepared teachers or degree-holders, or persons of an equivalent cultural level. But
religion teachers in general are sadly lacking in scientific pedagogico-
didactical training. Consequently special courses in such work, chiefly
given in the summer, help to remove this deficiency. Of course, sum-
mer-school work can never adequately substitute for professional preparation perduring throughout an entire academic year.

Article 36 of the Concordat of February 11, 1929 between the
Holy See and Italy is explicit on the entire matter of the integration
of religion into other areas of the curriculum:

Italy considers the teaching of Christian doctrine according to the form
received from Catholic tradition as both the foundation and the crowning

of public instruction. Hence it authorizes that the religious instruction as presently given in the government elementary schools should receive further development in the (lower and upper) secondary schools, according to programs to be established by agreement between the Holy See and the State.

In actual fact the teaching programs established by the Decrees (No. 584 for the nursery-kindergarten schools, and No. 503 for the primary schools) place the teaching of religion, given by one and the same instructor, at the very heart of the whole educational process. Decree No. 503 stipulated that:

The teaching of religion should be considered as the foundation and the crowning of the whole educational process. Each day the life of the school should begin with prayer, followed by the rendition of a short religious hymn or by listening to a simple passage of sacred music.

Religious education should be inspired by the life and by the teaching of Jesus, as expounded in the Gospels. A religious life should flow from the soul's deep-felt conformity to the principles of the Gospel and from the reasonableness of the relationship between such principles and the application of the moral and civil law.

To implement this infusion of religion into other curricular areas, the Higher Ecclesiastical Commission for the Revision of Texts on Religion publishes a "Guide for the Teaching of Religion in Elementary Schools."

For the nursery-kindergarten schools and the primary schools, the religious convictions of the teachers, integrated by the priest in the primary school, usually allow for the substantial integration of religion into the total school program. Nevertheless, in the Decree of April 24, 1963, dealing with the curriculum of the *scuola media*, and in other decrees governing the upper secondary level, it is stipulated that religion be considered simply as one of the disciplines to be taught, rather than a pervasive force permeating the entire curriculum. Interestingly enough, religion as a separate subject does not fall into the ordinary classification as necessary for advancement to (or exclusion from) the succeeding grade level. Nor do the regulations insist on its being considered as "the foundation and crowning of public instruction."

The lack of any organic, unifying integration of religion into the curriculum of the Italian secondary schools has had damaging effects on the religious life of the students. Neither in the government secondary schools nor in the universities is there either a chaplain or a spiritual director. Consequently it is the religion teachers who must freely take the initiative in matters involving certain acts of worship, such as the fulfilling of the Easter Duty. Thus it can be seen that religious guidance in government secondary schools is, on an organized schoolwide basis, almost nonexistent.

On the other hand, in Catholic schools there are spiritual directors (in the technical sense of the term) who are available for the free guidance of the students according to the various age groups; at the very least there is a priest who is responsible for collective acts of worship.

A notable influence is exercised in the government (and also Catholic) secondary schools by students who are members of the extracurricular Student Youth Movement (*Gioventù Studentesca*). These student movements involving both sexes are official branches of Catholic Action. A similar Catholic influence is brought to the universities by the Federation of Italian Catholic University students (*Federazione Universitaria Cattolici Italiani*, FUCI).

It should be noted that the government school system is not denominational, and the presence of instructors and students of every religious persuasion and of every ideology—including atheists, laicists, Marxists, Communists—scarcely allows for a common cultural or pedagogical orientation of education.

It is true that the Italians do indicate that they wish to have a religious education program in government schools, since most of the parents, including the non-Catholic parents, do not seek to have their children exempted from such instruction, even though the law allows this. It is also true that the religion teacher is almost always a priest—for either pastoral or salary reasons. Yet it cannot be denied that the role of the priest in the cultural and moral formation of the students in the school could certainly be extended and broadened. On the other hand, it is also true that religion enters the curriculum of the *scuola media* and of the upper secondary schools merely as one of the many disciplines and that the priest is but one among many instructors—appreciated or otherwise, backed up or ostracized, supported or impeded, as the case may be.

In the Italian Catholic schools at all levels, all the teachers are of the same faith, which they all more or less practice. But even here, unfortunately, there is usually no systematic integration of religion into the other disciplines, with the exception of those instances in which the religion teacher, priest or frequently religious, teaches other subjects such as philosophy or pedagogy. Religion forms the natural fabric which the history of art, of literature, and of political events of Italy has woven with the Church, with her history and her doctrine. For the alert teacher, integration is thus quite natural. Yet much remains to be done to bring about such integration in a systematic fashion rather than leaving it to the initiative of the individual teachers.

Church control over religious instruction functions at three levels. Since 1923 a Central Catechetical Office has been in existence. This office is a branch of the Sacred Congregation of the Council. In 1960 the National Catechetical Office of the Italian Episcopal Conference was established, and since 1929 there has been a diocesan catechetical office in every diocese.

Supervision of religious instruction rests completely in the hands of the central and diocesan ecclesiastical authorities and is exercised by means of appropriate agreements made with school officials. The curricula and general directives of the religious education program and its supervision emanate from the central Vatican authorities; the diocesan authorities execute and otherwise implement these directives through the local catechetical office. (The norms for the religious education program and its supervision may be found in A. Balocco, *Le religione nelle scuole italiane*. Rome: CENAC, 1962.)

In addition to the local diocesan supervisors of religious instruction, there are also three regional inspectors for northern, central, and southern Italy, respectively, appointed by the Sacred Congregation of the Council. Unfortunately, however, there is no regular corps of supervisors with a specialized university pedagogico-didactical professional preparation. Such a corps of supervisors would afford a regular and competent supervisory force which could upgrade religious education programs through ongoing vigilance and control.

In a related connection, there is a strong national movement for the professional preparation of religion teachers. Such a movement is primarily the result of the existence of the National Catechetical Office (*Ufficio Catechistico Nazionale*, UCN) in Rome, established in 1961 by the Italian Episcopal Conference. The National Catechetical Office looks after the preparation of dossiers and promotes pedagogical study and practice; it also works through the regional and diocesan catechetical offices. A 1965 volume entitled *Pastorale e scuola secondaria* (edited by UCN) contains the proceedings of the first national congress on this subject. This volume sheds much light on the whole problem of catechetics and of religious education in secondary schools. (Other valuable works on the state of religious education in Italy include *L'Ufficio Catechistico Diocesano;* the publications of the Christian Doctrine Bookshop (Libreria Dottrina Cristiana, LDC); and those of the Higher Institute of Catechetics of the Pontifical Salesian Atheneum.

Besides the diocesan catechetical centers, the institutes of religious men and women who operate schools also maintain catechetical centers (*Centri Catechistici*). However, in the entire matter of regular supervision by pedagogical experts for the promotion of teaching excellence, religious institutes suffer from the same defects as do their diocesan counterparts. An overall official view of the general state of affairs on religious education in Italy may be found in G. Frumento, *La Catechesi nei documenti della S. Sede* (Religious Education in the Documents of the Holy See). This 1965 book contains directives from Pius X to Paul VI, particularly in regard to the preparation of religion teachers.

Catholic schools follow the usual acts of worship during the liturgical year. Students are not forced to attend the sacraments. The practice of daily Mass for nonboarding pupils is rapidly declining; even in boarding schools attendance at daily Mass is on the wane.

The academic performance of the pupils of Catholic schools compared with the national average of examination success is generally at the same level as that of government schools, according to the Central Institute of Statistics.

With regard to maturity of personality and the resultant impact on the subsequent life of the students, there are few research data available. (See P. G. Grasso's 1954 and 1966 monographs.) Former Catholic school students of both sexes are numerous in the ranks of militant Catholics. But there are also many former Catholic school students among the leaders of all political parties without distinction, even those most hostile to Catholicism.

With regard to the educational attainment of pupils in Catholic schools compared with those in the corresponding government schools, the evidence seems to indicate that the Catholic school pupils in the primary and in the lower and upper secondary grades achieve better scholastically than do their counterparts in the government schools. (These data, the sole available evidence covering large numbers of pupils, were gathered in a scientific manner by the Higher Institute for Education of the Pontifical Atheneum Salesianum.)

The reason for this lies in the threefold selection process involved in the admission of children to Catholic schools: first, financial, since

Catholic schools, unlike the government schools, charge tuition; second, social because the families which send their children to Catholic schools usually belong to the upper achievement classes, such as professional men, managers, businessmen, or white-collar workers, rather than to the category of farmers, laborers, or tradesmen; third, religious-moral, inasmuch as parents who send their children to Catholic schools are concerned with a Catholic education for their offspring, even if they themselves are not always exemplary Catholics. Catholic school students usually have more highly developed verbal skills than do their counterparts in government schools.

The Catholic schools usually do not play a very active role in the life of the parish, primarily because the students come from different parishes and attend Sunday Mass with their families. It is difficult to ascertain to what extent the Catholic school tries to make its students parish-minded.

Student Personnel
and Guidance Services

An organized, systematic program of well-developed and comprehensive personnel and guidance services such as exist in advanced American government schools is unknown in Italian education.

Italian schools do offer some types of remedial work, especially in the areas of reading and in allied forms of psychopedagogical assistance.

There is some vocational guidance, chiefly through the government rather than through the school system. The Ministry for Public Instruction controls and operates approximately 100 centers linked with associations of technical education (*consorzi per l'istruzione tecnica*). In addition, these associations may be coordinated with the National Accident Prevention Bureau (*Ente Nazionale Prevenzione Infortuni*). Moreover, there are dozens of medical and psychopedagogical consulters, and some Italian schools have recourse to these. To date, however, there is no vocational guidance service on a national level. Catholic schools have at their disposal certain scientifically organized guidance centers, but there are far too few of these.

In general there are no official regulations for government schools which prescribe the development of an organized school testing program or even the use of standardized tests, except for placement of students in the differential classes of the primary and intermediate schools. For this purpose, the Gille and Goodenough tests are used. Other tests used in these schools include the Terman-Stanford, the Terman-Merrill, and the Wechsler.

Regular class achievement tests are given at the end of each trimester; standardized instruments are commonly given once a year.

The National Union of Technical Instruction Organizations (*Unione Nazionale Consorzi Istruzione Tecnica*, UNCIT) regularly administers aptitude tests to pupils of Class III of the *scuola media* for guidance purposes. The National Accident Prevention Bureau (*Ente Nazionale Prevenzione Infortuni*, ENPI), also for guidance purposes, supervises the testing of students enrolled in preparatory courses (*Corsi di addestramento*).

In addition to interviews, many other forms of tests and questionnaires are used, including the following: Differential Aptitude Test; Primary Mental Abilities; *Batterie du Centre Recherches*; Rogers; 16 Cattell P.F.; Minnesota Multiphasic Personality Inventory; Bernreuter P. I.; Revised Minnesota Paper Form Board Test; Otis; Progressives Matrices; Domino 48; and so forth.

Special Organizations (*Organizzazioni Speciali*) in Florence is the national distributor of standardized tests. Their catalog gives the list of tests used in Italy. The Higher Institute of Pedagogy of the Pontifical Salesian Atheneum has provided Italy with many tests which were developed for government and nongovernment schools. A description of the latter can be found in the educational review *Orientiamenti Pedagogici* and in the various volumes edited by the Institute. (See, for example, L. Calonghi, *Reattivi nella scuola*, 1961; L. Calonghi, *Sussidi per la conoscenza dell'alunno*, 1963; P. G. Grasso, *I giovani stanno cambiando*, 1966; P. G. Grasso, *Personalità giovanile in transizione*, 1964; and G. Lutte, *L'adolescente e il suo gruppo*, 1964.

Discipline in Catholic schools follows traditional lines. According to some, it is still rather strict. In practice, only in very exceptional cases are the disciplinary sanctions set down in the official school regulations applied. These sanctions include official warnings, suspension from lectures, exclusion from the first sitting in examinations, and expulsion.

The Staff of the Catholic Schools

The number of clerical and religious personnel in the operation of the Italian Catholic school system is very high. FIDAE estimates that on a proportionate basis, 92 per cent of all the teachers in Catholic nursery schools and kindergartens are priests or religious. Seventy-five per cent of all teachers in Catholic elementary schools and 67 per cent of all teachers in Catholic secondary schools are priests or religious. In general, the higher the salary, the greater is the percentage of lay teachers in a given Catholic school.

The law requires special professional preparation to teach in government or Catholic schools. To teach in nursery school and kindergarten, a teacher must hold a diploma from a special teacher-training school (scuola magistrale). A diploma from the Istituto Magistrale is required for teaching in elementary schools, and secondary school teachers must possess a diploma which permits them to give instruction at this level. This diploma is obtained by first completing the doctorate in the university faculty for the subject to be taught in secondary school and then by passing a government examination in this subject. [Editor's note: An Italian doctorate represents a different level of educational attainment than a doctorate from other countries.] All members of the teaching staffs in Catholic schools, including religious and clergy, hold the legal teaching license appropriate to their level of school service. In some schools there are faculty members who do not possess the requisite teaching license, but such persons are employed only in emergency situations.

A serious defect in the professional preparation of Italian schoolteachers is the absence at the university level of any faculties for pedagogical or didactical training. Also, the Italian school system has no provision for professional appreticeship, internship, or student teaching, whereby the persons studying to become teachers have the opportunity to be guided jointly by master teachers in the field and by university supervisors in both the pedagogical and subject fields. Only the subuniversity level teacher-training schools (Istituto Magistrale) offer such preparation. This lack of university course work in education affects teachers in both government and Catholic schools; indeed, Catholic schoolteachers in one sense are more adversely affected by this lacuna since they further lack that pedagogical and didactical preparation peculiar to Catholic education over and above the common core of education courses.

Academic freedom for school personnel at all levels is spelled out in their contracts. These staff members bind themselves in their contracts to "collaborate in the specific educational mission" of the particular school. Consequently behavior judged contrary to this contract is deemed a just cause for dismissal. Insofar as the person or board which judges such misbehavior is concerned, academic freedom might be said to vary.

There are teacher associations at all levels to assist Catholic school-teachers to become more professional. In some instances the thrust of such associations is realized in meetings and activities, in others through publication media. Because most of the teachers in government elementary schools are Catholic, the Italian Association of Catholic Teachers (*Associazione Italiana Maestri Cattolici*, AIMC) is very influential in the elementary schools. Similarly, the Movement of Teachers of Catholic Action (*Movimento Maestri di Azione Cattolica*, MMAC) and the National Union for Elementary Schools (*Sindacato Nazionale Scuola Elementare*, SINASCEL) play important roles. Of special importance for the constant improvement of elementary education is the widely read Catholic review, *Scuola Italiana Moderna*, published by *La Scuola* of Brescia. This review celebrated its seventy-fifth year of publication in 1966. It plays a major role in assisting the teaching profession all over the world in the area of didactical methodology.

Other influential professional groups include the editors of *La Scuola Moderna*, launched in 1914 by the Catholic publisher *La Scuola* of Brescia. The Catholic Italian Educational Association (*Associazione Educatrice Italiana*), founded in 1927, is professionally influential, as is the National Teaching Center for Nursery Schools (*Centro Didattico Nazionale per la Scuola materna*) in Brescia. The latter is an official institution for promoting the development of pedagogy and educational theory for the kindergartens. Other *Centri Didattici Nazionali* (National Teaching Centers) perform the same function for the elementary schools, for *licei*, for technical and professional education, for lower secondary schools (*secondaria inferiore*), for art schools, schools of physical education, for relations between school and family, and for educational guidance. These centers are affiliated with the Office of Teaching Centers (*Ufficio Centri Didattici*) of the Ministry for Public Instruction. All of them have Catholics on their boards of directors. The work of these centers in effecting the progress of teaching methods and practice by means of books and reviews has a noticeable impact on both government and Catholic schools.

An important force in Catholic secondary education is the Movement of Clubs for Teaching (*Movimento Circoli della Didattica*). The Movement publishes a monthly review called the *Ricerche Didattiche* (Teaching Research), which promotes among teachers the development of teaching study, research, and experimentation. This kind of research is all the more needed because secondary school-teachers begin their teaching without benefit of any university course work in pedagogy or didactics.

The Parents
and the
Catholic School

There is meager and scant parent-teacher contact in Italian Catholic schools. Many causes might be given for this unfortunate phenomenon, including a passiveness of the laity. Since the end of World War II, Catholic school people have utilized a variety of devices to involve parents in collaborating in the educational process through committees, associations, parent-teacher meetings, and so forth. But any national form of parent-school organization has not evolved from these efforts, nor has any procedural methodology been devised as a guideline for effecting home-school collaboration.

Special Educational
Problems Facing
Catholic Schools in Italy

To assess accurately the problems and opportunities of the Catholic school system in Italy, it is necessary to situate these institutions in the context of the national school system. To be sure, the total school system is entirely dominated by the government schools. In the primary and lower secondary schools, 92 per cent of Italian pupils attend government schools, and the figure for the upper secondary school is 85 per cent.

The government schools at all levels are nondenominational, open to all teachers and all pupils without religious distinction. In practice, however, Catholics wield considerable influence in government schools at every level, both in administration and in teaching. Such influence extends not only to the pupils but to their families as well. Added to this is the influence the Church wields through compulsory religious instruction given in government and Catholic schools alike.

Consequently the Church, militant Catholics, and parents, in particular, view the problem of religious education primarily in terms of the government schools with their more than seven million Catholic pupils. This is pointed up by the fact that there is freedom of choice as to what school a parent may send his child. It must be remembered also that government schools are free and so do not involve any additional expense to parents.

The Catholic school system, therefore, as a sectarian system retains in principle its essential validity. However, the expansion and development of the Catholic school system is not seriously considered either by the clergy, by lay Catholics, or by public opinion, as a major problem of conscience.

On the other hand, the very existence of a separate Catholic school system is the result largely of the survival of an element of nineteenth-century anticlericalism. Therefore the system is often the target of violent hostility from certain political parties who use every legal and factual opening to extend the scope of the government schools. The ultimate intention of these parties is to extend the government school system to encompass all education and all students at government expense. Leaders of these parties hope to be able from year to year to whittle away the *Lebensraum* of the Catholic schools. Meanwhile the imbalance between the tuition-free government schools and the Catholic schools continues to grow larger. The Christian Democrat Party, which is fighting a lone battle on the school question and which by the mid-1960's had only a relative majority in the parliament, is powerless to do anything to ameliorate the situation.

In Catholic circles, discussion revolves around two major problems of Catholic education, the educational and the economic. As noted earlier in this essay, the difficulty in providing better pedagogical and didactical standards arises from the absence of any national effort toward experimental research on education and teaching methodology. As a result, Catholic schools suffer from the lack of a scientific procedural system for making exact checks on the educational and didactical situation. This prevents any attempt at framing working hypotheses with a view either to improving the current situation or to acquiring the raw data necessary to that end. The few attempts being made in this area give ground for hope; nevertheless, concrete results will be evident only over the long term.

The economic difficulties arising from the incapacity or the reluctance of parents to bear the whole cost of Catholic education—understandable in the presence of the free government system—can only be overcome if one of four possibilities comes about. The first possibility is for the burden of teaching to be borne entirely or almost entirely by the religious staffs. A second possibility is for a large part of the expenses to be covered from public revenue as, for instance, for vocational training, where a part of the expense is currently subsidized by the government. A third possibility would be a felicitous development whereby for the period of compulsory education the government would reverse its current unjustified interpretation of Article 35 of the Constitution and observe the clear meaning of this Article's text which makes the years of compulsory education (six to fourteen years of age) tuition-free no matter what kind of approved school is concerned. The fourth possibility is for Catholic schools to abandon the teaching of poorer children and turn instead to educating families with an income sufficient to bear the whole cost of Catholic education. Obviously the Catholic Church and religious institutes would never permit Catholic schools to be socially segregated, which would be the result of this possibility.

A second major problem facing Italian Catholic education (and government education as well) is the archaic school system. In this essay it was noted that the school regulations prevailing in Italy are binding on the Catholic schools equally with the others. This situation dates back to the *risorgimento*, the national resurgence of 1848–70. The result is that the entire Italian school system, government and Catholic, although undoubtedly making gains over the decades, has suffered from the basic weaknesses inherent in the very system itself.

Foremost among these defects is the maintenance of the skeleton of the 1859 Casati administrative legislation, which has been kept intact until today despite the enormous transformations that have taken place in the national community and in the developments in school systems around the world. The isolation of various types of schools under different General Departments, such as the humanities, technology, the professional, or artistic, is one of its basic defects. In the French school system, all the schools, including universities, are controlled by the *Direction Générale de l'organisation et des programmes scolaires*. Also, the many and diverse traditional secondary schools have been replaced for the first four years (ages twelve to sixteen) by the comprehensive, uniform, and flexible *premier cycle*. (See J. Minot: *L'administration de l'education nationale*. Paris: Institut Pédagogique National, 1964, p. 358.) To be sure, it was in the United States that the comprehensive secondary school was pioneered, and alert European and Asian countries are following America's lead.

The centralization of authority in Italian education—a centralization for which there could have been a reason in the last century during the struggles and resistance that opposed national unification—has stifled the very soul of the school system. It has smothered the free and responsible initiative of the teaching profession. It has subjected teachers to the rule of bureaucrats. It has created a school system estranged from the parents, with whom it has never had any organized collaboration. Finally, it is largely divorced from the economic and social development of the country.

This archaic, overcentralized Italian school system, copied from the French model, has in the century between 1861, when the nation of Italy was born, and 1961 revealed the anomaly of making a complex and delicate living organism like the school system depend on one central bureaucracy. The situation is exactly contrary to what has happened in the Anglo-Saxon countries, where the school system— with its own, yet minor, drawbacks—is based on districts with corresponding teachers and local communities. Similarly, the German system is decentralized, being based on the different *Länder*.

It is true that Article 5 of the 1948 Constitution calls for government decentralization and establishes regions (Article 117). These regional units are supposed to have certain powers over the schools. However, the centralization continues or, rather, is being increased with the establishment of the new government *scuola materna*, although these *scuola materna* could and should be left to local initiative.

This jealous guarding by the state of all direct control over the national schools (92 per cent of all elementary and secondary pupils are in government schools) has seriously damaged the national education program inasmuch as it has placed the whole fiscal burden of the schools on the government (with the exception of certain contributions imposed on provinces and municipalities. These contributions all go to government schools). Thus public territorial public bodies such as the regions, provinces, and municipalities were excluded from direct involvement in the schools when it suited the ruling class or dominant party (Liberals first and later the Fascists). The result was a lack of interest, especially economic, in the schools and the effective cutting off of what are usually fruitful sources of fiscal support for noncentralized schools. Such sources include public bodies, associations, and private interest groups and individuals. This kind of government monopoly has uprooted the school system from its most fertile soil, the local population and the students' families, by reducing their participation in the life and formative contribution of the school. By so doing the state has entirely eliminated the local economic contribution, which is all the more generous and self-sacrificing when the school administration is local and close at hand.

Another outcome of the centralization of the school system has been the ossification of the entire nongovernment school network, including the resources of the Catholic community. This has been effected by the imposition of the *pareggiamento* and the *parificazione* for legal recognition of studies made at Catholic schools. If Catholic schools were to adopt their own distinctive educational programs, they would be punished by not being recognized by the state. Hence there is a total absence in Italy of free university colleges on the style of those in the United States. Also, universities refuse to face up to modern technological demands: vocational education is necessarily limited to the type of school approved by the state. Another case in point is the school reform of Minister Gentile, which in 1923 downgraded experimental science in government schools and consequently in nongovernment schools. Pedagogy and didactical science in Italian schools still have not recovered from this blunder, a blunder possible only because of the hypercentralization of the Italian school system.

A related educational defect is the overall classicist ground plan of the school system, dating back to 1859 and organized solely on the traditional *ginnasio-liceo* axis destined for preparing the political ruling class, civil servants, the military, and the teaching profession. Such an aristocratic system is too slow to open its doors to the technical professions or even to throw open all the secondary schools to the entire school-age population.

Fortunately for Italian secondary education a reform attempt was made in 1962 with the establishment of the comprehensive *scuola media* to provide a school adapted to all youths. However, the system, even if broadened to include the four types of secondary schools (humanistic, technical, professional, artistic), still retains the old rigidity. There are to date no less than seventeen separate parallel secondary schools to which three others have been added so far, The Linguistic Lyceum, The Technical Institute for Tourism, and The Technical Institute for Company Secretaries.

It is the rigidity and archaism of the punctilious Italian school system which creates insoluble economic and human problems. Is it really necessary to multiply so many different types of schools all over the country? Such a plethora of schools impedes guiding students in

the proper choice of one school among many. It is all the more difficult when it is a question of fourteen-year-olds, for whom the definitive choice of a career is not only difficult but often psychologically
impossible. Moreover, scientifically functioning guidance services such
as are prevalent in American schools are scarcely off the ground.
Indeed, in most instances such services are restricted to vocational
and scholastic guidance. Each of the twenty types of schools has its
own academic program for the first fourteen to sixteen biennium. An
effort is being made by some to harmonize the program of certain
bienniums—the *licei* among themselves and the technical institutes
among themselves. But such an effort is putting patches on old wine-
skins rather than solving the basic structural problem.

Within this antiquated school system, Catholic schools have also
followed the mainstream, giving themselves over particularly to the
humanities and to the training of teachers for the elementary and
nursery schools. Only a few religious institutes, such as the Salesians
of Don Bosco and the Brothers of the Christian Schools (de la Salle),
have developed professional schools. Indeed, it was not until about
1950 that Catholic schools really faced the professional training of
youth. But this was done outside the regular school program, in the
Corsi di Addestramento Professionale (CAP), operated under the
Ministry of Work.

A third major problem facing Catholic education in Italy is the
lack of effective Catholic influence on national school legislation and
school control proportionate to the numbers and strength of Italian
Catholics.

The circumstances in which Italian Catholics found themselves in
1945 were still governed by the nineteenth-century mentality formed
during the war against the papacy and against all ecclesiastical institutions for the unification of Italy. This mentality was hardened by
the domination of an anticlerical *Zeitgeist* in public life. Catholics
were forbidden by papal command to enter public life or to take public office. It is true that Catholics lacked any historical experience in
government since the establishment of the unified Kingdom of Italy.
Such inexperience arose chiefly as a result of the occupation of the
Papal States by the new Italian state. The state restricted political
liberty. The Church established the norm *nè eletti nè elettori* (neither
elected nor electors), a norm formally sanctioned by the famous *non
expedit* (it is not fitting that Catholics should participate in political
elections) issued by the Sacred Penetentiary in 1868. This *non expedit*
was confirmed by the Pope himself in 1874 and was declared binding

by a decree of the Holy Office in 1886 which declared: *non expedit prohibitionem importat.* The *non expedit* implied, of course, a pro-hibition upon Catholics vis-à-vis public life in the Italian government.

The result of the *non expedit* was that political power became monopolized above and outside all Catholic influence—opposed on the one side and abstaining on the other, first by the Liberals and later by the Fascists. The sole exception was the too short interval of 1919–1925, when the *Partito Popolare* of Don Luigi Sturzo was repre-sented in the parliament, but even then only as a minority.

Consequently at the end of World War II, when Catholics found themselves faced with the sad task of rehabilitating the country from the sink of military defeat, economic collapse, and political and social confusion, they came to power with a majority not yet tried or sea-soned in responsible democracy. Catholics assuming power at that time were angry at the fatal excesses of the former political and mili-tary leaders and were seduced by myths of their own. They found themselves alone in the struggle against militant secularist tendencies. From the right they were attacked by the newly organized forces of neo-Fascists, Monarchists, and Liberals, while from the left they were confronted by the Communists and Socialists, who had grown enor-mously strong during the war and the anti-Fascist struggle. The Cath-olics themselves, with the exception of a small group formerly of the Popular Party, were totally lacking in high caliber political and socio-economic training, especially in that political maturity which only develops with long association with political power.

In the stormy climate which has beset Italian politics since the war, it has been quite impossible to take any action whatsoever with regard to the schools except within the existing legal framework with all its defects. All that could be done and what in fact was done was the numerical extension of the schools. The thousands of millions of Lire spent on the schools jumped from 124 in 1949 to 306 in 1956, 487 in 1960, and 1317 in 1966. Italy certainly is committed to education. By 1966 almost 20 per cent of the national budget was ear-marked for education. The stalemate in school reform also had reper-cussions on the nongovernment schools which were still under the same rigid educational thinking. Not only was legal conformism still imposed, but also economic difficulties increased. Moreover, teachers —ecclesiastics, male and female religious, and laity—were virtually all trained in government universities and so all suffered the same lack of pedagogical and didactical study and initiation.

Still another factor which strongly hampered the action of Catholics in both government and nongovernment schools was the lack of coordination of forces. In certain powerful formally Catholic or Catholic-dominated associations there was even open conflict about educational problems of national importance. Hence in spite of the impressive number of Catholic organizations, a result in particular of the vision and energy of Pius XII, and in spite of the undeniable speed with which these organizations acted, the impact of Catholic associations on the national educational system fell far short of the realizable potential of the energy expended. The Catholic Educational Institute (*Istituto Cattolico dell'Educazione*, ICE), which includes all Catholic forces active in education and schooling, has never succeeded in producing an effective coordinated effort. In addition, there was a lack of interested public opinion.

For some years now, however, a more acute awareness of the problem has been emerging, and the clergy are showing more concern. New hopes have been awakened for action in the cultural and educational fields. Leadership in these areas might well come from the Italian Episcopal Conference, in accordance with the decrees promulgated at Vatican Council II.

Another hopeful omen is that since about 1958 there has been a revival of national interest in the extension and reform of the schools. Today all political parties have become advocates of this reform, translating the aspirations of the public into economic terms with the plan for scholastic development for 1966–70. Also under way is a general revision of the upper secondary schools, and several proposed laws are currently being discussed in the parliament.

Selected
Bibliography

AA. vari. *La nuova scuola media*. Rome: MCD, via G. Carini 28, 1964.

Annuario Cattolico d'Italia. Rome: ed. Treveri, v. Vigliena 10, 1965.

Di Stefano, Gioacchino. *Raccolta delle disposizioni legislative e amministrative sulla scuola media*. Rome: MCD, via G. Carini 28, 1966. Indice analitico.

Froio, F. *Una scuola da rinnovare*. Milan: ed. Comunita, 1964. Tavole. Bibliografia. Panorama della scuola italiana. Indirizzo laicista.

Giannarelli, R. *Compendio di leggi e regolamenti sull'istruzione secondaria*. Florence: Le Monnier, 1965. Indici cronologico e analitico.

Ministero della P. I. *Annuario degli Istituti non statali di istruzione secondaria.* Rome: 1961. Leggi, Decreti, Circolari, Elenco Scuole.
Sinistrero, V. *La politica scolastica 1945–1965 e la scuola cattolica.* Rome: FIDAE, 1966.
Sinistrero, V. *La scuola cattolica: diritti e cifre.* Turin: SEI, 1961.
Sinistrero, V. *Scuola e formazione professionale nel mondo.* Rome: LAS, via Ateneo Salesiano 1, 1963. Grafici. Contiene i sistemi scolastici USA, Inghilterra, Germania-RF, URSS, Francia, Italia, India, Giappone, Argentina e i Piani per l'America Latina e l'Africa.
Sinistrero, V. *Il Vaticano II e l'Educazione—Testi e commento.* Rome: LDC, 1967.
Ufficio scolastico Centrale della Sacra Congregazione dei Seminari e delle Università degli Studi. *Istituti di Istruzione Secondaria dipendenti dall'Autorità Ecclesiastica in Italia.* Rome: Poliglotta Vaticana, 1955.
Zanobini, L. *Codice delle leggi sulla Pubblica Istruzione.* Milan, Giuffrè, 1966. Vol. 1: Istruzione primaria; Vol. 2: Istruzione secondaria.

Publications Which Reflect Catholic Thought and Practice About Education and the Schools

AA. vari, Professori dell'Istituto Superiore di Pedagogia del Pontificio Ateneo Salesiano, *Educare—Sommario di scienze pedagogiche;* vol. 1°—Pedagogia e didattica, p. 600; vol. 2°—Psicologia, p. 510; vol. 3°—Metodologia della Catechesi, Roma, Libreria Ateneo Salesiano, LAS, via Ateneo Salesiano 1, 1962–65, v. il catalogo della LAS con pubblicazioni e ricerche su tutte le scienze psico-socio-pedagogiche.
Le edizioni di *Vita e Pensiero.* Milan, Largo Gemelli e de *La Scuola,* Brescia, via Cadorna 11.
Orientamenti Pedagogici, a cura dei Professori dell'Istituto Superiore di Pedagogia del PAS; Rivista Internazionale di scienze dell'educazione. Turin: SEI, Corso Regina Margherita 176, Anna XII–1966, bimestrale.
Scuola viva. Rivista didattica per gli insegnanti in 3 edizioni: SM, per la scuola media; LM, per i licei e gli Istituti magistrali; TP, per le scuole tecniche e professionali. Turin: SEI.

Catholic Organizations Involved in Education and Schools

(All addresses in Rome)

Associazione Educatrice Italiana—AEI, via Trinità dei Pellegrini-16
Associazione Gestori Istituti Dipendenti dall'Autorità Ecclesiastica— AGIDAE, via Chiabrera-97

Associazione Italiana Ascoltatori Radio Telespettatori—AIART, via Federico Cesi-44

Associazione Medici Cattolici Italiani—AMCI, via della Conciliazione-15

Associazione Scautistica Cattolica Italiana—ASCI, piazza Pasquale Paoli-18

Associazioni Cristiane Lavoratori Italiani—ACLI, via Monte della Farina-64

Centro Nazionale Attività Catechistiche—CENAC, via della Conciliazione-1

Centro Italiano Femminile—CIF, via Boezio-21

Centro Sportivo Italiano—CSI, via della Conciliazione-1

Centro Turistico Giovanile—CTG, via Alberico II-35

Comitato Docenti Universitari—CDU, via della Conciliazione-4d

Federazione Attività Ricreative Italiane—FARI, via Aurelia-481

Federazione Istituti Dipendenti dall'Autorità Ecclesiastica—FIDAE, via dell'Umilta-36

Federazione Universitaria Cattolica Italiana—FUCI, via Conciliazione-4d

Gioventù Femminile di Azione Cattolica Italiana—GFACI, via Aurelia-481

Gioventù Maschile Azione Cattolica Italiana—GMACI, via Conciliazione-1

Istituto Cattolico Attivita Sociali—ICAS, via Conciliazione-1

Istituto Cattolico Educazione—ICE, via Conciliazione-1

Movimento Laureati Azione Cattolica Italiana—MLACI, via Conciliazione-4d

Movimento Maestri di Azione Cattolica Italiana—MMAC, via Conciliazione-3

Scuole Superiori di Servizio Sociale, presso ONARMO, via Placido Riccardi-41

Unione Cattolica Artisti Italiani—UCAI, via Conciliazione-4d

Unione Cattolica Farmacisti Italiani—UCFI, via Conciliazione-4d

Unione Cattolica Infermieri—UCI, via Gregorio VII-111

Unione Cattolica Italiana Tecnini—UCIT, via Conciliazione-4d

Unione Cristiana Imprenditori e Dirigenti—UCID, via Tritone-201

Unione Donne Azione Cattolica Italiana—UDACI, Circonvallazione Aurelia-50

Unione Editori Cattolici Italiani—UECI, via Porta Angelica-63

Unione Giuristi Cattolici Italiani—UGCI, via Conciliazione-4d

Unione Uomini Azione Cattolica Italiana—UUACI, via Conciliazione-4d

Università Internazionale degli Studi Sociali "Pro Deo," viale Pola-12

Catholic Education
in England

by John P. White

A Short History
of English
Catholic Education

Before the Reformation

There is no cause to doubt that the Church played her part in educating the inhabitants of the British Isles from the earlier times of Christendom, and the fifth century in particular was a flourishing period for English culture—and therefore for an education that was at least partly Christian in emphasis—but it was not until the landing of St. Augustine upon English shores in 597 that the wholesale christianization of England began. Indeed, it was probably St. Augustine himself who established the first English Catholic school, the King's School at Canterbury.

St. Augustine had landed in Kent. But in the seventh and eighth centuries English culture found its focus, not in the south, but in the northeast quarter of the land. St. Wilfrid (634?–709), St. Benedict Bishop (628?–690), and St. Bede (672?–735), all noted for their influence as scholars and teachers, were associated with Wearmouth and Jarrow. In the ninth century King Alfred (reigned 891–901), who did more than any man before him to weld England into one nation, combined brilliant military talents with a fiery religious and educational zeal. It is to Alfred, ruling the kingdom of Wessex in the south of England, that indebtedness belongs for the inspiration for the first official use of the English tongue—in contrast with Latin—as a serious educational medium.

Between the time of Alfred and the Reformation it was the religious houses that for 600 years were the principal perpetuators of learning. The universities of Oxford and Cambridge were monastic foundations. The monastic schools, forerunners of the present-day grammar and public schools—so called because they were open to all and not merely to the sons of a particular group or guild—were widely famed.

Reformation and Decline

The political, theological, and economic forces and motives which operated to bring about the Reformation in England are still a source of confusion and debate to historians of the period. Nonetheless it is generally conceded that the change from a Catholic to a Protestant England was effected in a remarkably short time, roughly between the beginning of Edward VI's reign (1547) to the end of Elizabeth's in 1603. During this half century the monastic houses passed almost entirely into the hands of the state or of private individuals. Catholic schools, except in some pockets far removed from London, the capital city, virtually ceased to exist.

Where the Catholic religion flowered at all, it flowered almost invisibly. The same held true for Catholic education: severe penalties were attached to the practice of either. The Catholic mass, and consequently the Catholic school, found a home only on the Continent, except for a very few Catholic families whose members clung tenaciously to the traditions of the faith. Cardinal Allen—one of the few among the English hierarchy who would not conform to the new religion—founded in 1579 the famous College at Douai in Belgium, where English Catholics driven into exile were able to find an education for their sons. The English Jesuits founded schools for a similar purpose at Rheims, Pont le Mousson, Verdun, and St. Omers.

The seventeenth century in England was marked by the Act of Uniformity (1662), one of the main effects of which was to close education, particularly higher education, to those who would not offer their formal assent to the Thirty-Nine Articles (a summary of doctrine) of the Church of England Established. This act had as its target, not so much Catholics (who were automatically inhibited by proscription from achieving any legal or civil status) as Nonconformists. Only later was the force of this act felt by Catholics, who were to be categorized, with their "brethren" the Nonconformists, as Dissenters.

James II, who reigned very briefly (1685–88), was an avowed Catholic. While he was on the throne, Catholics were for a time, if not popular, at least not so violently persecuted as they had been during the previous three-quarters of a century. But this short breathing space left no time for shouts of triumph. The most that can be said is that the nonconformist Dissenters, partly freed from suspicion by the general tolerance which James II was obliged to extend to them in order to preserve tolerance for Roman Dissenters, took strong political advantage from their enhanced prestige at the end of the seventeenth and the beginning of the eighteenth century. It was their efforts, their success in achieving official recognition, that paved the way for a full acknowledgement of Catholic rights, both in religious and in educational matters.

In any case, English education in general declined markedly as the eighteenth century grew older. John Wesley (1703–91), the founder of Methodism, was one of several men outside the pale of the Anglican Church who displayed their educational zeal by founding schools financed from private sources. (The Act of Uniformity prevented any public funds from reaching those who would not conform to the state religion.) Meanwhile Catholics would have many years to wait before their schools could once again flourish on native soil.

Revolution and Return

The decline in Catholic prestige in England was arrested toward the end of the eighteenth century by an odd side-effect of the French Revolution. England set herself resolutely against the atheistic spirit of the revolutionaries. The logical result was that the French Catholic emigrées sought and received a haven in England, much as English Catholics had been forced into exile to France over a hundred years before and had been befriended there. The English nationalist spirit smiled benevolently even upon Catholics when they were persecuted by Britain's worst enemy.

While the English air became easier for Catholics to breathe, the Industrial Revolution, with its effect of pressing crowds of human beings into large conurbations—especially in the Midlands and the North of England—emphasized the national need for better teaching of children.

In 1829 the Catholic Emancipation Act was passed. Catholics were then permitted to exercise their religious and civil functions without penalty or restriction. The slow but steady rise in Catholic status can be dated from 1829. By 1845 a Catholic Institute had come into being; its responsibilities embraced the care of Catholic children, for whom there were by now as many as 220 schools. Most of these schools were small and by comparison with the total number of schools insignificant. In 1847 the Catholic Poor School Committee was established. This body entered into negotiations with the government concerning financial aid to Catholic schools. A year later the Catholic Church was granted relief from taxation. By 1870 there were 770 Catholic elementary schools, of which 350 received some financial support from the state.

From that time until the present day Catholic schools have increased in number, size, and efficiency. Despite the continuing debate about the legal rights of Catholic taxpayers who affirm that they possess a moral right to send their children to nonfee-paying schools of their choice, the present position may be described as one of slightly uneasy truce, in which the Church is recognized as a distinct body, with opinions, powers, and rights. The discussion, sometimes fierce, currently centers not on whether the state should contribute toward the cost of Catholic schools but on how much the Church should be compelled to add. Catholic prestige and influence in Britain are higher now than at any time since before the Reformation. It remains to be seen whether Catholics can bear the grave financial burden imposed upon them, not so much by a tyrannical state as by a rapidly increasing Catholic population.

The Purpose of Catholic Schools in England

The Stated Purpose

To be [a Catholic school] it is necessary that all the teaching and whole organisation of the school, and its teachers, syllabus, and textbooks in every branch, be regulated by the Christian spirit, under the direction and maternal supervision of the Church; so that Religion may be in very truth the foundation and crown of the youth's entire training; and this in every grade of school, not only in the elementary, but the intermediate and higher institutions of learning as well.

The words of Pope Pius XI in his encyclical The Christian Education of Youth would be accepted in their entirety by most English Catholic educationists. The declared purpose of Catholic education in England is by cooperating with the good influence of the home to raise up children to love God and to serve him, through all the secular learning offered, and above all through the religious instruction which forms a regular part of the Catholic school curriculum. This education must found itself on a doctrinal basis; in Archbishop Beck's words, "Without a dogmatic basis, moral education cannot be enduring."

The Real Purpose

Many Catholic schools fulfill the spirit of the above-mentioned pronouncements. There are unfortunately still more where dogma is held not simply as a basis but as a restricting framework fencing in human growth. In such schools teachers, far from showing the possibility of Christian witness in a pluralist society, rather induce an attitude of withdrawal. Such schools build walls fully as much if not more than opening doors. But if there are Catholic schools whose chief aim seems to be to foster a ghetto mentality, there are increasingly frequent signs that Catholics are awakening to their positive responsibilities.

The Relationship of Catholic Schools to Government Schools

Government Legislation Which Has Affected Catholic Schools

The development of the relationships between government schools and Catholic schools can be traced through the British Government reports and enactments which have emerged from London since 1880, when education was for the first time made compulsory for all English children.

The first important enactment of the present century was the Balfour Act (1902), by which schools were divided into two distinct categories. The first group was termed "maintained schools," and were controlled by the local education authorities. The second broad classification was "voluntary" or "non-provided" schools, which were free to appoint their own teachers and to offer religious teaching according to their own denomination. Catholic schools fell under the second classification.

The Hadow Report of 1926 recommended the raising of the compulsory school age from fourteen to fifteen years. This report further envisaged the provision of two other types of school besides the grammar school with its highly academic syllabus—the "technical school," with its thrust toward the teaching of practical skills, and the "modern school," which was intended to adapt the general academic curriculum more to the needs of students not intending to go to the university. No particular recommendation was made in this report for financial help for schools desiring to preserve their religious independence, as Catholic schools. The suggestion was that if Catholic parents wished their children to have a Catholic education they should be prepared to pay full fees. If they wanted to take advantage of the free education now offered by the state, then they must be content with the facilities for occasional religious (Catholic) instruction to be given by the visiting clergy, say, from outside the school.

Ten years later a law was introduced offering help to denominational interests that desired to take part in the three-level reorganization. Local authorities were to pay half the cost of reconstruction, and either the local education authority or the central government might provide another quarter; the churches themselves were to raise the remaining 25 per cent. By availing themselves of this offer and by providing funds, the English Catholic hierarchy managed to contribute to a system which both preserved the religious independence of Catholic schools and at the same time enabled most Catholic children to attend a Catholic school without paying fees.

English education is now controlled by the Butler Act of 1944. This act, which was an attempt to rationalize the relationship between local and central government, on the one hand, and the schools— religious and secular—on the other, provides for two main kinds of schools, independent schools and state-subsidized schools. There are three categories of the latter, aided schools, controlled schools, and special agreement schools. These will be discussed in detail later in this essay. Suffice it to say that most Catholic schools are aided schools.

Comparison of Catholic Schools with Government Schools as to Quality

The best Catholic schools produce students as strong academically as those in the government schools. The worst are poorer than the poorest of the state schools. One reason for this is that many Catholic schools are run by clergy or sisters, who themselves being bound to obedience consequently expect and demand a like docility from their staff. A second reason is that the institutional nature of the Church makes for conservatism in teaching methods. Third, there is a shortage of Catholic teachers, so that any Catholic who is professionally qualified, at however low a standard, will find it easy to obtain employment in a Catholic school. This factor constitutes a problem in non-

Catholic schools as well. In this connection, however, there is another element: Catholic appointing bodies will naturally maintain that piety and the regular practice of religion is a factor of equal (if not greater) importance with the professional qualifications of a teacher. It is unfortunate that piety and professional ability are not always associated.

The final reasons why Catholic schools find it difficult to maintain good academic standards are distinct from the three mentioned above. Since most Catholic schools must draw financial aid from already seriously burdened diocesan funds, equipment and special salary allowances for senior members of staff are hard to come by. Consequently Catholic teachers tend to shy away from employment in Catholic schools when they can acquire better salaries and working conditions in government schools.

Finally, the Catholic schools exist to serve the Catholic community. Since these schools are few and far between, they are forced—with some notable exceptions—to enroll all the Catholic children in the area, regardless of intellectual ability. If they do not take in every Catholic child who applies, then those children will be sent to government schools, a step which is not in accordance with official Catholic policy. Government schools, which find it somewhat easier than Catholic schools to obtain well-qualified staffs, also have more choice in the pupils they select, but it is probably true that few schools of any kind are entirely satisfied with the selection of children actually sent to them.

The Present Form of Catholic Schools in England

The Organizational Level

The English Catholic schools—in all but one important instance, the seminary school—follow the pattern which has grown up in English education as a whole. Formal schooling is compulsory from the ages of five through fifteen years. There are some Catholic nursery schools (that is, for children from about two to five years) attached to schools which work at the compulsory level, but these are exceptional. A child who attends a Catholic school will generally start at the age of five in a primary school. This school will give him instruction from the age of five to the age of seven years called the "infant level" and then from the age of seven to about eleven, called the junior level." At some time during his eleventh year the child will sit for a test called the "eleven plus," which comprises tests in arithmetic and English and an intelligence test. (In some parts of England however, the "eleven plus" examination is being modified or dropped altogether.) On the basis of the results of this test the student will be sent into one of several different types of secondary schools. A student whose test scores reveal that he is academically superior will be sent to a grammer school, where he will stay until the age of fifteen at least, and probably longer—finishing perhaps with entry to a university or a teacher-training college. A child whose test scores show that he is of inferior academic ability will be placed in a so-called "modern school," where the curriculum includes subjects of a more practical nature. The student whose test scores reveal that he has high technical aptitude will be sent to a technical school, where he will be taught specific skills, along with a certain amount of humanistic subjects. Thus this test is a screening device for determining what path a student will follow in secondary school.

All the schools described so far fall into the government school system. Catholic schools which fit into this system educate their pupils with no direct cost to the parents—at least for the formal part of their studies. All wage-earners pay the taxes (government levy) and rates (local authority levy) which fiscally support the schools, and Catholic parents are legally entitled to demand that their children be educated in a Catholic school, though they do not have the right to specify which type of school, whether grammar, modern, or technical. On the other hand, those parents who can afford the money may send their children to a nongovernment school where they pay full fees. The pattern is slightly different from that in the public sector. At the age of five the child may be sent to an approved kindergarten or private junior school where he is taught the three R's. At eight or thereabouts he is sent to a preparatory school where he stays until he is twelve. At the age of twelve he takes a fairly undemanding examination called "common entrance." If he passes this examination, he gains admission to a public school. (In English education a public school is in fact a private school, independent of the state, and subsisting on fees and on endowments from previous ages. Government schools in England are never called public schools.) There are about twenty Catholic public schools in England, mostly controlled by priests or members of religious orders. Some of them, like the Benedictine Ampleforth and Downside, and the Jesuit Stonyhurst, are nationally renowned.

England is notorious for the rigidity of its social class structure, and Catholic education reflects this rigidity. Public schools exist for children of almost any ability level whose parents have the money to pay the fees. The government schools are free of charge. There is very little cooperation between the government schools and public schools. Between the various parts of the government school system, however, there is some cooperation. The British government school system, in fact, allows for considerable mobility.

The entire structure of the government school system described has been found unsatisfactory for two principal reasons. First, the "eleven plus" examination is only about ninety per cent reliable as a predictor of a child's bent and abilities. Second, the determination of whether a child will be sent to a grammar school, for example, is arrived at not simply by his own academic ability, but also by the academic ability of the hundreds of other children who will be sitting for the "eleven plus" at the same time, and further on the availability of places in the local grammar school. The "eleven plus" is, in other words, competitive and often not justly competitive.

It is an unspoken (and sometimes a spoken) assumption that a grammar school education leading to a job as a white-collar worker is the most desirable socially; a child's failure to obtain a grammar school place can sometimes lead to bitterness and disappointment in the family, which stirs up anxieties in the child himself.

As one answer to the problems connected with the "eleven plus," the Ministry of Education has introduced two new kinds of schools at the secondary level: the bilateral school and the comprehensive school. Catholic schools are to be found among these schools, just as they are represented among other types of government schools. The bilateral school has under one roof both the grammar and the modern patterns. A comprehensive school embraces the grammar, modern, and technical patterns. The result of such organization is that if a child is, according to his performance in the "eleven plus," assigned to the modern pattern he can easily make the transition to the grammar pattern if he later displays considerable academic ability. This transition is generally made during the child's fourteenth year. To transform all schools, including religious schools, into comprehensive ones is the aim of the British government. By the end of 1966 there were definite plans for incorporating all schools, even the public schools, into the comprehensive system, either by enlarging them or by merging them administratively with schools of another type in the same district.

There is one kind of school within the private sector which is likely to retain its independence longer than most other types, that is the seminary school. Each diocese and religious institute is responsible for training priests, brothers, and sisters for service in the diocese or institute. To this end there is in each diocese a seminary for that training. Quite often, though not always, there is attached to this seminary as an integral part of its structure a seminary school, enrolling boys from about twelve years (like the public schools). Boys who show some signs of interest in a priestly vocation are admitted and given a general education, but with a bias toward theological subjects. Although there is no compulsion upon any boy when he reaches the age of eighteen or so to transfer to the seminary proper, many of the boys who attend seminary schools do in fact proceed to the seminary and start full time studies for the priesthood.

If there is any link that binds almost all the types of schools together, including even the public and seminary schools, it is the system of public examinations. There are many of these examinations, but two deserve mention. These are (1) general certificate of education at ordinary level, and (2) the general certificate of education at advanced level. The ordinary level examination is usually taken at the age of fifteen, in as many subjects as the student or his teacher decides, usually about four or five. A student who is successful in this examination will often choose not to leave school but to go on studying until he is seventeen or eighteen years old. At this later stage he may sit—usually in about three subjects—for the advanced level examination. Success here means that he is in a strong position to apply for admission to a university or a teacher-training college. These institutions of higher learning have as a minimum entrance requirement at least five passes at ordinary level. In fact, competition being what it is, very few of them will accept a student unless he has acquired two or more passes at advanced level. These two examinations are not only taken in most schools, including Catholic schools; they are set and marked externally and are therefore often accepted as a criterion of scholastic ability.

A Catholic student who graduates from school approximately at the age of eighteen to an institution of higher learning may be able to enter one of the dozen Catholic teacher-training colleges. He will not, however, find his way into a Catholic university, for there are none in England. There have been none since the Middle Ages, when all universities were under the patronage of both the Church and the Crown.

Control Structure of the Catholic School System

Catholic schools which are integrated into the government system have imposed upon them one or more of three kinds of control. First, they are responsible to the Ministry of Education both for the maintenance of the proper standards of education and the general operation of the school. The Ministry issues a certificate to the school confirming that it is "efficient" in the Ministry's sense of the term. The schools are thus open to inspection by Ministry inspectors, who are appointed on a regional basis and make occasional visitations to the school to check the work.

The individual school is also responsible, at a parochial level, to a board of governors. This board consists of the head teacher of the school, representatives from the local education authority, senior members of the Catholic community, and the local parish priest. General decisions about policy—buildings to be erected, numbers of students to be admitted, appointment of staff, content of the religious life of the school, and so on—are always made at this level.

Further, the individual school will be responsible to the diocesan schools inspector, a priest appointed by the bishop. It is his task to ensure that the religious teaching of the school is being carried out properly. Consequently one of his main functions is to examine the children in religious knowledge.

The board of governors and the diocesan inspector are, in the final analysis, responsible to the bishop himself, who maintains control over the general operation of the Catholic schools in his diocese. A body known as the Catholic Education Council acts as a kind of benevolent overseer of education throughout the country, and offers guidance in policymaking at the diocesan level to those who need it. The Council concerns itself particularly with the dealings that take place between the hierarchy and the state. Some educational institutions are under the direct control of the Council—for example, St. Mary's Teacher Training College near London; but in general the Council, whose chairman is a specially appointed bishop, acts in a coordinating and advisory capacity only.

In the private sector the Catholic schools are controlled by priests, brothers, or sisters. These priests and religious must sustain their responsibility to the Ministry of Education in order to hold the certificate of efficiency. Notwithstanding, their final obligation is to the superior of the religious institute. The preparatory schools sometimes associated with these schools are often run by laymen.

At the secondary level, both in the public and the private sectors, the head teacher of the Catholic school is usually a religious. Acting under the head teacher will be the deputy head, who is more often than not a member of the laity. Since World War II, with the increasing numbers of children in need of a Catholic education, with the diminishing numbers of postulants for the religious institutes, and with the growing need for priests in the parishes and the mission field, there has been a tendency for Catholic schools and teacher-training colleges to be staffed by laymen. At present the change from predominantly religious to predominantly lay control of schools is accelerating. Indeed there are already several Catholic secondary modern schools whose head teacher and deputy are both laymen. Such schools still serve the parish and the diocese, but the day-to-day operation of affairs involves the presence of a priest only as a teacher of religious knowledge, to hear confessions, and to say the special masses which the school may arrange. In the schools operated by religious institutes —the proportion of these is diminishing—the head teacher will always be a religious, though not necessarily the superior of the institute to which he or she belongs.

In general the clerical hegemony in education is slowly giving way to lay leadership.

Some Statistics on Catholic Schools

The table below presents figures showing the numerical relationship between Catholic and government schools at primary and secondary levels.

Figures are not available to show the increase in the number of Catholic schools since 1900 as a continuous record. Suffice it to say that there were 1100 such schools in 1900; the figure rose to 1900 by 1950 and 2300 by 1964. No accurate figures are available to show what proportion of Catholic children attend a Catholic school; but in February, 1947 Bishop Beck (now Archbishop Beck, Chairman of the Catholic Education Council) indicated that one child out of four was not at a Catholic school, as compared with one child out of five before World War II.

The English school year begins sometime in September and ends in the following July. Government primary and secondary schools begin the first week in September, whereas nongovernment schools and teacher-training colleges begin about September 20. Universities begin the fall term at the very end of September. The school year is divided into three terms, each of which lasts about ten or twelve

Statistical Summary, Catholic and Government Schools*

	Government Schools 1964	Catholic Schools 1964
Total schools, primary	14,000	1,800
Total schools, secondary	5,000	500
Total teacher-training colleges	128	13
Total universities	31	0
Total students primary	2,997,100	434,700
Total students secondary	2,437,700	18,530
Total students teacher-training colleges	35,240	5,640
Total students universities	95,800	0
Median school enrollment primary	210	240
Median school enrollment secondary	490	400
Median school enrollment teacher-training colleges	280	430
Median school enrollment universities	3,100	0
Median pupil class size primary	30	32
Median pupil class size secondary	20	27
Median pupil class size teacher-training colleges	10	10
Median pupil class size universities	10	0

* Based on data compiled from statistics of the Catholic Education Council and from the Education Committee's *Yearbook, 1965-1966.*

1. These data are for England and Wales.
2. All figures are rounded off to the nearest hundred or to the nearest ten.
3. For purposes of this table, government schools excludes schools operated by non-Catholic religious denominations (principally sponsored by the Church of England), whether or not they receive some State fiscal support.
4. The median pupil class size for the teacher-training colleges and the universities is a somewhat misleading figure. The average teacher-training college size dictated by the Ministry of Education is 11, while that for universities is not officially fixed. Rather the 5.6 figure was calculated by dividing the number of instructors into the number of students.

weeks. Each term is divided by a midterm holiday, which lasts up to one week. There are three major vacation periods; the first comes at Christmas time, with a three-week vacation from just before Christmas until the first half of January. The second is at Eastertide, the duration of which varies according to the date of Easter. The summer vacation lasts from the end of July until the beginning of the new school year in September.

The school day, in both Catholic and government schools, begins at about 9:15 A.M. with a religious service and an assembly period for announcements by the head teacher. Lessons begin at about 9:30

A.M. At 10:30 there is a recess of fifteen minutes. Work then proceeds until noon or 12:30 P.M. The lunch period lasts for an hour or an hour and a half. After lunch, primary schools continue until about 3:30 P.M., whereas secondary schools continue until about 4:15 P.M. In teacher-training colleges and the universities the school day varies and is in no way subject to the type of time-blocks utilized in the lower schools.

In the primary schools the teaching periods, as they are called, last for half an hour, with a double period sometimes for a subject like art, which requires preparation and cleaning up. In secondary schools and in most colleges of education the periods are longer, with forty-five minutes as the usual maximum.

The recent increase in the number of English schools of all types has benefited the Catholic community, especially in the area of school architecture. Many new Catholic schools are being erected, and most of them incorporate the more progressive thinking of English architects. Although a number of Catholic children are still taught in bleak, chocolate-colored, badly lit classrooms, the more fortunate are accommodated in a bright, spacious, generously glazed building on one or two floors, with wide corridors and good amenities. These amenities, for secondary schools, include well-equipped laboratories and lecture theatres, an engineering workshop, art studios, a library, a gymnasium (which must sometimes do duty as an assembly hall), perhaps a theatre, and even, occasionally, facilities for closed circuit educational television.

Nearly all new schools, even in urban areas, are surrounded by playing fields, which have the incidental advantage of insulating the buildings from the noise of passing traffic.

But despite these advances, there is still a shortage of money. For this reason, and because those in positions of authority still tend to be conservative, most classrooms will be as large as possible, and rectangular in shape, with the teacher installed at one end, sometimes on a dais, facing the class. The bigger rooms can sometimes be divided by sliding partitions to accommodate two classes without mutual disturbance. Desks, usually of modern design, can be cleared away for a drama lesson or for a class in movement.

Staff facilities are rarely more than adequate. The head teacher and the deputy head generally have private offices; other members of staff share one common room.

Because the state will not contribute toward the cost of erecting buildings used essentially for religious purposes, most schools, even if they are not directly attached to a parish church, tend to use the nearest church for special masses. Other services are sometimes held in the assembly hall.

Financial Support of Catholic Schools in England

The financing of the English Catholic schools is not only the most complex of all the questions facing Catholic educationists and administrators, it is also the question which arouses the bitterest feelings among both Catholics and non-Catholics. The fundamental position from which Catholic authorities argue is something like the following: Catholic schools not only have a moral right to exist, but indeed they must continue to exist to foster the growing intellects of the faithful. Further, every time a Catholic school puts the name of a Catholic child on its roll there remains one child fewer for the state to educate. Therefore the state should provide some, if not all, of the cost of building and operating Catholic schools—so long as these schools meet the requirements of the state for educational efficiency.

To these arguments the state replies that no parent is compelled to send his child to a Catholic school, when the state provides education free of charge for all children. Moreover, it would not be correct —so the state's argument runs—to spend state money on denominational schools which would not be approved by the majority of citizens who pay the rates and taxes which support them.

If Catholic schools are to be entirely supported by the state, either at local level (by the local education authorities) or at the national level (by the Ministry of Education), then the state demands that two conditions must be fulfilled. First, as in government schools, the state must have the right to appoint the teachers. Second, the religious instruction given in the Catholic schools must, on at least three days a week, consist of the so-called "agreed syllabus"; that is a syllabus of general Christian doctrine, pleasing to all parties and given in government schools (sometimes by teachers who confessedly are not Christians themselves).

The Catholic schools, fortified by a long tradition of independence and jealous of their moral rights, but in fact finding it increasingly difficult to carry the heavy financial burden imposed upon them by their obligations toward Catholic students, argue from principle that the second of these two conditions at any rate, if not the first, is unacceptable. If the Catholic Church in England were to accept both clauses in the fullness of their implications, Catholic education could immediately become entirely supported by the state—and would cease to exist.

As usual in England, some kind of compromise has been reached, with renewed arguments from the Catholic side to gain moral as well as financial support for what is held to be an inalienable right for children to be educated in accordance with the wishes of their parents.

The present situation is as follows (it is necessary to simplify the issues greatly; it must be remembered that they are complex, depending a great deal on case law and precedent as well as on statute law; and that they vary from area to area according to the interests and sympathies of the local education committees).

There is a considerable group of Catholic schools which are entirely independent of state fiscal support. These schools are financed in one or more of four different ways. First, and principally, these Catholic schools are financed by tuition paid by the students' parents, who also pay rates and taxes which contribute to the state-supported schools in the area in which they reside. The second source of revenue comes from funds made available from various sources by the religious institutes which often conduct these schools. Funds also come from endowments, outright gifts, bequests, alumni donations and so forth, and occasionally by grants made by bodies such as the Catholic Education Council. These Catholic schools will in all probability be absorbed eventually into the comprehensive system of schooling desired by the national government.

The Education Act of 1936 permitted 50 to 75 per cent of the total cost to be borne by the state for new senior schools (for students aged twelve to eighteen years). This provision extended to all types of schools, including Catholic schools, falling under this category. Then the 1944 (Butler) Education Act made provision for three types of state support for schools which are already in existence: (1) aided schools, in which the group operating the institution pays half the maintenance costs, the Ministry of Education the other half, with the local school's board of governors controlling the institution; (2) controlled schools, in which the local civil education authority pays all the costs for these schools, but assumes complete control over the general administration and policymaking of the school; (3) special agreement schools, in which any sum up to 75 per cent of the total maintenance costs could be (though need not necessarily be) paid by the local civil education authority.

Clearly, Catholic schools could not under any circumstance become controlled schools. As a result most Catholic schools are aided schools or special agreement schools, the large majority aided schools. Despite the neatness of the percentages offered, the variation in the *actual* percentage of the running costs paid by the state is considerable and makes it difficult to generalize about the proportions carried by any of the three bodies, Church, state, and local education authority.

The 1944 Butler Act and its amendments enacted in 1946 and in 1948 made provision for payment by the local education authority for Catholic and other voluntary schools to receive grants to meet the cost of such amenities as playing fields, religious books, medical dispensaries, and student dining halls.

Two recent innovations to reduce expense in the building and operation of Catholic schools should be mentioned. The first is the Catholic National Building Office, founded in 1960. The Office examines allocations of cost involved in new Catholic schools and offers recommendations as to how these costs might be reduced. The second is the Diocesan Purchasing Service, established primarily, though not exclusively, to assist independent schools. Arrangements are made for bulk buying of essential equipment direct from manufacturers at a good discount. The DPS has saved Catholic schools an enormous amount of money.

The chief difficulty facing the Roman Catholic Church in England is not so much the operation of schools already in existence, but rather the building of new schools to meet the needs of a Catholic population which is growing at a rate higher than the rate of population increase in the country as a whole. Financial grants for new schools are very difficult to obtain.

The Church's contribution to Catholic schools (apart from independent schools) comes almost entirely from the pockets of the faithful at Sunday masses. Sometimes the money will go directly to the parish school, but usually the funds are administered by the diocese.

Taking into account the high rates of interest demanded on money borrowed, a rough estimate would suggest that Catholics are now bearing between 50 to 75 per cent of all the money spent on Catholic schools. The state bears the rest.

All teachers in Catholic schools are paid from the source of the general finances of the schools, whether Church, state, or local education authority. The Burnham Scale is used as the minimum for salary gradients. The Burnham Scale was worked out by the Burnham Committee, which consisted of representatives from the Ministry of Education and from the teachers' associations. The scale starts at about £800 ($2240) per annum and rises by annual increments of about £50 ($140). There are under the Scale many special increments. A man who has a degree from a British university will receive an extra increment from the beginning of his teaching career. If he has also taken special pedagogical course work and preparation he will receive a further sum. Increments are also paid to teachers with special responsibilities, for example, teaching in the higher forms (grades) of secondary schools or for being chairman of an academic department. There are special salary scales for head teachers and deputy heads, the sum generally depending on the total number of students in the school. Special increments are based upon skill; in theory the best man for the job gets the job and the increment, even if this does not always work out in practice. The annual salary increment for service is automatic.

Independent schools tend to pay salaries slightly higher than the Burnham Scale and can therefore be more selective in their choice of staff. When there are religious as teachers in a school their salary is still paid, but it is usually put straight into the common purse of the institute and is often paid back into the school funds for improvements and extensions to buildings and so forth.

There are few fringe benefits in teaching in England. All teachers contribute to a Ministry of Education Fund about 5 per cent of their salary, and on retirement at the age of sixty or sixty-five they are entitled to a modest pension, the amount of which depends on their length of service and their position at retirement. There are also widows' pensions.

Although private health insurance plans are offered at special rates to teachers, few teachers either wish or can afford to take advantage of them. All citizens pay for the National Health Service and are entitled thereby to free medical services when they or their dependents fall ill. Private insurance plans can sometimes make treatment more quickly available or provide a private room in hospital.

The Curriculum

The English belief in freedom, particularly academic freedom, has led to a great variety of subjects and other educational activities in all schools, including Catholic schools. Indeed, it is impossible to summarize with any exactness the range of class and extraclass activities. At the infant and junior stages the traditional topics are studies: English, arithmetic, reading, writing, drama, art, history, geography, nature study (that is, elementary botany and zoology), and singing. All these topics are taught by one or two teachers, who are assigned to a class rather than to a subject. Classes on the primary level are self-contained rather than departmentalized. In nongovernment (private) schools, curriculum and syllabus tend to be more formal, generally including Latin and French—since most public schools still demand knowledge of Latin or another foreign language for entrance. At the primary level, both in the private and in the government schools, every student must attend all classes, since there are no electives of any sort.

The more educationally alert of the Catholic primary schools have thriving clubs and societies run by the staff. Playlets and small concerts are an important feature of school life. And with travel to the Continent becoming progressively less expensive and increasingly popular, there are more and more educational trips abroad arranged by schools for parties of children. No primary school is considered to be doing its job properly if it omits these activities and such others as field trips to museums and art galleries, which can provoke in the children a felt need for the cultural adventures which can later enrich their adult lives. Games are taken seriously. Boys engage in cricket and swimming in the summer, and in the winter their attention is on association or rugby football. Girls play tennis and volleyball in the summer and hockey or lacrosse in the winter months.

At the secondary level the curricular pattern becomes differentiated. All students are streamed into the grammar school curriculum, the modern curriculum, or the technical curriculum. The grammar school curriculum includes the classical formal subjects in the pure structural form such as mathematics and English. All students begin to specialize in at least three different tracks at the age of fifteen or earlier. The first track is classics, Latin and Greek, though fewer and fewer now choose this track. The second is modern languages, particularly French, German, and Spanish. The third track is in science, physics, chemistry, and the biological sciences. This specialization tends to occur in the public schools as well, even though many of the students will not be suited to the academic rigors incumbent upon the students in the grammar schools.

In the modern curriculum pattern there is a much more liberal approach to learning for children who are less able academically. Some foreign language work is done, usually French, but the study of this and other topics is pursued much less rigorously, more informally, and at a lower scholastic level. Subjects tend to be more integrated with one another; for example, a history project might involve the geography and the English departments for a student learning experience which has need of knowledges and understandings from those areas related to his project.

In the technical secondary schools or in the technical streams of the secondary modern schools, there will be a strong stress on practical subjects such as woodwork, metalwork, cooking, technical drawing, and engineering. Where academic subjects are studied, they will be considered in their applications rather than in their intrinsic structure. For example, mathematics teachers in technical schools are involved in helping students with the applied mathematics needed for specialized technical subjects. Some technical schools take "day release" students, that is boys over fifteen who, having left school and taken factory jobs, are released from work one or two days a week to continue their technical studies at a theoretical level. This program is somewhat similar to the work-study program in American secondary schools.

Games still loom large, even outside the public schools. Principal sports activities for boys include football and cricket. Physical education is an important school function. Formal instruction, exercise, and movement in the gymnasium constitute an essential part of all curricula at the secondary and the primary level.

In general Catholic schools, particularly the grammar and public schools, have been slow to use any kind of curricular design except the subject-centered. Most Catholic schools encourage a spirit of human community; few concern themselves with the equally vital "community of topic." The Core curriculum is relatively unknown. However, as noted, in government modern schools, some curricular integration among the subjects, albeit informal, does occur.

Since the end of World War II, there has been more stress on the study of science in its various forms. Another post-war curricular development is that the old formal teaching of English language and literature has yielded to a freer approach which attempts to involve the whole being of the student in the kind of work he can most succeed at, that is creative writing, where he genuinely handles his own experience in poetic, narrative, or dramatic form.

These and other curricular innovations are partly the result of a wider conception of what education means, partly the effect of teaching children whose scholastic ability is not congruent with the old formal methods and subjects and partly the issue of academic research at University Institutes of Education. Although certain Catholics have contributed to the widening of the curriculum, most of the progress in educational theory at curriculum level has been engendered by men who are not Catholics; as a matter of fact, these advances in curriculum theory have been received lethargically by Catholic schools.

In English Catholic schools the syllabus varies from school to school, with the exception of the syllabus for religious knowledge, which is typically prescribed by the diocese. Within the school the recommended syllabus is a general schema rather than a rigid structure—divided into weeks or terms—which the teacher must follow. Scheduling needs and the availability of staff does determine the scope and variety of the syllabus. Yet each instructor is free to teach the course in whatever order or fashion he wishes, limited only by the following considerations: first, the head teacher decides what subjects shall be studied in the school; second, the planner of the schedule (generally the deputy head) determines how there can be a varied instructional pattern among the subjects chosen, so that the children are moved frequently from one topic to another; third, demands made by external examinations must be considered, especially the general certificate of education at ordinary level and advanced level, and the certificate of secondary education (a more recent and a more informal examination for secondary modern students at the age of about fifteen).

There is therefore a good deal of freedom allowed to teachers at the week-to-week level, leaving space both for profitable digressions by the class and for meeting the individual interests of the children. The nearer the public examinations loom, the more closely the teacher will follow the syllabus which these examinations prescribe. Obvious exceptions to this are the mathematical and scientific subjects: here, since each stage depends upon the one before it, the progression tends to follow the logical structure of the scientific argument.

Apart from primary schools, where for obvious reasons there must be a great deal of speech and movement, and apart from the technical schools, where activity such as problem-solving, designing, engineering practice, and so forth is built into the demands of the subject the syllabus tends to be extremely bookish. Bookish here is used in two senses: in the sense that the teacher will rely to a large extent upon the textbook that happens to be available, or which his head teacher or head of department has specified, and bookish in the sense that a large number of the exercises are unrelated to the kind of activities in which the students actually engage during their out-of-school hours. Even scientific subjects are still treated in an abstract and historical way, rather than in a way which shows their relationship to the life human beings really need and lead. There are signs that in mathematics, geography, English, and drama, students are being helped to see the connection between academic work and the world they find outside the classroom. Fieldwork, map-making, the enactment of real-life situations are beginning to contribute to a more lively and a more genuinely educational kind of lesson.

Instruction

Two concepts underlie teaching methods in English Catholic schools. One view holds that the teacher is king; the other is that classroom education is primarily a process of acquiring knowledge. Despite the protests of educational writers and the perpetual emphasis in teacher-training colleges, most teaching in elementary schools, in secondary schools, and particularly in universities follows the first of these two principles, even where teachers themselves will not admit it. The reason is simple: to dominate a class and to fill children with information is easy. Most teachers take the easy course.

Except in certain subjects, particularly history and geography, it is not quite true to say that the teacher is a lecturer, properly so called. Most teachers make some concession to the needs of the children and will use at least a question and answer method. The typical teacher is midway between lecturer and group leader, with a tendency to the side of lecturing.

Happily, attitudes are changing. Like most positive improvements in teaching methodology, these changes derive from the primary schools. In these schools the teacher usually teaches in a self-contained classroom and hence teaches one class for all subjects. This enables him to get down to real education, that is to encouraging the students to discover not simply what there is to be known about a subject but also what topics they might profitably pursue and the underlying causes for such activity. In some of the more progressive Catholic primary schools, a visitor finds children of mixed intellectual ability sitting in groups of four or five around separate tables, working on different projects. The teacher, instead of addressing the class from one area of the room, will move about, listening, watching, and giving individual attention where it is needed.

A word should be said about the term "project." The teacher will suggest a theme, transport, for example. Each group of four or five children will then discuss, perhaps with the help of the teacher, those aspects of the theme which might interest them. In a given group one child might set about finding and annotating pictures of different kinds of transport, land, sea, and air. Another might delve into the history of transport. A third might write some poems about journeys he has made. A fourth might inquire into methods of propulsion, drawing diagrams of different kinds of power sources which men have used. Another might make an imaginative jump and do some research into modes of animal movement. Here, it will be seen, all "subjects" are included: the children *become* mathematicians, historians, geographers, artists, writers, and so on. Unfortunately children who have been fortunate enough to work under such a plan are sorely disappointed when they leave the primary school and discover that the secondary school is organized around the old lecture method. Too little pedagogical experimentation has been carried out at the secondary level. This unhappy situation is partly because teachers are timid, partly because school authorities think (quite wrongly) that the project method militates against good examination results, and partly because most secondary pupils are divided by intellectual ability into streams (tracks) and taught by specialists, who are loath to drop the university style of teaching by which they themselves have acquired their skills.

If Catholic schools are unenterprising here, they do not lag behind in the use of audiovisual aids. The excellent programs put out on sound and vision by the British Broadcasting Corporation and the Independent Television Authority are received in many schools, both primary and secondary. The filmstrip projector and the tape recorder are occasional allies of the teacher. Yet it is true that few teachers understand the possibilities inherent in these machines: equipment merely transforms a lecture into an illustrated lecture. There are signs, however, that the next generation of teachers will be more alert to these aids and will use them more creatively, really involving the children in the lesson. Teaching machines are slowly being introduced —against a backwash of conservative hostility. At the moment the programs are too few and too little used to say with certainty whether teaching machines will revolutionize classroom techniques. In general English teachers are wary of audiovisual aids and will use them primarily because they perceive it is the "proper" thing to do.

Role-playing, that dynamic pedagogical tool, is seldom used in English Catholic schools. Panels, symposia, and cell methodologies also are rarities.

At the primary level few children are given homework or any formal out-of-school assignments to complete. At the secondary level homework looms large. Some grammar schools require three hours' work every evening. As students grow older they are invited to use textbooks with increasing frequency to reinforce what they have been taught. Only at the senior level, however, are students encouraged to do any peripheral reading. Lessons are textbook-centered. Field trips, especially for historians and geographers, are becoming steadily more common, and these expeditions are often well integrated into the teaching program of the school.

Motivation is a concern of most English teachers. Punishment, particularly corporal punishment, is becoming less and less used—although Catholic schools are slower to abjure the deterrents. Prizes are given annually at most schools for good conduct or scholastic achievement. In primary schools "stars" and other symbols of approval are presented to the "better" children. In some Catholic schools a more positive attitude toward motivation is developing: not simply the carrot instead of the stick, but lessons where a pupil can hardly help cooperating because of genuine interest and genuine respect. To academically inclined students the pressure of external examinations remains a strong stimulus.

In primary schools competitive instincts are channelled into outdoor sports. Because classes include pupils of varying abilities, the emphasis is on motivating the child to compete only with himself. At the secondary level the sense of competition is stronger. However this competition is not so much between individuals as between "houses." This system, borrowed from the public schools, assigns each student to a group of about sixty, called a house. To this group he owes his primary loyalty, contributing "credits" for work and sports. The system has not really transplanted well to modern schools. In Catholic schools cooperation rather than competition is encouraged. The traditional British emphasis on teamwork as exemplified in the British military service provides a positive cultural framework by which cooperation rather than competition in schools is encouraged.

The focus of evaluation in Catholic and other schools in England is the essay or other exercise handed in, marked, and handed back. Other methods of evaluation include terminal examinations, weekly tests, and "mock" examinations preceding external examinations. These devices are used by most teachers, but the process of testing is usually thought of as being independent of the process of learning, and is usually carried out under the conditions of a public examination, invigilated and solemn. Students are not encouraged, except by the superior teachers, to evaluate their own work or to engage in joint teacher-pupil evaluation of the course.

Apart from the external examinations such as the "eleven plus," achievement tests in English schools have three characteristics. First, they are teacher-composed. This has the disadvantage that it continues the restricting process which one teacher's method must impose upon the material of his lessons. Second, the typical teacher-constructed test demands correct information rather than the use of judgment. Third, testing is seen as a necessary evil, amputated from the process of education. Few teachers in English Catholic schools seem to have thought at all about the process of examining and its function in the educational process as a whole; lessons are "interrupted" for a test before the next block of "real" teaching begins.

Parents are informed at the end of each term of their child's performance in a written report. Usually each teacher of a subject indicates a mark for scholastic achievement and adds a short comment. Then the report card is signed by the head teacher.

There is no formal channel of communication by which parents can discuss a child's work with the teachers. Parents are invited to call upon members of staff in school, but this visiting is informal and occurs only when some special problem arises, for example, about the child's career. Teacher-student discussion of the report is almost unknown.

The head teacher will make occasional visits to a classroom to inspect a teacher, particularly a new teacher, but these visits are rare. The state has the right to inspect and supervise teaching in *all* schools, (except teacher-training colleges). Supervisory visitations are infrequent, and advance notice is always given. Supervision, then, falls into a dichotomy: it is either very informal or very formal. Catholic schools receive occasional visits from the diocesan inspector, whose first concern is with the program of religious education: In cases in which the school is operated by a religious institute it is very unusual for the local or regional superior of the institute to interfere with the work done in the school.

Supervision of teachers is considered to be advisory. The aim of supervision is to help teachers in their work, perhaps to criticize them adversely at times but never to make firm rulings which an individual teacher is bound to follow. After a formal inspection a full written report will be sent to the head teacher. It is then up to the head teacher to make whatever changes he thinks desirable. One of the very few areas in which ministry inspectors can issue a mandate is in the matter of amenities: cloakrooms, teaching space, and equipment.

There are three kinds of control over standards of instruction. The first is by the prudent appointment of staff. The second is by the results obtained in external examinations: poor marks sometimes mean inefficient teaching. The third is the arrangement of the syllabus of the various courses. Here a head of department can help his colleagues by discussing what topics they should cover. But there are few sanctions. It is difficult to dismiss a teacher (members of a religious institute, can, of course, be transferred; there is so great shortage of teachers in Catholic schools that a head teacher would be loath to dismiss a teacher, even for poor teaching or for educational inefficiency in general).

The Program of Religious Education

Under English law *all* primary and secondary schools must begin the day with a short religious service. In Catholic schools this service, which may include a short instruction, may be considered as part of the program of religious education. The formal instruction in religion —called religious instruction or religious knowledge—must occupy in every Catholic school certain minimum time as required by the diocese. This is usually about four periods a week. At the primary level the period lasts about half an hour, at the higher levels roughly forty minutes. In short, approximately 12 and 10 per cent, respectively, of the school day is spent in religious instruction.

A teacher who presents his material in a dull manner in mathematics or history will present a dull religious instruction lesson. Professional preparation of those who are to teach religion is more far reaching, though, than for those who teach other subjects. For example, it is impressed upon teachers during their professional preparation that the religion lesson should be permeated with a friendly atmosphere. Every lesson should promote a "knowledge end"—the child should learn the truths of his faith; an "action end"—the child should behave differently because of what he has learned; and sometimes a devotion end—the child's sense of worship should be evoked and encouraged.

But too often, the religious instruction lesson is a burden for the teacher, therefore a penance for the pupil. Too often mere instruction —information—is purveyed without any attempt at discussion or at inquiries about why a doctrine must be what it is. Too often the approach is excessively angled toward apologetics: "Prove that the Church possesses the four marks: unity, holiness, catholicity, and apostolicity," for example. The children learn the proofs, but they do not become better apostles thereby.

The following are some of the pedagogical methods used in the religious instruction lesson: reference to (and rote learning of) the penny catechism, with explanation of the point that comes appropriately for the lesson of the day; stories from Scripture, especially those relating events in the life of Our Lord; a lecture, showing "answers" to "difficulties"; a survey of the Commandments—with the sixth and ninth commonly omitted, even in secondary schools; illustrated descriptions of the various parts of the mass. These methods clearly vary in their usefulness.

There are some happy modern emphases which are gradually changing the face of religious education in English schools. The first of these is the increased emphasis on Scripture: seeing the narrative for what it is, then allowing the pupils themselves to draw the conclusion which follows naturally rather than forcing them to memorize the conclusion drawn out by theologians. The second is the use of filmstrips and motion pictures depicting some aspect of bible history, or of the mass, or of daily conduct. The third is the fuller discussion of moral and doctrinal questions connected with actual living—real discussion, led but not limited by the teacher. The fourth is the dramatization of situations in and outside church—for example, a detailed performance of the baptismal ceremony upon a doll for ten-year old girls and boys. The fifth is the commentary, not too intrusive, given during mass or benediction itself, while the action is going on in the children's presence. There are hopes that these and other methods will become increasingly current in Catholic schools during the next twenty years; in any case there is no doubt that England is faced with something like a revolution in catechetical method. The fruits are to come.

Except in schools conducted by religious institutes, most religious teaching is done by laymen, who hold the religious teaching certificate granted to them at the teacher-training college by the diocesan authorities. However teachers-in-training are slow to see the relevance of the catechetics classes which they must attend to qualify for the religious teaching certificate. Unhappily, many teachers-in-training acquire the certificate at the end of their course even when they have not proved genuine competence in the field. Much teaching of religion, at any rate in Catholic secondary modern and comprehensive schools, is done by teachers whose specialty is something other than theology. Standards are inevitably low.

Catholic schools in England are still a minority and are conscious of their Catholic status. Students in schools operated by religious institutes are constantly reminded of the religious life by the simple fact that most of their teachers are living it. In these and in other Catholic schools, a short prayer usually precedes each lesson or at least at the beginning of the morning and the afternoon sessions. Holydays and patronal feasts are celebrated in the local church with a special mass. Nevertheless it is not wholly unjust to state that in most Catholic schools the practice and atmosphere of the faith are elements superadded to what must look to an outsider very much like any other school. This is believed by some to possess certain advantages: delicate subjects like biology (with evolution) and history (with Reformation) are no longer felt to be loaded with risk; further, the mentality which could conceive the existence of subjects like Catholic mathematics or Catholic poetry is fast dying. But little has taken the place of the old postures. Religion is not integrated into the teaching program. It remains a special subject and, as has been observed, a subject not very well handled.

The man who bears the greatest responsibility for supervising religious instruction is the parish priest. Indeed, he himself will often teach religion in the school. Moreover he will generally be one of the school governors and will be responsible, under his bishop, for the general policy in the matter of religious instruction. His responsibility is particularly marked when children are being prepared at school for first communion and confession, or for confirmation. In these instances he himself will conduct special classes. Theoretically the diocesan inspector holds a supervisory role in Catholic schools, but the parish priest exercises the greater control.

In Catholic boarding schools (mostly public schools) the community life involves confession and mass as regular desiderata. Some such schools will bind their students by rule to attend confession every so often and will make mass attendance compulsory. In a day school the situation is more complex. A feast day will find the children trooping to mass together, with lessons cancelled for the religious exercises. This applies particularly to primary schools. At the secondary level there is an increasing voluntarism, together with a larger provision of opportunities for those who wish to avail themselves of the special programs for devotion.

Little empirical research has been done on the comparative results of Catholic and government schooling, and it is difficult to say accurately whether Catholic schools offer a better education than they once did. Probably they do. But before World War II a Catholic at a Catholic school had a poorer opportunity for scholastic actualization or for attaining the next educational level than did his contemporary at a government school. One reason is that most Catholic schools were operated by clergy and sisters, most of whom were Irish. These religious were educated under a system which did not promote wide knowledge, discouraged intellectual inquiry, and tended to scorn modern teaching methods. The intellect was felt to be almost the enemy of the soul. Only as the supply of clergy and sisters in schools dwindle does England see a new picture emerging, that of schools largely staffed by laymen, who are more alert to the possibilities of modern psychology, of the ontological richness of the teaching process, and the classroom implications of both. But even now there is no Catholic school in England known to the present writer which seems likely to generate a distinguished tradition of intellectual leadership.

A recent statistical comparison between the religious practices of Catholics who attended Catholic schools and Catholics who were educated elsewhere shows no significant difference between the two groups. One must, however, accept the results with caution—even though one might have guessed them—since the study covered only just over a thousand persons.

There is some evidence, however, that Catholics who have attended a Catholic school are better integrated into the visible life of the Church than those who have not—even if only because they know more of what the Church has to offer at her margins: the sodalities, clubs, and societies which exist at parochial and diocesan level. Whether they are better Christians is very doubtful. They are more rigid in their attitudes and more institutionally oriented. One way of putting it is to say that Catholics with Catholic schooling have the faith firmly but not flexibly, whereas Catholics who have mixed with children of all denominations have a wider tolerance but are less clear about the content of the faith.

240   Catholic Education in the Western World

The official Catholic ideal in England is that in each parish there should be at least a primary school specifically for Catholic children. This ideal is sometimes attained; sometimes, indeed, the school meets in the church hall. There are few secondary schools attached to parishes. One reason for this is that the catchment area for a Catholic school extends some distance beyond the bounds of the parish.

But even where there is a close geographical and statistical relationship between parish and school there is generally a very thin existential relationship. It is only rarely that a Catholic school makes a perceptible contribution to the Catholic community surrounding it.

Nevertheless there are signs that pupils at Catholic secondary schools are beginning to make their contribution to the welfare of the society, Catholic and non-Catholic, in which they move: visiting the sick and elderly, doing free house repairs, and so on. But in England, particularly in urban areas, the sense of what the parish *is* has almost been lost. Consequently, while a Catholic school is an identifiable unit, having its own place, times, and relationships, the parish too often means no more than the church building and the presbytery, existing without an ecology. Any relationship is at best tenuous when there is no clear realization of what the relationship is with.

Pupil Personnel and
Guidance Services

Although the nonscholastic guidance a Catholic school student receives is desultory, the regular visits by doctors, nurses, and dentists —at least to schools which receive some state support—are important features of school life. The student's general welfare is the head teacher's responsibility, which he delegates in the following ways. First, all students are attached to a class teacher, who acts as a kind of personal tutor to them. Second, a "careers master" (or mistress) is available to show a student the possibilities open to him when he leaves school. Third, any pupil with personal or emotional problems which need clinical assistance will be invited to attend, together with his parents, the Child Guidance Clinic, where there is a school psychologist on duty. The psychologist refers a student for treatment if necessary. Finally, the school chaplain has regular sessions in the school.

Group guidance is not a formal feature of life in Catholic or government schools in England, although experts in certain fields occasionally do address the whole school or a selected group of older students. Two kinds of guidance (apart from the specifically religious) are slowly being introduced into Catholic schools. One is a regular visit from a health visitor (female clinical-social worker), who gives instruction and advice to girls, in groups or singly, on matters of health, makeup, and general appearance. The health visitor also discusses personal problems. The other consists in the one-day visits by a team of speakers from the Catholic Marriage Advisory Council. These speakers discuss questions in the whole area of sexuality (not only or primarily moral questions) with school-leavers. Usually no special rooms are available for these meetings; rather, they take place in classrooms. In both these kinds of guidance the work is arduous, the experts are few, and the school authorities are often uninformed or suspicious.

The original "eleven plus" examination to determine what kind of school a child should attend was basically an intelligence test. Recent research has shown that intelligence is a complicated concept to deal with. The testing program still includes intelligence, special ability, and personality tests, but the decision about a child's class placement is now made not only from test results, but also incorporates the teachers' opinion, and parental wishes. Indeed, some authorities have stopped standardized objective testing at the age of eleven. Only when a student shows marked abnormalities will he be sent to a psychologist and subjected to standardized clinical tests.

A compliment paid by non-Catholics to Catholic schools is that the children's behavior is better than the deportment of other school children. The compliment is often justified. Sometimes a greater docility arises from the children's respect for the clergy and religious who teach them, sometimes from something less worthy: fear. While no teacher in an English Catholic school would deny that discipline is primarily an inward quality, too few Catholic teachers—particularly in secondary schools—subscribe in their practice to that view. Corporal punishment is more widespread in Catholic than in other schools. Overcrowded classes (particularly marked in Catholic schools) often generate a regime which is strict even by English standards.

Although Catholic teachers are implicitly responsible for the spiritual welfare of their students, few of them have received any pastoral training except a little psychology and a little moral theology. The influence of the head teacher and the chaplain are therefore vital. At worst, students inhabit an atmosphere of generalized piety having no relevance to their real problems; at best, the chaplain will play a vigorous role in the school, joining positively in the students' concerns, genuinely interesting himself in their ambitions, and giving prudent and charitable counsel. Unquestionably he is the key to the religious guidance program.

The Staff of the Catholic Schools

There were in England and Wales at the beginning of 1964, 202 secular priests teaching full time in Catholic primary and secondary schools, 969 male religious, 4517 female religious, and 21,803 laymen and laywomen. The table below shows the qualifications of these full-time teachers by status.

Distribution of Teachers in English Catholic Schools, 1964*

Qualifications	Status	Primary	Secondary	All Independent Schools	TOTAL
University Trained Graduates	Secular Clergy	—	28	30	58
	Religious (Male)	—	94	140	234
	Religious (Female)	25	289	389	703
	Lay (Male and Female)	386	2,261	598	3,245
University Untrained Graduates	Secular Clergy	—	16	69	85
	Religious (Male)	1	95	246	342
	Religious (Female)	3	68	159	230
	Lay (Male and Female)	93	649	330	1,072
Teacher Training College Graduates	Secular Clergy	—	7	8	15
	Religious (Male)	1	72	119	192
	Religious (Female)	1,457	349	1,032	2,838
	Lay (Male and Female)	10,229	4,861	901	15,991
Non-graduates of University or Teacher Training College	Secular Clergy	—	5	39	44
	Religious (Male)	1	29	171	201
	Religious (Female)	66	49	631	746
	Lay (Male and Female)	811	215	469	1,495

* Data from the Catholic Education Council.

There are four categories in the table. The university-trained graduates hold a bachelor's degree from a British university and have also taken at least one year of course work in education. The university untrained graduates hold merely a degree, with no further course work in education. Teacher-training college graduates comprise the largest single group. The teachers in this category possess a teacher's certificate, gained after three (previously two) years' study at a teacher-training college. At the college they made an academic study of one or two major subject areas and were given a fairly thorough training in instructional methodology and the teaching process, including about four months' practice teaching in schools. In the final category, untrained nongraduates of university or teacher-training college, there are about 1000 clergy or religious and about 1500 laymen who hold no qualifications at all.

The category described in the table as "all independent schools" deserves special mention. This special category covers Catholic schools at all levels which receive no help at all from the state, but subsist entirely on tuition, gifts, and endowments. It should be noted that there are as many sisters (about 2200) teaching in such schools as there are laymen. Almost all Catholic independent schools for girls, particularly at the senior level, are convent schools.

The degree of academic freedom permitted to students and staff in Catholic educational establishments varies widely and depends upon two factors. The first is the attitude of the head teacher, especially in respect to the degree of permissiveness he shows toward the approach and methods of the members of his staff. The second is the kind of obedience owed by religious members of staff to their institute.

When there is censorship in Catholic schools, it tends to be indirect and tactful and to operate in terms of appeals to personal loyalties. Yet a person may perhaps miss promotion or a new appointment because his views are not felt to be "safe." There are very few direct administrative reprisals in the form of dismissal of a teacher, at least among lay staff. (It must be noted that the rights of the teacher are very jealously guarded in England; it is extremely difficult for a teacher to be dismissed from a school or college.) The same applies to students in a school. Only if a student's conduct is outrageous by standards that any liberal would be likely to approve will he be expelled from a school. Persuasion and oblique attack are preferred in England. Even the isolated pockets of administration or teacher intolerance seem to be weakening.

There are three main teacher associations to which a Catholic may belong. The first is the Catholic Teachers' Federation, which acts as a consortium of like-minded persons to discuss points of educational concern, to make pronouncements, and to publish the results of research on current problems. The other two groups more closely resemble trade unions and include teachers of all religious persuasions. One is the National Association of Schoolmasters (for men only); the other is the National Union of Teachers. The last is the largest body of the three; it negotiates with the state about salaries and working conditions for teachers.

The Parents
and the
Catholic School

There are two large organizations which forward the interests of the parents of schoolchildren: the Confederation for the Advancement of State Education and the National Federation of Parent-Teacher Associations. Few Catholic parents would commit themselves to all the aims of the former; very few belong to the latter, and only one in a hundred parents has heard of either.

Most parents tend to regard teachers with suspicion (they remember how they were taught). Yet at the same time (human nature being inconsistent) parents sense that things are more agreeable at school than they were when they were children—perhaps, indeed, too agreeable! There is a sense of puzzlement at some of the new teaching methods used, for example in mathematics and English. To this is added a general feeling that the education of the child is best left entirely to the teachers. This is a view which teachers, particularly members of religious institutes, tend to encourage with vigor. For the lay teacher's part, treasured independence of the professional man or woman extends to a feeling that parents really know little about their children. Formal contacts between parents and school are minimal.

The main official line of contact between parents and teachers is the Parent-Teacher Association (P.T.A.). Some schools hold regular meetings where points of common interest such as teaching methods, the future of Catholic schools, and the like, can be discussed, or where a visiting speaker may address parents and staff together. There are few Catholic schools where the P.T.A. is a thriving concern.

Other occasions when parents meet teachers are at a preliminary interview prior to the child's entering school; at what might be called parental visits of problem to protest—for example, when a parent thinks that his child has been unjustly punished, or has too much homework to do; when it becomes a head teacher's duty to soothe parental worries about the "eleven plus" or other external examinations; or to discuss a student's future career.

Most Catholic schools give a religious concert at Christmas time, to which parents are invited. Most schools welcome parents to the summer sports day, when informal—if glancing—contact is more readily possible. Catholic schools will often organize a bazaar or fête to raise funds. Mothers usually serve at stalls or help in other ways.

Many schools have a special day, generally in the summer term, when parents are encouraged to visit the school and inspect the work which students have done.

There is one more serious experiment which a few convent schools have been conducting recently. This is in the matter of sex education. A series of booklets for girls has been written by some of the sisters. These books are sent to the parents, talks are given at school, and parents are asked to attend discussions about the most effective method of giving sociosexual guidance to their daughters. As of 1967 this experiment is a cry in the wilderness: the real relationship between parents and Catholic schools, despite social contacts, is thin.

Special Educational Problems Facing Catholic Schools in England

It is a naked commonplace that questions about education can be answered only with reference to the aims of the society in which the students are being educated. Yet there is in current discussions about Catholic education in England very little consideration of the social —and the sociological—issues involved. For four hundred years the Roman Catholic Church in England has lived under persecution or penalty; sometimes to be a Catholic has been to risk one's life. But this is all changing. Catholics are now respected for the firmness of their beliefs and the sureness of their sense of direction, or pitied for the aura of superstition in which they are felt to exist. In any case they are left unharmed, except in a few extremist areas. The days of religious conflict are dead.

Unfortunately many Catholics, particularly those from old-established Catholic families or from Ireland (the Irish too have suffered their persecutions), tend to conduct their lives according to a tired but still fierce jingoism: my Church, right or wrong. The spirit of nationalism has shrivelled to an ecclesiastical loyalty. Those who move for vigorous reform inside the Church are felt to be traitors in the camp; on the other hand, radicals view those who prefer the status quo as diehard reactionaries, uninterested in the true life of the Church.

Although the tension between radicalism and conservatism is worldwide, it is probably felt as bitterly in England as in any other country. And it has an unhappy effect in that it tends to dispossess a man of his integrity. If a person announces that some profound change is needed, he is immediately categorized as a "left-wing firebrand" bent on destroying the Church itself. If, on the contrary, one commits himself to the view that certain changes are undesirable, such a person earns the soubriquet of "stuffy conservative," longing to see the Church die of inanition. A party spirit prevails. Yet it is a truism that those who incline by temperament or conviction to desire the old ways actually become more conservative under the pressure of opposition; those who yearn for a root-and-branch policy sometimes become irresponsible rebels, bishop-baiting, out for blood. It appears at times that there is more charity from both conservatives and radicals for those outside the Church than there is for those who are her members.

Catholic parents must give their children—for whom they will answer on Judgment Day—a Catholic education. But, it may be asked, what is a Catholic education—at least in England?

Two answers present themselves as extremes. One view argues for the retention of the kind of school of which many convent and other religious schools are the paradigm: a total institution, a closed society in which faith and good manners, courtesy and an established (generally upper middle-class) way of life are purveyed in bright rooms between gleaming parquet corridors smelling of their daily application of beeswax; where order, tradition, and the penny catechism triumph. The other extreme view holds up for emulation the government schools, where students of all religions and no religion mix freely, where there are the discussion group and the mutual influence, where a catechist (probably a layman) visits three or four times a week to give religious instruction to the Catholics, instruction which will be open-ended, based on the Bible rather than on formal theology, where there is an existential rather than an essentialist approach to the teaching of religion. These extremes are social and political rather than religious.

The previous paragraphs serve as the prologomenal context for an examination of current problems besetting English Catholic education. With the broad sociocultural framework, there are a few ineluctable facts which present a problem to all concerned with the future of Catholic education in England, and therefore with the whole future of the Catholic Church in England.

The first major problem can be elaborated in the following manner. There are few Catholic schools in England. Of that few, a great many are headed by religious. Consequently the chances of a layman obtaining a senior teaching post are thin. There is at the moment an explosive bitterness among Catholic laymen about this situation. The best of them will tend to gravitate to a school where there is a strong opportunity for their rising in rank. This will not be a Catholic school. Justly or unjustly, there is a felt sense of discrimination in favor of the religious, whether or not these religious are more highly qualified academically and pedagogically.

The regrettable situation is exacerbated by the increasing shortage of vocations to the priesthood and the religious institutes. As a result there is greater probability today than there was fifty years ago that the appointment of a religious to a head teacher's post will be an inappropriate appointment, since there are fewer from which to choose. Some of the religious institutes are being forced into a kind of ghetto situation, with their attitudes hardening as lay protests mount. Laymen, on the other hand, are twisted into a posture of anticlericalism which their consciences do not really approve.

One can understand the attitude of the religious. After centuries of intellectual superiority they are discovering that many of the laity are as well, or better, educated than themselves. After hundreds of years during which they made sacrifices to establish and maintain schools, they are suffering the feeling that they are no longer wanted. It is not uncommon for a sister to describe Catholic schools operated by religious institutes as "our" (the institute's) schools. Outside the historical context the claim is fantastic; within the context of history it seems moderate. From one angle the continued occupation by the religious of English Catholic education appears to be flinty stubbornness; from another view it looks like a noble resoluteness to perform a duty to which there has been a clear calling.

One might conjecture as to what would result if tomorrow all the religious institutes in England were to relinquish teaching. Apart from the loss of manpower, there would be a specific problem, which is the shortage of trained catechists. As noted earlier, the laity are already assuming a large share of religion teaching in English Catholic schools, and, most of them are ill-trained. Recent disclosures about the blinkered life led by many seminarists show beyond doubt that many priests also are not taught, or not well taught, how to teach religion. Priests do not appear to have been shown in their seminary careers the relevance of the faith to the daily world in which most lay Catholics find themselves.

Notwithstanding, there is a powerhouse of pedagogical energy inside the clerical domain and the religious institutes. Such a source must continue to be used. The fact remains that both clergy and laity must be taught better how to teach all subjects, especially religion. New ventures like the recently founded Catechetical Centre in London, which conducts courses for catechists, clerical and lay, give positive witness that the problem can be solved. But it will be a long business.

A second major contextual problem confronting Catholic education in England is that the intellectual standard of Catholic life in England is still deplorably low. One need only look at the table inside the vestibule of any Catholic church. Most of the papers for sale have poor layout and wretched content, larded over with smugly provincial attitudes. There is only one weekly English Catholic journal which makes any pretensions to intellectual standards, and that has a small circulation and deeply conservative commitments. There are one or two lively monthlies which would appeal to an educated Catholic reader and one bimonthly journal which can be recommended, even though it shows a spirit of political party rather than a spirit of impartial inquiry. Catholic journalism, which acts as a diagram of other features of English Catholic cultural life, is at a low level.

This fact results from a tension, a philosophical tension, which is at least as ancient as Montaigne: how can the encouragement of disinterested intellectual inquiry—surely one of the mainsprings of education—be reconciled with the provision of dogmatic teaching? How many teachers, religious or lay, have seriously considered the problem? Here is a difficult question with no final answer, but recent studies have shown that some teachers at any rate are valuing the virtues of intellectual clarity and honesty more highly than they were valued fifty years ago.

The third major problem confronting English Catholic education is that of a shortage of money. The section in this essay dealing with finance has given some indication of the financial burden under which English Catholics labor, and one is bound to ask whether all the expenditure is worthwhile. The simple answer is that any expense whatever is worthwhile to nourish the faith in English children. But the question then arises whether the Catholic schools are in fact nourishing that faith. The English hierarchy at any rate is committed to an expansionist policy; not eradication but reform is the official answer to those who cogently point out that Catholic schools are not as good as they might be.

It would be an error to suppose that the money saved by abolishing Catholic schools would necessarily be pure saving. The cost of sending skilled, professionally prepared catechists into government schools for a few periods per week would be much greater than is sometimes realized. Further, this abandonment of the Catholic school enterprise does not necessarily insure that the Catholic community at large would be better off or have more resources available for other apostolic work.

The solutions to these and other problems which have been implicitly raised in the earlier parts of this essay are difficult, complex, and inconclusive. The chief reason for this is that very little is known about the actual effects of Catholic schooling—whether, for example, students in Catholic schools really become better Catholics in later life. Another reason is that Catholics have for so long equated Catholic education with Catholic schooling, making it difficult to ascertain what the superior alternative (if there is a superior alternative) would look like. There have as yet been no controlled empirical experiments.

One solution is indubitable: that Catholics should pay much more attention to academic and professional standards. Too often piety or the traditional role of the religious is judged to be sufficient cause for a cleric or religious to be a teacher. The veiled nepotism of the religious institutes—and the writer does not forget the devoted work they have been doing and are still doing—produces nothing but bitterness inside the Church and contempt outside it. The best positions should go to the best teachers, irrespective of their canonical status.

Second, there should be much more extensive research investigations into the sociological structure of the Catholic community, to find its real potential and its real needs. Some years ago the "Newman Demographic Survey" was instituted, with a staff of professional sociologists and statisticians whose mission was to examine the sort of questions that thoughtful Catholic educationists are raising. In the early 1960's the Survey scandalously collapsed for lack of funds. Many

English Catholics are open to the rebuke of Matthew Arnold that too much is spent acting and not enough time thinking.

Third, there must be more emphasis on the role of the parents in the education of the child. This is an age when responsibility after responsibility is being handed over to the schools; small wonder that they are unable to bear the burden of their new obligations. What is urgently needed is a program of education for adults. A far deeper sense of the possible liaison between home and school must be nurtured in Catholic parents. Indeed, there is a case for gradually phasing out the primary schools and concentrating the best ability of Catholic teachers into the channels of secondary and adult education. This means that new ideas of the nature and relevancy of the parish must be discovered. It is the parish priest who can and must help to bring about the new liaison between Church and school on the one hand, and between Church and home on the other.

Last, and most important of all, English Catholics must discover what they wish the term "Catholic education" to mean. Clearly English Catholics are not to go the way of the world, investing themselves with its standards, so that the dough controls the yeast. But are English Catholics to retain the "closed" concept of the Catholic school, conducted by committed but otherworldly Catholics, inducing irrelevant pieties that will not survive the actual pressures brought to bear by the world? The yeast is inert unless it enters and permeates the dough.

Catholic education in England cannot identify with and must not withdraw from the world. How to find a new way of continuing is not only a pressing problem; it is a problem which every adult Catholic in England should be eager to help solve.

Selected Bibliography

Beales, A. C. F. *Education under Penalty: English Catholic Education from the Reformation to the Fall of James II.* London: University of London Press, 1963.

Beck, George Andrew, A. C. F. Beales, et al. *The Case for Catholic Schools.* London: Catholic Education Council for England and Wales, 1955.

Brothers, Joan. *Church and School: A Study of the Impact of Education on Religion.* Liverpool: Social Research Series, Liverpool University Press, 1964.

Catholic Education Council for England and Wales. *Catholic Education: A Handbook*. London: CEC, published biannually.

Cruickshank, Marjorie. *Church and State in English Education 1870 to the Present Day*. London: Macmillan, 1963.

Evennett, H. O. *The Catholic Schools of England and Wales*. Cambridge: Cambridge University Press, 1944.

Hulme, Anthony. *School in Church and State*. London: St. Paul Publications, 1959.

Leetham, Claude. *Catholic Education: Some Notes for Parents*. Abington: Catholic Social Guild, 1964.

Marnane, M. T. *A Guide for Catholic Teachers*. Dublin: Gill and Co. Ltd., 1959.

Murphy, James. *The Religious Problem in English Education: The Crucial Experiment*. Liverpool: Liverpool University Press, 1959.

Catholic Education
in the United States

by James Michael Lee

A Short History
of American
Catholic Education

Colonial Period, 1513–1789

The Franciscan missionaries established elementary schools in the Spanish colonies of Florida and of the American southwest as early as the sixteenth century. In the French colonies located along the Mississippi Valley, Catholic elementary schools were established a century later. But the situation was quite different in the English settlements. Indeed, until the conclusion of the American Revolutionary War, the Church was persecuted in every one of the thirteen colonies except Pennsylvania. By the end of that war Catholics still numbered only 1 per cent of the population.

Because of the hostility toward the Church, extremely few Catholic elementary schools were founded during this period. These institutions were erected sporadically, were hidden, and were of short life. Only two known Catholic secondary schools were established in this period, one in the seventeenth and the other in the eighteenth century. Both were erected and staffed by English Jesuits. Each school had but two faculty members. The purpose of these short-lived boarding schools was to prepare their students to pursue higher education in Europe, particularly at St. Omer's. The curriculum was classical, and the schools were supported by student tuition. No Catholic colleges or universities were founded during this period.

The Young Republic, 1789–1865

Throughout this period Catholics still remained a small though growing minority group. Not until 1840 did the Catholic population reach the million mark. Despite persecution in some localities, the Church as a whole enjoyed complete freedom, thanks to the provisions of the United States Constitution.

With the establishment in 1801 of the first Catholic elementary school in the United States operated by women religious, Catholic

elementary schools began to grow slowly but steadily. In 1809 the
first free parochial school for both boys and girls opened also in Maryland. In the late 1840's many women teaching religious were forced to
flee Europe. These immigrants, together with the native clergy and
religious, began opening up many elementary and secondary schools.
The latter either were patterned after the lycées in France or were
operated as finishing schools to educate the girls in the manner of pre-
Revolutionary France.

The first Catholic college was founded by the Jesuits at George-
town, Maryland in 1789. Throughout this period, all-male colleges
and secondary schools were typically operated as combined institutions. From 1840–1860, sixty new all-male colleges were established.
These schools averaged about fifty students each. Only about twenty
of these colleges are still in existence.

The discipline in Catholic schools at all levels was Jansenistically
severe. The school year spanned ten to eleven months. Practically all
of the teachers were religious or priests. The schools were supported
by student tuition and by the contributed services of the clerical and
religious staff.

The Sovereign Industrialized Union, 1865–1918

This period saw the rapid rise of the Catholic population, in no
small measure a result of the great waves of immigration from Southern Europe in the 1880's and 1890's. Although the attitude toward
the Church was often hostile in a preponderantly Protestant America,
local acts of violence against Catholics had by and large subsided.

The First and Second Plenary Councils of Baltimore (1852 and
1866 respectively) officially exhorted all Catholic parents to send their
children to Catholic schools at all levels. But it was the highly influential and decisive Third Plenary Council of Baltimore (1884) which
formally decreed that every pastor must build a parish school and that
parents must send their children to Catholic schools.

Catholic elementary schools began to be built apace. Catholic
secondary schools expanded in this period, though not so rapidly as
did the elementary schools. Most secondary schools were small and
typically located in urban centers of concentrated Catholic population. The growth of parochial Catholic high schools was stimulated
by the Third Plenary Council. This period also witnessed the relatively widespread growth of private Catholic secondary schools, that
is those operated by religious institutes. The first central diocesan secondary school was erected in Philadelphia in 1890. Catholic all-female

academies began to develop into four-year secondary schools, thus
evolving from the former finishing school pattern of one to two years.
During this period the American hierarchy and clergy vocally but
unofficially opposed the establishment of tax-supported government
secondary schools. Indeed, churchmen publicly argued that education
belonged to the home and to the Church and therefore should not
be sponsored by the government. Occasional dissenters like Father
Thomas Bouquillon of The Catholic University of America were
silenced (Butts and Cremin).

By the end of this period the clear-cut separation of Catholic secondary schools and colleges had occurred. The first Catholic institution of higher learning exclusively for women, Trinity College, was
established in the first decade of the twentieth century.

There was little professional preparation for teachers, except sporadically by certain communities of women religious. Discipline at all
school levels was still rather harsh—somewhat deliberately imitative
of seminaries and novitiates of the time. The curricula of all schools
by and large remained traditional.

The Second Plenary Council of Baltimore stated that as far as
possible all teachers in Catholic parish schools should be clergy and
religious. The lay teacher, consequently, was hired only in a dire
emergency.

The Modern Period, 1918–Present

During this period the government schools at all levels became
increasingly dereligionized and secularized. Despite the 1951 positive policy statement of the prestigious secular National Education
Association on moral and spiritual values in government schools, this
trend rapidly accelerated in the 1950's and 1960's. Consequently
Catholics started to expand their school system. Indeed, the rate of
Catholic school enrollment since World War II has jumped far more
rapidly than has the percentage of students enrolling in government
schools at all levels.

In 1925 the United States Supreme Court affirmed the legal right
of parents to send their children to the school of their choice, whether
government or nongovernment. In 1953 the Department of Health,
Education, and Welfare was instituted as a cabinet post. This action
had been opposed by the hierarchy and ranking Catholic clergy for
nearly a century. In 1954 the Supreme Court outlawed racial segrega-
tion in government schools. Officials of government schools in southern states delayed compliance; however, Catholic school leaders in

the South proved more vigorous in desegregating Catholic schools. In 1962 the hierarchy, in complete reversal of the stand they had maintained for over 150 years, officially began to demand federal financial aid to Catholic schools if such aid were given to government schools.

The Catholic elementary school witnessed moderate expansion before World War II. However, after the war, people began moving to the previously underpopulated suburbs. New churches sprang up there, and Catholic elementary schools started to mushroom.

There were building booms in Catholic secondary schools in the 1920's and again in the 1950's and 1960's. This period saw the rise of the central diocesan high school and the decline of parochial high schools. Catholic high schools became increasingly more intellectually restrictive and at the same time more expensive. Unlike the government secondary schools which offered comprehensive programs, the curriculum of the Catholic secondary school remained for the most part traditional and college preparatory.

Most contemporary Catholic all-women's colleges were founded in this period. Many religious institutes of women seemed impelled to erect their own college as the "crowning educational work" of their community in that region. The Jesuits had the largest number of colleges and universities (28 in 1967), typically located in the heart of metropolitan areas. The major Catholic universities expanded their curricula and faculties to include most of the wide spectrum of modern secular university offerings.

Because Catholic schools at all levels grew at a more rapid pace than the number of clerical and religious vocations, Catholic lay people were at first reluctantly taken into the system. Administrative positions, particularly at the elementary and secondary levels, remained the exclusive province of the clergy and religious. On the university level, however, laymen increasingly began to be employed in lower-echelon administrative posts and in some instances in intermediate-echelon posts. A mid-1960 survey conducted by the National Catholic Educational Association (NCEA) revealed that 95 per cent of Catholic secondary schools did not have a policy whereby laymen could become principals of the schools.

Government schools have always taken the lead in all spheres of professionalization, especially in experimentation, in guidance, and in instructional services. Catholic schools generally have lagged behind, criticizing government schools for their innovational practices and ending up by tardily accepting these improvements. After World War I, teacher preparation and inservice programs became increasingly professionalized; however, it was not until the 1950's and 1960's that Catholic schoolmen moved with vigor in this direction. Comprehensive organized school guidance services and testing programs were proceeding apace in government schools in the 1920's, only to be condemned as immoral by Catholic schoolmen (Lee and Pallone). It was not until the late 1950's and 1960's that Catholic schools moved seriously into guidance and testing, a move spearheaded in 1962 by the founding of the National Catholic Guidance Conference. Catholics were particularly opposed to the Progressive Education movement which changed the course of American education in the direction of student-centeredness and scientific pedagogy (Redden and Ryan). The celebrated Eight-Year Study conducted in the late 1930's proved that graduates from the newly evolved Core curriculum performed better in creative subjects, in leadership skills, in personal adjustment, and in traditional subject areas than did graduates from schools having traditional curricula. But Catholic schoolmen ignored these and related findings, as did many government schools. Following World War II, innovations swept the government schools. School buildings began to be constructed to adjust to various instructional and curricular patterns. Team teaching and teacher aides began to be utilized. In 1961 the Trump Report blueprinted a total new design for secondary schools in the years ahead. As a rule Catholic schools continued to proceed in the traditional ways, by and large failing to implement the new advances. By the mid 1960's, however, Catholic schools did begin to express interest in utilizing teacher aides and team teaching. A few venturesome Catholic schools embraced other innovations, thus becoming the pioneers of tomorrow.

In the 1960's Catholic school officials began extending the hand of cooperation to their colleagues in government schools. This perhaps augurs well for the day when there will be one school system with two affiliated divisions instead of the present two entirely separate systems.

The Purpose of Catholic Schools in the United States

The Stated Purpose

There is no one stated purpose formally binding on all American Catholic schools. This is doubtless a result of the autonomy of Catholic educational institutions both at the national and diocesan levels. Consequently, in a very real sense, the stated purpose of the Catholic school varies according to what each school's principal says it is.

The only nationally stated purpose of any consequence is the 1944 official statement of the Policies Commission of the NCEA. The stated ultimate purpose is that the Catholic school is intended "to guide, nourish, and stimulate the student's mind and heart." The stated primary proximate purpose is sevenfold: to develop intelligent Catholics, to develop spiritually vigorous Catholics, to develop cultured Catholics, to develop healthy Catholics, to develop vocationally prepared Catholics, to develop social-minded Catholics, and to develop American Catholics. This sevenfold purpose is clearly based on the 1917 document, *Seven Cardinal Principles of Secondary Education*, developed by and deeply influential on government schools. For the most part, Catholic school officials and teachers seem unaware of the existence of the NCEA's statement.

The Real Purpose

As with most organizations, the real purpose of American Catholic schools is not necessarily, nor even frequently, similar to the stated purpose. Convergence of the real and stated purposes of Catholic schools comes only in the ultimate goal; the primary proximate purpose varies.

Some of the more common real primary proximate purposes why dioceses or religious institutes operate Catholic schools at various levels include: to attract vocations to the institute or diocese (particularly at the secondary level); to prevent the student from losing his faith, something which is believed (albeit with scant supporting evidence) to be quite possible in a government school; to provide a God-centered education; to fulfill the educational apostolate charged to a particular religious institute by its constitution; to accede to pressure from the laity or from ecclesiastical officials to open a Catholic school.

Controversy exists as to what the real primary purpose of the Catholic school should be. Three major positions can be identified. The first, or moralist position, holds that the primary proximate goal of the Catholic school is to bring the students directly closer to Christ. This approach has been the traditional one in the United States. Some of its chief advocates include Monsignor G. A. Kelly,

Father K. O'Brien, C.Ss.R., and the late Professors J. D. Redden and F. A. Ryan. To Monsignor Kelly, moral teaching implies not only instruction in religious truths but the active encouragement of living a spiritual life. He maintains that the superior school is not the one with the best overall scholastic achievement but rather the one which best teaches the pupil the Christian position in his "relationship to his Creator, his fellow man and nature." Father O'Brien states that "knowledge without moral formation is simply a weapon in the hands of a criminal." He holds that the world should not worry so much about educating a poor, devout, but intellectually backward savage in some distant land because such a savage "has in his will charity, which is superior to all knowledge in this life."

The second major position, the intellectualist, holds that the primary proximate goal of the Catholic school is chiefly (and according to some, exclusively) the intellectual development of the student. This development is best achieved through exclusive instruction in what V. E. Smith terms "the teachable subjects," those intellectual disciplines which Aristotle identified as capable of being learned from an instructor. Nonintellectual areas, including Christian perfection, social needs, and so forth, do not really fall under the purview of the Catholic school; indeed, if the school does engage in certain nonintellectual functions, it does so incidentally rather than as an essential extension of its primary proximate objective. Although intellectualism is still the minority position in Catholic educational circles, there are definite signs of its increased acceptance. Prominent among its advocates are Fathers L. Reed, S.J., T. C. Donlan, O.P., T. McAvoy, C.S.C., and Professors H. L. Johnston and V. E. Smith.

The third major position, prudentialism, states that the primary proximate purpose of the Catholic school is to develop the student's intellect and will coequally. Akin to the basic thrust of the Scholastic virtue of prudence, it represents a middle, more inclusive, and, to its adherents, a more human position than either moralism or intellectualism. Prudentialists believe that exclusive emphasis on the will alone or on the intellect alone fragments the person and consequently is in practice an impossible educational task. As the intellect is rendered impotent without its externalization by the will, so too the will is rendered blind without the guidance of the intellect. Only very recently has this position of prudentialism been enunciated. Its principal advocates include J. M. Lee and J. J. Ryan.

The Relationship
of Catholic Schools
to Government Schools

Government Legislation
Which Has Affected Catholic Schools

In the United States government legislation emanates either from:
(1) federal, state, or local statutes enacted by the respective legislatures; (2) federal, state, or local courts passing on the constitutionality of an existing statute.

The first category of government legislation vis-à-vis the schools deals with the legitimacy of the existence of nongovernment educational institutions. The First Amendment to the United States Constitution provided that "Congress shall make no law respecting an establishment of religion, or prohibiting the free exercise thereof." Thus, constitutionally, church schools are permitted to exist; conversely however, the government is forbidden to assist them directly. The United States Supreme Court (1948 Everson decision) noted that this Amendment is a two-edged sword; if the government directly assists church schools it is simultaneously illegally supporting religion and unlawfully interfering with the free exercise of religion.

By the provisions of the Tenth Amendment to the Constitution, the state and local governments, rather than the federal government, have legal control over both government and church-related schools. American schools, government and nongovernment alike, are not nationally controlled.

In 1819 the Supreme Court held that the governance of a state-chartered private university (Dartmouth) cannot be wholly or partially wrested from university trustees without the consent of those trustees. (All United States government and Catholic universities, both private and government-operated, are state chartered). But the Magna Carta for private schools came in 1925 when the Supreme Court ruled (Pierce decision) that a state government law which forbade parents to send their children to nongovernment schools was unconstitutional.

The second category of government legislation vis-à-vis the schools concerns the increasing government restriction of the degree of religionism in government schools. This is an important issue because the more secularistic government schools become, the more Catholics recognize the need for erecting a separate Catholic school system.

For several decades after the American Revolutionary War, government schools were in reality Protestant schools, with Protestant doctrine and morals more or less openly taught. For this reason Catholics sought their own separate schools. In 1873 in Poughkeepsie, New York, and a little later in Faribault, Minnesota, the local town government leased the government school to the Catholic Church, and nuns taught in this leased government school. Despite the fact that religious instruction was given outside the regular school hours of the leased school, this plan was held by the government to be illegal. Thereafter Catholics utilized a practice known as released time. Released time means that the government school dismisses its pupils early on a designated school day so that these pupils can receive religious instruction from their respective clergymen. In 1948 (McCollum decision) the Supreme Court ruled that it was unconstitutional to have released-time instruction on government school premises. Thereafter pupils had to go to their respective churches to receive released-time instruction, a practice ruled constitutional in 1952 (Zorach decision). In 1962 (Engel decision), the Supreme Court declared that no state could compose an official prayer for use in government schools. The following year, the same court declared (Schempp decision) that public bible reading was forbidden in government schools.

Because of the lack of involvement of the federal government in education, American government and Catholic schools have been heavily influenced by private agencies, particularly accrediting associations and teachers' associations. Voluntary accrediting agencies, organized on a broad regional level, examine government and Catholic schools by both submitted reports and visiting teams of specialists. If the school meets the educational standards established by the agency it is said to be accredited. But accreditation only indicates that a bare minimum of educational quality has been met by the particular school. Hence accreditation is only a crude index of a school's quality. Teachers' associations, especially the National Education Association, have throughout the years issued reports and recommendations which have profoundly affected the course of American education.

Comparison of Quality of Catholic Schools and Government Schools

Notwithstanding the fact that there are no formal research investigations on this subject, broadly considered, government schools are typically superior to Catholic schools at every level—with, of course, many notable exceptions. Administrators, teachers, and guidance workers in government schools are typically better prepared professionally than their Catholic school counterparts. The pupil-teacher ratio in Catholic schools, particularly at the elementary level, is frightfully high. There is an almost unbelievable shortage of qualified guidance counselors. Too high a percentage of Catholic secondary schools are not regionally accredited. Diocesan school officials allow either the local Catholic school official or the diocesan superintendent to license Catholic school personnel, which means virtually all applicants are licensed to teach or to be an administrator. Government schools, on the other hand, have rather strict licensing procedures for their personnel. However, since 1955 the quality of Catholic schools has been rising dramatically on all fronts. Catholic schools, in a conscientious effort drastically to improve their quality, are more and more modeling themselves after government schools. Although this is admirable in many respects—in class size and professional preparation—many Catholics believe that by so doing Catholic schools are losing their distinctiveness and are becoming carbon copies of the government schools.

The Present Form
of Catholic Schools
in the United States

The Organizational Level

In the loosest sense of the term "system," there is an American Catholic system of education encompassing a network of Church-operated schools which meet the needs of Catholics in nearly every age bracket. At the very center of the system stand the elementary, secondary, and higher educational institutions, levels almost identically paralleling those of the government schools. The elementary schools admit students from the first through the eighth grade, ages approximately six to fourteen. Secondary schools enroll students from the ninth through the twelfth grade, ages fourteen to eighteen. Universities are divided into two distinct levels, undergraduate and graduate. The undergraduate division enrolls students from the thirteenth through the sixteenth grade, ages eighteen to twenty-two. The graduate division enrolls students who wish to pursue a master's or a doctor's degree. In the graduate division there are no formal grade levels, since the student may attend part time or full time. The customary length of time for acquiring a master's degree is one and one-half years of full-time study after the bachelor's degree; for the doctor's degree, from two to four years of full-time study beyond the master's degree.

Some of the more traditional government school systems (usually in rural areas) and almost all the Catholic school systems have retained the 8–4 pattern for their elementary and secondary schools, respectively. However, many advanced government systems, notably in the cities and in suburbia are organized on a 6-3-3 basis. Elementary school continues through the sixth grade (age eleven). Secondary school is divided into two divisions in separate buildings and different locations. Junior high school accommodates students from grades seven through nine (ages twelve to fifteen); senior high school accepts youths from grade ten through twelve (ages fifteen to eighteen). This 6-3-3 organization is based on the psychological maturation of the students.

On the university level the Catholic and the government systems are organized similarly.

Throughout these three basic levels of schooling (excluding graduate school), the word "grade" is used to designate a student's particular educational level. The duration of a student's stay in each grade is customarily one year. After this year he is promoted to the next grade if his scholastic achievement is satisfactory or kept back if it is substantially deficient. It is possible for a student in elementary school to have to repeat an entire year if his work is unsatisfactory; however, in secondary school and in undergraduate university education, the student customarily repeats only those subjects in which he has exhibited deficient performance, and he advances in the other subjects to the next higher grade. Only if he fails too many subjects is he kept in his grade level at the end of the year.

The Catholic school at all levels—elementary, secondary, and university—awards a diploma to those students who successfully complete the basic requirements. This diploma is recognized without restriction by the government and in every way is legally the equivalent of a diploma from a government school of the same level. Each government and Catholic school confers its own diploma; the only difference in quality of diploma is in the subjective judgment of persons as to which particular school offers the strongest educational program. A student can not obtain a government-school diploma unless he attends a government school. In any event there is no such thing as a government diploma; there is only a school diploma.

At the perimeter of the Catholic school system stand a variety of Catholic educational institutions. In some localities the Church operates preschool educational institutions. Customarily these institutions are kindergartens, enrolling children aged five or in the year immediately preceding elementary school. In a few instances the Church operates nursery schools for toddlers from three to five. A few private Catholic schools, chiefly under lay auspices rather than conducted by religious institutes, follow the Montessori approach. Such schools are either exclusively nursery schools, or a combination of nursery school and kindergarten, or a combination of nursery school, kindergarten, and elementary school. Catholics are the pioneers in America in establishing Montessori schools; such schools operated by the government are almost nonexistent, and, in fact, Montessori schools have become automatically regarded as under Catholic auspices. The Church is active in some localities in sponsoring adult education classes for postschool persons who wish to learn one special field or other (Keeler). These adult classes are usually in theology, or in theology-related areas, and are typically operated in conjunction with a Catholic university. However, usually no university credit is given for successful completion of these courses, which are commonly held in the evening hours. On the elementary and secondary levels, the Church very vigorously sponsors released-time classes in religious instruction for Catholic students attending non-Catholic schools. This program is that of the Confraternity of Christian Doctrine. Parallel to this the Church maintains religious education centers on the campuses of non-Catholic secondary and higher educational institutions. These centers, called Newman Clubs in honor of the celebrated English Cardinal, offer formal noncredit classes, lecture series, and social activities. The Church, moreover, operates a number of elementary and secondary schools for special education. These schools enroll exclusively the mentally and physically handicapped students, endeavoring to assist them to adjust to "normal" living. Finally, the Church operates seminaries, novitiates, and convents for the preparation of its future priests, brothers, and sisters. These institutions are almost always totally separated in every way from Catholic schools for lay students, although there is a happy trend away from this isolationism.

The so-called Catholic "system" of educational institutions is not very systematic. It is more a loosely organized, poorly connected network of schools under the auspices of one or other Church group than a well-integrated, unified complex. Catholic schools are basically atomistic organizational structures. They enjoy a unity only in ultimate commitment. There is little vertical articulation between schools on different levels. Surprisingly, this is true even in localities in which the same religious institute or diocesan authority conducts schools at each of the three educational levels. Also, there is little horizontal articulation among Catholic schools of the same educational level. Each Catholic school is operated with almost total independence; each is a little empire unto itself.

At the secondary and the university levels, there are differentiated patterns in American education. At the secondary level there are two basic curricular divisions, the vocational and the academic. Within the vocational division there are four areas of specialization: industrial arts (for example, school of automotive trades), agriculture, business education, and home economics. The academic division has two principal categories, the college preparatory, designed exclusively to prepare the students to enter the university, and the general curriculum, in which the students who cannot qualify for any one of the secondary curricula mentioned take a modified college preparatory course to improve their cultural background. Those secondary schools which include under one roof two or more of the types of curricula mentioned are called comprehensive secondary schools. Catholic secondary schools typically include all but the industrial arts and the agriculture curricula. However, Catholic secondary schools usually admit students of superior intelligence (and who can pay the tuition); consequently Catholic secondary schools are typically college-preparatory rather than comprehensive.

On the postsecondary school level there are innumerable types of faculties within the university, including the traditional arts and science faculties, and more recently the engineering faculty, the business faculty, the law faculty, and so on. The majority of the small Catholic colleges have only the arts and science faculties; however, the Catholic universities have almost every type of postsecondary faculty.

Many government school educators, such as J. B. Conant, together with many secularists, such as J. L. Childs, have asserted that the Catholic school system, which presently is totally separate from the government school system, is divisive in terms of the formation of a single American consciousness and character. In 1965 a carefully conducted empirical research study of American Catholic schools found no confirmation of this allegation (Greeley and Rossi). But it must be admitted that there is an unbelievable amount of duplication of educational energies, resources, and gain between the two "rival" systems. This fact is most discernible in communities where Catholic and government school buildings often are located literally less than a few thousand feet from each other. Such competitive situations usually redound to the second-class showing of Catholic schools, which typically have less-developed plants, weaker instructional and guidance facilities, poorer libraries, and fewer qualified teachers and administrative personnel.

The desire to unify the educational efforts of both school systems has resulted in programs of shared time, an educational innovation which bids fair perhaps to hasten the day when the two separate school systems are eliminated and in their places will be a single school system with two coordinated but integral divisions, the government school division and the private school division. Shared time is a system of programming some private school students into the government school program to fulfill certain aspects of their education (Friedlander). Shared time is the first educational device involving the Catholic school student in the government school program during the actual school day. No matter how many hours are spent at the government school, he is still considered a student of the Catholic school. Typically the classes most shared are vocational trades courses, physical education courses utilizing gymnasium facilities, and science courses (particularly those involving laboratory work).

Shared time is usually considered as aid to private schools which are too poor in personnel or in facilities to maintain adequate total educational programs of their own. But in a deeper dimension, shared time is really assistance to students, rather than aid to schools. Neither government schools nor private schools benefit directly from shared time; rather, it is the individual student who is aided. Thus many educationists prefer to use the term dual enrollment rather than shared time, because the former term places the proper emphasis on the fact that the pupil is spending his time in two schools instead of one, with the stress on the student instead of the place where he learns.

Many Catholics enthusiastically favor shared time. Protestants are cautiously in favor, government school officials watchful, and the secularists bitterly opposed. Unfortunately, not a few Catholics who favor shared time seem to do so more in terms of financial savings rather than in terms of providing students with a richer education.

In 1965 over one-third of all American dioceses had one or more schools engaged in some form of shared-time activity with the nearby government school. A total of 252 Catholic elementary schools and 182 Catholic schools had at least a minimum program of shared time in operation, with some programs quietly in existence for decades. Certain Catholic educators are fearful that shared time will render the Church-related school a satellite of the government school. Surely one problem of shared time is that religion cannot be integrated into all areas of the Catholic school curriculum, since some of the curriculum will no longer be taught in the Catholic school. However, it must be remembered that dynamic, meaningful, and conscious structural curricular integration is not especially widespread in Catholic elementary and, particularly, secondary schools, and hence not too much is lost in this area. Monsignor J. B. McDowell, a diocesan superintendent, contends that "it is better to have 2000 students receive a religiously oriented education in subjects directly connected with value content and ideas than to have 1000 receive no Catholic education at all." Shared time also eliminates the ghettoism of the Catholic school milieu. As of 1967 the constitutionality of shared-time programs had not been tested in the courts.

At the college and university level there is an increasing trend toward interinstitutional cooperation of secular and Catholic universities. Almost all Catholic colleges and a heavy proportion of Catholic universities are woefully underdeveloped in library facilities, outstanding faculty, and plant facilities. There is an unbelievable proliferation of small, inconsequential Catholic colleges and universities. New York City has nine separate Catholic colleges and universities, Chicago five, and Erie, Pa. (population 130,000) three. Because of the fragmentation of Catholic institutions of higher learning, exchange of faculty and students, together with shared library and other learning facilities is becoming increasingly popular and necessary. By 1965 one Catholic college in three had some sort of shared facilities and/or faculty. Two-thirds of these shared programs did not exist prior to 1960 (NCEA). Many of these programs are, perhaps, heralds of the day when Catholic colleges and universities will face up to educational realities, phase themselves out of existence, and become separate colleges within the larger secular universities of stature.

Compulsory education laws in most states require a student to attend school full time from the age of six until the age of sixteen. Hence virtually all youths complete elementary school and attend secondary school. By 1967 three-fourths of all youth entering secondary school will graduate. Admission to Catholic elementary school is customarily contingent on three qualifications: residence in the parish operating the school, ability to pay the nominal tuition, and a bare minimum of scholastic aptitude. Admission to the Catholic secondary school and to the Catholic university requires successful completion of the previous level, attested to by a diploma; scrutiny of the quality of academic ability; and ability to pay the usually high tuition. Because the student demand exceeds the supply of Catholic schools, the average student in the Catholic secondary school and university is more intelligent than the scholastically lowest one-third of the corresponding government school.

Government schools at all levels are usually coeducational. Catholic schools, on the other hand, have a quiltlike pattern. Most elementary schools are coeducational. On the secondary level, 16 per cent of all Catholic schools enroll males only; 34 per cent, females only; 46 per cent, males and females (coeducational). The remaining 4 per cent are coinstitutional, that is a single school building having two separate units, one for males and the other for females (Neuwien). On the undergraduate university level, 45 per cent enroll females only, 20 per cent males only, and 35 per cent are coeducational. Practically all graduate university classes are totally coeducational.

Control Structure of the Catholic School System

Because there is no national system of government or Catholic education, control of Catholic schools rests more or less at the local level. At the national level, the Department of Education of the National Catholic Welfare Conference, through its executive secretary, is supposed to represent the will of the American bishops in matters educational. However, the NCWC really has no concrete power over individual Catholic schools. All it actually can do is to make recommendations. The National Catholic Educational Association (NCEA), a separate organization, is basically a forum for discussion. Most of its activities have traditionally centered around its annual convention. However, in the early 1960's, thanks to the efforts of one of NCEA's officials, Father C. Albert Koob, O. Praem., the NCEA began to move dynamically in assisting and promoting American Catholic education. Organizationally, NCEA has a president general (always a bishop), vice presidents general (always monsignori), a general executive board (mostly monsignori and clergy, with a small sprinkling of brothers and sisters, and recently an occasional layman), seven departments, one separate section, and two consultantships. The departments are: major seminary department; minor seminary department; college and university department, containing three sections, the section on teacher education, the sister formation section, and the Newman education section; school superintendents' department, containing one section, the supervisors' section; elementary school department; and the special education department. There is a separate vocation section. The two consultantship posts are the consultant for guidance services and the evaluation consultant. As of 1966 six of the seven department presidents were priests, the seventh a sister. Three of the four affiliated section chairmen were sisters, the other a priest. The vocation section chairman and the consultant for guidance services were priests, and the evaluation section chairman was a brother. As can be seen, NCEA is clerically dominated, with a smattering of sisters and brothers. Laymen have virtually no role in the organization.

In general there are three types of control of Catholic schools: (1) parochial—administered educationally and financially by the individual parish and usually open only to students within that parish; (2) central or diocesan—administered educationally and financially by the diocese and usually open to all qualified students in that diocese; (3) private—administered educationally and financially by religious institutes more or less independently of parish or diocese. By and large Catholic elementary schools are parochial; no colleges or universities are parochial. On the secondary level, approximately 40 per cent are parochial, 20 per cent central, and 40 per cent private (Neuwien). At this level there is a definite trend toward an increasingly larger percentage of central schools. At the college and university level, 5 per cent are diocesan and 95 per cent private. At each level schools operated by laymen are negligible.

In parochial elementary and secondary schools, the seat of power lies with the pastor, who is often the principal (nominally, at least) of the school. The control is thus closely knit, subject only to extremely loose and usually vague diocesan control. In central or diocesan secondary schools, the bishop is the seat of power. In theory the bishop delegates his power to the diocesan school board (elementary and secondary levels), which is commonly composed chiefly of the clergy and religious. The board has little real power; its actual function is to serve as advisor to the episcopally appointed diocesan superintendent of schools, who is always a diocesan priest. The superintendent delegates power to the individual principal. The superintendent's power over parochial elementary schools and central secondary schools is often severely limited in that the religious faculty and administrators

are typically the local motherhouse and the religious community instructional supervisor rather than the superintendent. In diocesan colleges, the board of trustees has the power. Members of the board are
almost always clergy. In private schools the provincial superior is the
seat of power; this power is delegated in turn to the regional superior,
to the local superior, and finally to the chief building officer, either
principal or president. Professionally minded religious institutes have
discontinued the practice of having the local superior serve as chief
building officer in order that the latter not be bound by the canonical
limitation on term of office. The executive council of the school or
college, typically composed exclusively of religious, governs with the
principal or president. Private schools at every level are not under
the authority of the diocesan superintendent or bishop, except in a
very loose way.

In the main, American Catholic education is heavily and tightly
controlled by the clergy and religious. However, there are definite
signs of change. There is a growing feeling that priests should be full-
time priests and consequently should leave such directly nonpastoral
functions as school work to the laity. A move by conservative clerical
diocesan superintendents of schools to amend the Code of Canon Law
to require this office to be held exclusively by a cleric was defeated
in a secret meeting of superintendents. Laymen are rising to some
positions of influence in Catholic educational institutions, notably
universities. Diocesan school boards are increasingly including laymen
as members. Recently a very few laymen have been appointed as
assistant superintendents of schools, a practice begun in the 1960's.
An occasional layman rises to executive office in the National Catholic
Educational Association. But the day still seems distant when laymen
rather than clerics and religious will have a strong voice in, much less
control of, American Catholic education.

Some Statistics on Catholic Schools

The following table presents pertinent comparative data on government and Catholic schools at all educational levels.

The proportion of children and youth in American Catholic
schools is highest at the elementary school level, where one in every
eight pupils in the United States attends a Catholic school. In secondary schools and in colleges and universities, the figure is one in
every twelve students (NCEA).

On the elementary level the number of Catholic schools is increas-

Statistical Summary, Catholic and Government Schools*

	1965 Government schools	Catholic schools	1935 Government schools	Catholic schools
Total schools elementary	82,000	10,836	232,174	7,442
Total schools secondary	25,000	2,460	23,213	1,134 (a)
Total colleges and universities	700	314	549	186
Total students elementary	28,000,000	4,465,000	20,477,964	2,209,673
Total students secondary	10,000,000	1,095,000	5,340,563	186,948 (a)
Total students college	3,025,000	417,115	530,000	n.d.
Median school enrollment elementary	n.d.	380	n.d.	n.d.
Median school enrollment secondary	n.d.	240	n.d.	n.d.
Median school enrollment higher	n.d.	n.d.	n.d.	n.d.
Median pupil class size elementary	n.d.	37	n.d.	n.d.
Median pupil class size secondary	n.d.	34(b)	n.d.	n.d.
Median pupil class size higher	n.d.	n.d.	n.d.	n.d.
Median school size in rooms elementary	n.d.	8	n.d.	n.d.
Median school size in rooms secondary	n.d.	11	n.d.	n.d.
Median school size in rooms higher	n.d.	n.d.	n.d.	n.d.

* Many figures are stated in round numbers.
(a) Data excluded so-called girls academies, of which many were secondary schools.
(b) NCEA figures place this number at 20.
    Elementary schools are here defined as comprising grades 1–8. Secondary schools are here defined as comprising grades 9–12. In the American pattern, the private college and university, i.e. nongovernment and non-Catholic, are the most important single factors in higher education. There are 1,000 private colleges and universities. On the elementary and secondary level, 90 per cent of all nongovernment schools are Catholic.
n.d. signifies no data available.
* Table is based on data from the following sources: NEA, NCEA, Neuwlen, *Catholic Directory*, *Biennial Survey of Education.*

ing annually, as suburban communities mushroom all over the country. Some critics are alarmed by this trend, since such building occurs at the very time when the advisability of retaining Catholic elementary schools is being seriously questioned by forward-looking Catholic educationists such as J. M. Lee and Monsignor Carl Ryan. Indeed, some dioceses have already dropped the first grade from their elementary school system, an increasing practice in individual parochial schools throughout the nation. A happy development, still too small to be called a trend, is the practice in some dioceses such as Gary,

Indiana, whereby several parish elementary schools are consolidated into larger interparochial elementary schools. With larger schools, the instructional program, particularly with regard to student tracking, can be made much richer and more differentiated. Although there are more schools year by year on the elementary level, there is a steady decrease annually in the total number of pupils enrolled as diocese after diocese tightens its restrictions on class size. One of the scandals of American Catholic elementary education has been the unbelievably large class size—in not a few cases ranging from sixty to one hundred pupils in a single elementary school classroom (in contrast to twenty to thirty in comparable government schools). With the increased professionalization of Catholic education, diocesan superintendents and religious superiors are reducing the pupil-teacher ratio to approach optimum pedagogical levels more closely.

On the Catholic secondary school level there is a definite trend toward consolidation of small parish secondary schools into larger central or interparochial secondary schools. The result is that, despite the opening of many completely new Catholic secondary schools annually, the total number of Catholic secondary schools is slowly declining year by year.

The number of non-Catholic students attending Catholic schools at all levels is not known. On the basis of incomplete NCEA surveys, however, it is conservatively estimated that there are at least 80,000 such students in Catholic schools. Thus in 1965, 101 dioceses reported 53,100 non-Catholic children in their elementary schools, and 10,300 in their secondary schools. The totals would have been significantly larger had all dioceses been able to report, since the forty dioceses unable to supply data included many of the largest ones. In seven dioceses, the number of non-Catholic children in elementary schools comprised from 12 to 50 per cent of the total enrollment, a figure duplicated for secondary schools in five dioceses. Almost all the dioceses with very large percentages of non-Catholic students enrolled were located in the South. On the college and university level, the percentage of non-Catholic students varies from very small in the typical small Catholic women's college to very large in those metropolitan Catholic universities whose academic standards might be described as weak. Indeed, one such institution recently reported that it could not use Catholic textbooks or a thorough-going Catholic approach to subject matter for fear of "offending the large number of non-Catholic students" in that institution.

In both government and Catholic schools on the elementary and secondary levels, the school year begins sometime during the first two weeks of September and continues until sometime in late May or early June, depending on the section of the country in which the school is located. On the university level, school opens slightly later and closes slightly earlier. The school year is customarily divided into two equal semesters. The first semester terminates at the end of January and the new semester begins a few days later. A small number of universities divide their school year into thirds or quarters instead of semesters. Schools at all levels have three principal vacation periods: the Christmas holiday, lasting approximately two weeks; the Easter holiday of about ten days; and the summer vacation of from two to three and one-half months, depending on the school. Many government and Catholic secondary schools and most government and Catholic universities hold intensive classes of six to eight weeks' duration in the summer for students who wish to take additional classes, either because they hope in that way to graduate from the school earlier than is usual or because they wish to make up a course which they have failed. A summer session is customarily the equivalent of a semester's work. The state, which established the legal minimum number of days which all pupils must spend in government schools, typically requires from 175–190 school days at the elementary and secondary level. The number varies from state to state. Customarily, Catholic schools try to come close to this number, though usually they require less. This figure not infrequently varies from about five to ten days less in schools conducted by the diocese to about thirty to forty in secondary schools operated by religious institutes. In addition, many Catholic schools even go below the diocesan or institute legal minimum. Thus, for example, one typical Catholic elementary school recently investigated gave a free day to students not only for religious holydays but also for the pastor's name day, principal's name day, funeral for nun's father, parish patron saint day, first communion honor day, and two furnace failure days (Curran in *Ave Maria,* April, 1966).

In both government and Catholic schools on the elementary and secondary levels, the school day lasts from between 8:30 to 9:00 in the morning until between 3:00 to 3:30 in the afternoon, five days per week. On the university level students attend from fifteen to twenty hours of class per week, at different times over five and sometimes six days. On the secondary level, students often remain in school after 3:30 to participate in teacher-moderated special interest clubs, referred to as extracurricular activities. On the elementary level, the students study the various subjects in the same room continuously, with a fifteen-minute break at about 10:15 A.M. and another at about 2:00 P.M. There is a lunch period usually from about 12:00 to 1:00 P.M. On the secondary level, the students study their various subjects under different teachers in separate time divisions called periods. Each period consumes about fifty minutes, with five minutes allowed for the students to move from one room to another. Laboratory classes customarily are allotted two continuous periods. At the university day classes usually are also divided into fifty- or fifty-five-minute periods; evening classes typically utilize the double period. In both the day and the evening classes laboratory classes are double periods.

The typical Catholic elementary and secondary school building is the traditional multistoried boxlike structure with immovable walls dividing the rooms. The older, unremodeled Catholic school buildings have the students' seats securely bolted to the floor; the newer and remodeled plants have movable furniture, so that the seating arrangement is sufficiently flexible to accommodate a variety of combinations of student groupings required by different instructional methods. (In practice, the lecture method is almost completely used in Catholic secondary schools and recitation method in elementary schools so that there is little or no use made of this flexibility.) Nearly all educationists, as well as most specialists in the architecture of school buildings, recommend flexible construction, especially movable walls for altering class size when dictated by instructional needs. Some new government schools, but very few new or remodeled Catholic schools, have implemented these suggestions. Most new government elementary and secondary schools are built exclusively on one floor because this permits more flexibility in the use of instructional space. Most new Catholic elementary schools and some new Catholic secondary schools are similarly one-floor plants.

The greater number of all Catholic schools have auditoriums for assembly periods and student theatrical productions. Athletic gymnasiums are features of almost all Catholic schools; in some of the newer Catholic secondary schools the athletic gymnasium is the most imposing single architectural aspect. Most schools have a central library; some have a cafeteria where hot meals are prepared and sold to students. In the newer schools there is at least one faculty lounge, and there is usually an administrative suite with the principal's office and a records office. There is an office for the guidance counselor in some of the newer or remodeled and more forward-looking secondary schools. The parish church is the place of worship for most of the elementary and parochial secondary schools, whereas in the major portion of the larger central and private secondary schools the chapel is located in the school itself.

Typically, Catholic elementary and secondary schools are considerably smaller than their government counterparts. One-third of the Catholic elementary schools have six rooms or less, three-fourths have twelve or less, and nine-tenths have eighteen or less. On the secondary level, nearly one-half of all Catholic schools have less than ten rooms, and four-fifths have less than twenty rooms (Neuwien). The small size of schools is the result of a lack of consolidation among Catholic schools.

Since World War II, specialists in educational architecture have devised many new learning-centered building designs, such as the campus plan and the school-within-a-school or little-school design. With few exceptions, Catholic elementary and secondary schools have not utilized these designs. In general, the learning program in Catholic schools is structured to meet the exigencies of the school building, rather than vice-versa, as educationists urge. In this respect government schools, by and large, are similar to Catholic schools.

On the university level most of the buildings are campus style with numerous buildings. Excluding certain Catholic universities located in metropolitan areas, these campuses have residence halls where the students live under the supervision of the university. All universities have cafeterias, auditoriums, gymnasiums, guidance counselor suites, administrative offices; many have athletic stadiums, radio stations, and so forth. The larger universities have separate buildings to house various academic departments.

Financial Support
of Catholic Schools
in the United States

By virtue of the Tenth Amendment to the United States Constitution, each state must assume total fiscal support of the government schools within its boundaries. The state delegates much of this financial obligation to each local community having a school district. Because of the gross differences in wealth from state to state and from local school district to local school district within a state, there are considerable variations in the fiscal support from state to state and from school district to school district.

By the First Amendment to the Constitution, no government,

federal, state, or local, can legally support any or all religions in any way. Consequently Catholic schools as such are not directly supported financially by any of these governments. However, all governments, federal, state, and local, do grant to Catholic schools and to lands upon which these schools are built complete exemption from taxation.

Income for government schools is classified under two broad categories, revenue receipts and nonrevenue receipts. Revenue receipts which constitute the major portion of school income, are primarily derived from three specific sources. In 1963 approximately 4 per cent of the income of an individual government elementary and secondary

Patterns of Fiscal Support*

Catholic Elementary Schools

Locus of Support	Rate of Support				
	none	0-25%	26-50%	51-75%	76-100%
Parish support					
1. Parish schools (95%)	8	8	17	15	52
2. Private schools (5%)	91	6	2	1	0
Diocesan support					
1. Parish schools (95%)	98	2	0	0	0
2. Private schools (5%)	99	1	0	0	0

Catholic Secondary Schools

Locus of Support	Rate of Support				
	none	0-25%	26-50%	51-75%	76-100%
Parish support					
1. Parish schools (46%)	18	13	21	18	30
2. Central schools (17%)	41	14	25	9	11
3. Private schools (37%)	94	5	1	0	0
Diocesan support					
1. Parish schools (46%)	97	2	1	0	0
2. Central schools (17%)	57	22	14	3	4
3. Private schools (37%)	98	2	0	0	0
Religious institute support					
1. Parish schools (46%)	97	2	1	0	0
2. Central schools (17%)	97	2	1	0	0
3. Private schools (37%)	63	18	10	4	5

* Data derived from Neuwien study.

school came from the federal government, 40 per cent from the state government, and 56 per cent from the local community. The property tax is the chief source of revenue for local school districts. Government universities are supported in part by the federal government but principally by the state government. There is no local district financial support for government universities. Tuition is charged at all these institutions. Nonrevenue receipts come from the periodic sale of public bonds to support the school system, from the sale of property purchased from capital funds, and/or from philanthropic support of corporate foundations (Lee).

Catholic schools are financed in quite a different manner. The chief sources for financing the Catholic school are parish support, diocesan support, tuition, fees, contributed services of religious and lay school staff, and fund-raising. The degree of support from each of these sources varies because of many factors, chief of which is whether the school is under the control of a parish, of a diocese, or of a religious institute. The following table breaks down the patterns of fiscal support.

Catholic colleges and universities of all types receive negligible fiscal support from parishes, from the diocese, or from the religious institute.

The tables show that subsidization—parish, diocesan, religious institute—is woefully inadequate to support the Catholic schools. Consequently the bulk of the fiscal support comes from other sources, primarily from student tuition. The following table delineates the tuition picture.

On the college and university level tuition is extremely costly, since almost all of the revenue of the institution comes from this source.

There are compulsory fees, both general and specific, in addition to tuition, at most Catholic schools at all levels. Such fees include a general all-purpose fee levied on each student and special fees such as laboratory fees, athletic fees, locker room fees, and so forth. On the elementary level, 58 per cent of all schools have fees ranging up to twenty-five dollars. On the secondary level, 80 per cent of all institutions have fees, ranging up to one hundred dollars and in a few cases even higher (Neuwien). Catholic colleges and universities, with few exceptions, have rather heavy student fees. Government schools at all levels also have student fees.

Contributed services of clerical, religious, and lay staff constitute another, though less visible, form of Catholic school support. Contrib-

Tuition in Catholic Schools*

Catholic Elementary Schools

Type School	Dollar Rates per Annum in Percentages						
	$0	$1-25	$26-50	$51-75	$76-100	$101-200	$201 and over
Parish (95%)	50	20	21	6	3	0	0
Private (5%)	26	6	8	8	11	19	22

Catholic Secondary Schools

Type School	Dollar Rates per Annum in Percentages						
	$0	$1-50	$51-100	$101-200	$201-300	$301-400	$401 and over
Parish (46%)	36	27	26	11	0	0	0
Central (17%)	19	11	35	35	0	0	0
Private (37%)	9	5	12	40	19	6	9

* Data derived from Neuwien study.

uted services represent the difference between the total compensation which Catholic school personnel receive and the higher amounts which they would receive were they working in a comparable government school. Of the lay teachers in Catholic elementary schools, 22 per cent receive less than $2000 salary annually, 41 per cent less than $3000, and 61 per cent less than $3500. Only 2 per cent receive more than $4500, the common salary for beginning teachers in government schools in the same localities. On the secondary level 72 per cent of the Catholic teachers earned under $5000 annually, and less than 10 per cent received an annual salary in excess of $6000 (Neuwien). Further, the vital fringe benefits such as retirement plans, health insurance, and so forth are either nonexistent or, at best, relatively meager. Contrary to popular assumption, the religious are only 10-15 per cent less costly than the lay teachers on the elementary and secondary levels (Seidl).

Voluntary fund-raising activities conducted by Catholic school parents and others provide supplementary revenue. Such activities include cake sales, chance books, raffles, diverse entertainments, and most especially the gambling game called "bingo."

On the university level, some of the institutions of stature have endowment funds for the university as a whole, for certain programs, and for designated chaired professorships. Recently the federal government and private corporate foundations have awarded Catholic university scholars substantial financial grants to pursue worthwhile research projects.

Federal financial support to a rapidly accelerating degree (and state support to some though not as great a degree) has been increasing to Catholic and especially to government schools. The basic principle which the state and federal governments have applied when giving financial support to Catholic school students is known as the "child benefit principle." This means that funds disbursed by the federal or state government are not and constitutionally cannot benefit the Catholic Church directly via the Catholic school; rather these funds must assist the Catholic student as American citizen. If, in the latter instance, federal or state financial assistance in any form does indirectly or secondarily assist the Catholic school, this is permissible. Militant secularists have bitterly contested the child benefit principle. However, the state and federal courts have upheld its legality.

There have been three phases in the state and federal government's indirect assistance to Catholic students in Catholic schools, loans, auxiliary services, and outright aid. The federal government has lent money to Catholic students at lower than commercial rates to enable them to defray the cost of their university education. The federal government has also lent money to Catholic universities to build additions to their plants.

Auxiliary services are numerous. A few states and local school districts provide free textbooks from public funds to students in Catholic schools, a practice ruled constitutional by the Supreme Court in 1930 (Cochran decision). Quite a few states and local school districts provide free transportation for Catholic school students, a procedure ruled constitutional by the Court in 1947 (Everson decision). Since 1946 many Catholic schoolchildren have received lunches subsidized by the federal government.

Outright aid to students in Catholic schools first came in 1944 with the famous Serviceman's Readjustment Act. This act provided for free tuition, books, and living expenses to all honorably discharged war veterans who wished to continue their education in a secondary school or university of their choice, including Catholic institutions. This act, renewed many times, remains in force today. In 1958 the National Defense Education Act was passed. Renewed and broadened in 1965, this act provided stipends and tuition to Catholic secondary schoolteachers attending approved institutes in guidance and foreign language teaching at Catholic or government universities. In 1965 the Elementary and Secondary Education Act provided for outright aid to students in all schools, both government and Catholic, provided these students come from an economically underprivileged background. This aid is to be administered per modum the government school system.

The Curriculum

In the main, Catholic schoolmen at all levels—except perhaps in the extreme classical schools—agree with government schoolmen that the curriculum comprises all areas of learning for which the school has responsibility. Thus the curriculum is broader than merely the specific things learned in the classroom.

In the elementary grades the academic subjects commonly studied for the first three years (the primary grades) include reading, writing, arithmetic, religion, speaking, art, music, and games. At the fourth-grade level the following subjects are usually added: social studies (an integrated amalgam comprising history, civics, geography, and economics); English grammar; American and English literature; and science. In some of the more progressive elementary schools, a foreign language is studied from the third or fourth grade on.

Differentiation of curriculum begins at the secondary level. No longer must all students take the same classes with the same group of students. Courses are divided into two basic groups, required courses and elective courses. Required courses are of two kinds, those prescribed for all students and those prescribed for certain groups of students, for example those majoring in business education. Required courses of the first kind are generally those which give the student a broad base of general education. Required courses of the second kind, and also elective courses, are usually designed to develop the student's special interests, abilities, or vocational objectives. Catholic secondary schools, which are overwhelmingly university-preparatory, typically have a much larger required course sequence and fewer elective courses than do government secondary schools. Those Catholic secondary schools (usually for girls) which are business-vocational offer much the same sequence of commercial courses as do the comparable business departments in the government comprehensive secondary schools.

The curriculum of all American secondary schools, government and Catholic alike, is divided into so-called "Carnegie units." The Carnegie unit, named after the work of a 1906 private secular educational committee, consists of a class period of at least forty minutes' duration, meeting five times each week for at least thirty-six weeks. Laboratory classes meet for a slightly longer time—280 minutes per week. Successful completion of sixteen Carnegie units is required for graduation. Catholic high school curricula typically consist of two to four units of Latin, two units of a foreign language, four units of English grammar and literature, two to four units of mathematics, two to four units of science, two to four units of social studies, four half-units of religion, and four half-units of health and physical education.

The undergraduate division of an American university is considerably different from its counterpart in certain foreign countries, insofar as it is conceived as a school of general rather than of specialized education. This is particularly true of the first two years of the four-year undergraduate sequence, during which the typical student pursues much the same subject matter as he did in secondary school, only on a higher plane. In the third and fourth years of university work, the collegian begins to concentrate, though not exclusively, in his major field. It is only in the graduate school that the student works exclusively in a particular specialty.

Extracurricular activities comprise that sector of the school's educational program which takes place outside the classroom. Despite the designation extracurricular, these activities today are considered a vital part of the school's curriculum. Almost all government and Catholic secondary schools and universities have their school-sponsored and school-moderated extracurricular programs. Typical of these activities are the athletic program, student government, the social program, the school newspaper, religious activities programs (the Sodality, Young Christian Students, and so forth), and special interest clubs (German club, music club, dramatic club, history club).

Of course, curricular design is the pattern or framework or structural organization used in selecting, planning, and carrying forward educational experiences in the school. The subject-centered curriculum design utilizes bodies of information classified into intrinsically systematic branches of knowledge as both the organizing force in and center of learning; for example, the subject of history is taught chronologically. The Core design centers around interdisciplinary problems of both eternal and personal concern. Subject material is brought into the learning situation as it is needed to solve the problem under con-

sideration, without respect to precise subject boundaries. In spite of
the empirically proved superiority of the newer Core design in promoting a greater degree of student learning, Catholic schools at all
levels almost unanimously cling to the traditional subject-centered
approach (Lee). Most government schools similarly retain the outmoded subject-centered design, although more of these utilize Core
than do Catholic schools.

Since World War II there have been certain curricular innovations. These innovations have been pioneered chiefly by the government schools. The source of these innovations has not really been
teachers' committees or teacher-student planning, as urged by the
educationists. Rather, the source has been university-level specialists
who have concerned themselves with reforming the elementary school
curriculum. In some instances, however, teachers did assist these university professors in the planning. On the elementary and secondary
levels, the greatest curricular innovations have occurred in reading,
writing, foreign languages, the natural sciences, and mathematics.
Little if any new structural curricular changes are evident in religion;
however, much the reverse is true on the university level in the more
advanced Catholic institutions.

In marked contrast to government education, there is extremely
little experimental or theoretical research on curricular innovation
being done by Catholic educationists. A bit of theoretical thinking is
being done on this subject, however. This great neglect of curriculum
study and research by Catholic educationists is most regrettable insofar as it is the curriculum which forms the basic *raison d'être* of the
Catholic school's existence. As Bishop Ernest Primeau has stated: "It
is unfortunate that more people are not seriously concerned with the
subject of the [Catholic] school curriculum. Many want to talk about
class size, physical plant, and school organization. Important as these
may be, it is the curriculum which constitutes the primary means by
which the educational objectives of the school are attained."

A curriculum guide, called a syllabus, is an educational resource,
usually printed, which details for the teacher's use broad objectives,
desired outcomes, and suggested procedures for developing general
and specific classroom experiences. To all intents and purposes the
syllabus has become the curriculum, especially for the weaker teachers.
Government schools have detailed syllabi for the elementary and secondary schoolteacher to use in all subject areas. For the most part,
Catholic schools use these government syllabi, often adapting them to
their own situations. However, some of the more advanced archdio-

ceses and dioceses and some of the larger and more progressive religious institutes have created syllabi designed especially for Catholic schools. This is particularly true of religion courses. The teachers and students rarely have a voice in the construction of the Catholic-originated syllabi. Rather, the curriculum is commonly the product of a committee composed of persons of high repute in the religious institute and diocese, and of schoolpeople who have had experience teaching the course. Rarely are scholars from Catholic universities, parents, or laymen, regardless of their experience in Catholic schools, invited to participate in devising or revising a syllabus. Usually no syllabi exist at the university level. Each professor is relatively free to structure the curriculum for his course.

Traditional and classical as they are, Catholic school curricula are decidedly "bookish" rather than related to life and life-problems. Course work is viewed as a world unto itself, which would somehow be diluted if integrated into daily life. Thus, for example, the religion course is seldom integrated in the concrete existential situation with student involvement in the parish, in the social apostolate, and so forth. Homework assignments in all subjects are almost always bookish, instead of being aimed at extending the classroom learnings *in concreto* into community activities. Some perceptive Catholic educators, keenly aware of this pedagogically unhappy fact, hope to ameliorate the condition.

Instruction

Instruction in Catholic elementary schools takes place as it does in government elementary schools, that is in a self-contained classroom where all subjects are taught by the same teacher to the same group of students. On the secondary and university levels, instruction in both government and Catholic schools is departmentalized, that is each separate subject is taught by a different teacher, usually to a different group of students, and frequently in a different classroom. Some Catholic elementary schools follow the departmentalized system in the seventh and eighth grades, since in advanced government schools these grades are not part of the elementary school but are part of the junior high school.

Students at any given grade level in most Catholic and in the smaller government elementary schools are heterogeneous in intellectual ability as measured by standardized intelligence tests. On the secondary level most government schools and some Catholic schools group their students in the different classes at the same grade level homogeneously according to intellectual ability. There is heterogeneous grouping at the university level. In schools where homogeneous grouping is the policy there is usually a multiple-track system of instructional groups. The first track is designed for the intellectually superior students, the second track for the average students, and the third track for the weak students. Usually a given student will stay with his class in a given track for all his subjects; however, in more forward-looking schools, the student may stay in his basic track but move out of it for those subjects in which he is either more or less proficient.

In general, the elementary level in both government and Catholic schools features the most diverse, the most advanced, and the most experimental teaching processes and instructional methodologies. Typically, though by no means always, the higher the school level, the poorer the teaching. A notable exception is the government pilot secondary schools, in which teaching methodologies and instructional usances are diffuse and sophisticated.

Despite the empirical researches which have shown that the lecture is the weakest instructional method of all, it remains the principal pedagogical device in both government and Catholic schools at all levels. Catholic schoolteachers appear to make wider use of the lecture than the teachers in the government schools. Quite possibly the three most important reasons for this are the greater traditionalism, the greater authoritarianism, and the generally weaker pedagogical preparation of Catholic schoolteachers. A favorite allied device of the lecture is the practice of recitation, or "lesson-hearing," in which the teacher asks questions almost solely on what was presented in the previous lecture and/or in the preceding night's homework assignment.

Teacher-led discussion with the entire class is a pedagogical device which empirical research has shown to be vastly superior to the lecture, especially in the formation and alteration of student attitudes. Notwithstanding, Catholic schoolteachers do not appear to make sufficient use of this valuable pedagogical procedure, especially at the secondary and university levels.

Committee work, in which the class is divided into small groups to investigate intensively an educationally significant problem or topic under the supervision of the teacher is rarely utilized in Catholic schools. Government schools do use committee work but not with sufficient frequency.

Role-playing (sometimes called sociodrama) is an unrehearsed dramatization of a problem in which the members of the class, without scripts, extemporaneously portray how they would react in a given situation. As a pedagogical device role-playing has been of great value in assisting students to deepen and change their attitudes, particularly toward another group. Unfortunately role-playing is seldom used in Catholic schools.

The project is a learning activity which involves some sort of problem-oriented educative task to be performed by the student and is usually interdisciplinary in character. But such projects are rarely utilized by Catholic schoolteachers except some in forward-looking elementary schools. Unhappily the use of the project is declining in government schools, particularly at the secondary level.

Catholic schools are substantially superior to government schools at every level, except that of the university, in the use of most electric audiovisual instructional materials, such as motion pictures, filmstrips, and the like. Catholic schools are noticeably in the lead in the area of educational television. It has been hypothesized that the reason for this happy circumstance is that Catholic school administrators believe these audiovisual devices enable the school to instruct more students at less cost than with a "live" teacher.

Catholic schools in general do not make as much use as do the government schools of the electronic language laboratory, the exhibit, the display, the diorama, the specimen, the panel or symposium methods, or the new programmed instructional devices ("teaching machines"). Catholic schools feature virtually no teacher-student planning of the lesson or of curricular units. Much more attention is paid to the content of the lesson than to pedagogical procedures; indeed, most Catholic schoolteachers do not appear to have a deep knowledge of or respect for the science of pedagogy.

The cell is a learning activity in which a tightly knit group of students works together according to definitely organized procedures to solve a problem and subsequently to implement this solution in everyday living. It is different from committee work in that the cell technique consciously and overtly combines into one teaching-learning process both the intellective and the volitional faculties. Thus the basic purpose of the cell is twofold: deep, personal, meaningful, significant learning and subsequent utilization of this learning to transform one's milieu. The cell therefore coordinates knowledge and action, classroom experiences, and live situations. The basic cell technique consists of the three famous Jocist steps—observe, judge, act.

Almost no government schools and very few Catholic schools at any level use the cell method of teaching as part of the regular curriculum; a few Catholic schools use the cell technique in the extracurricular program.

Most of the courses in Catholic schools at all levels, including the university, are totally textbook courses, that is courses in which the sole required reading is the textbook. Relatively little use seems to be made of required supplementary or collateral reading assignments. Catholic textbooks have been developed and published for most courses in Catholic schools at every level. In the past many of these works overemphasized the achievements of Catholics or Catholic-related events. Thus, for example, a course in American literature might print a greater number of poems by a minor Catholic author than by a major secular poet (LaNoue). Integration of religion with subjects tended to be forced rather than flow according to natural, ontological lines; for example, in a mathematics textbook a problem might take the form of two nuns plus five nuns equal seven nuns. Religion textbooks, notably at the high school level, were legendary for their insipidness, artificiality, and pietism. In recent years, however, Catholic textbooks at every level have improved dramatically; in some areas, notably art and elementary school religion, Catholic textbooks are fully as good, if not better, in quality as government school textbooks in these fields. However, the violent reaction of many contemporary Catholic teachers to the old style Catholic textbooks has led them studiously to avoid the use of Catholic textbooks, even the new, high-quality ones.

Field trips are used to a lesser extent by Catholic schoolteachers than by government schoolteachers. Catholic schools typically require their students to do more homework than government schools do. One probable reason for this is the higher parental expectation for the Catholic school to assign more homework.

Several innovations in the teaching process, some of which impinge on the curricular structure of the school, have been pioneered by government schools. The first of these, introduced in 1957, is called team teaching. Team teaching is a combination of two or more teachers who work with variable-sized groups of prpils during an adjustable time period which covers two or more regular class sessions. Teaching teams fit no one pattern; they are of various sizes and compositions. Organizationally there are two chief types of team teaching, the coordinate and the associate. The coordinate pattern is that in which several classes are combined from time to time; the basic unit remains the regular classroom. The associate approach is that in which the basic unit is a large class under the direction of the team; this larger unit is periodically subdivided for separate group study in depth. The associate approach is true team teaching. Team teaching involves many different combinations of teachers and other staff personnel. In a large combined class the team teaches in an interdisciplinary fashion. This large class is then broken up periodically so that each team specialist meets in small class discussion groups with those students whose interests or course requirements call for probing more deeply the various areas of specialization. Still other types of teams use a masterteacher (with a regular teacher combination) who conducts the large-group lesson and the regular teachers give the instruction in the subdivided small group classes. Team teaching is becoming increasingly popular in Catholic secondary schools, although not infrequently what goes on there is not true team teaching but simply three teachers in the same room at the same time, with one lecturing.

Another innovation, also pioneered in government schools, is the nongraded school. In this system, the formal, lockstep, rigid grade levels are abolished, and in their place are substituted learning units jointly determined by the teacher and the pupil. These learning units are mastered by the student at his own level and at his own time. Promotion to the next advanced level is determined by "professional decision," that is the teacher, the guidance counselor, relevant staff personnel, and the student. The nongraded school plan is admirable in that it really tailors the school experience to the learner and not vice-versa, as is currently the case. The nongraded system was first used on the elementary level. Some experimental government secondary schools, such as Melbourne High School and Nova High School, both in Florida, have instituted the nongraded plan with apparent success. A few dynamic Catholic elementary school systems, notably in the dioceses of Pittsburgh and St. Louis, have partially or totally adopted the plan. Perhaps most exciting of all is the pilot nongraded Catholic secondary school operated by the dynamic Father L. J. Antoun, principal of Venango Christian High School in Oil City, Pennsylvania.

Another instructional innovation is that of flexible scheduling, recommended by the influential 1961 Trump Report. Based on evidence of successful pilot schools, this report urged elimination of class periods of equal length on the ground that certain subjects and lessons require greater or lesser lengths of formal class time than do others. The school day, proposed the report, will be divided into fifteen- or twenty-minute units, instead of equal periods. In this way the lengths of the classes can be changed constantly to adapt to the dynamics of the particular lesson or subject. The Trump Report states that a school adopting flexible scheduling adequately provides for individual differences, individual initiative, and accelerated individual growth as a replacement for the stagnant uniformity of teaching which characterizes most secondary schools. A very few Catholic secondary schools —for example, St. Mel High School in Chicago, under the leadership of Brother Kevin Mark, F.S.C.—have adopted flexible scheduling.

As a general rule, Catholic schools traditionally have at first been opposed to and, at best, reluctant to introduce pedagogical reforms. Thus in 1966 Father Koob, a highly placed official in the National Catholic Educational Association reported:

To be perfectly blunt about the problem of innovation and creative activity at the teacher level, we must admit a paucity of ideas from both our [Catholic school] administrators and our supervisors. Three separate questionnaires regarding new [educational] projects underway and planned were sent by NCEA to high school administrators, and they failed to disclose anything significant. Workshops on Catholic secondary school administration reveal a great deal of interest, a bit of "know-how," but not much that isn't being done better by a vast number of showcase government secondary schools.

Fear is still a prime motivational tool in Catholic schools—fear of expulsion, fear of failing a course, fear of being sent to an administrator (usually a cleric or religious), whose role is that of disciplinarian. Physical discipline has been officially outlawed in most Catholic school systems, but its practice is still more prevalent than in government schools. Social competition in academic subjects rather than cooperation with one's classmates is stressed. Incentives, such as higher class marks for superior work, are common motivational devices. But in general there has been a decided and discernible improvement in the type and quality of motivational practices used by Catholic schoolteachers over the past few years.

Though educationists have stressed that evaluation is a part of the student's integrated learning experience, evaluation in both government and Catholic schools is commonly conceived of as something done after the learning has been completed. Evaluation is commonly done at periodic intervals—at the middle and at the end of each semester and at designated intervals during these times, depending on the decisions of the teacher and the school. Despite the urging of educationists, evaluation is typically carried out with no cooperation or consultation with the student. Evaluation, in short, is done *on* rather than *with* the student.

Evaluation is usually accomplished by two principal devices, the teacher's subjective observation and written tests. Catholic school-teachers tend to utilize teacher-constructed achievement tests far more frequently than they do those achievement tests which measurement experts have standardized scientifically for validity and reliability for large groups of similar students. Reasons for this include the lack of appreciation of the value of standardized tests, the lack of pedagogical sophistication, and the cost of standardized tests. Nevertheless, the situation has improved markedly in the past two decades. Teacher-constructed tests commonly are not rigorously constructed in accord with the scientific canons of test construction. As a rule, teacher-constructed tests tend to measure rote memory and factual information rather than broad understanding of what was learned in class (Lee).

Catholic schools, like their government counterparts, utilize the report card as their principal and usually their sole reporting device to parents on the educational progress of their children. The report card usually contains two discrete sections: the first section is for the evaluation of the student's achievement in his various academic courses; the second notes the student's progress in selected non-academic behavioral areas which are deemed important—discipline, courteousness, effort, and so forth. Marks are typically in two forms, a percentage score in each subject or, even more commonly, a letter grade A (over 90 per cent); B (80–90 per cent), and so forth. Report cards which include explanatory teacher comments for each subject are the exception rather than the rule. Any mark which is a 60 per cent, or D represents successful completion of the course. Although urged by educationists as a requisite for effective evaluation, parent-teacher conferences to discuss the report card before and/or after it has been distributed are seldom held, except possibly for students who are performing very poorly. Teacher-student conferences to evolve or to discuss the report card are rare occurrences except for failing students.

Supervision of instruction in Catholic schools at all levels, as compared with that in government schools, is relatively chaotic and unorganized. As private, separatist schools, Catholic educational institutions have no government school supervisors or inspectors. The closest Catholic schools come to "outside" supervision is the inspection by voluntary associations for regional accreditation. On the secondary school level such evaluation is accomplished through the use of a very detailed and comprehensive instrument called the Evaluative Criteria. However, this device is more properly a self-evaluative tool than a supervisory one. Most dioceses leave supervision to the religious institutes which staff the various schools. The larger institutes have supervisors who make the rounds of the various schools; the smaller institutes usually have no supervisors. Few, if any, laymen have risen to supervisory posts in Catholic schools. Many Catholic school supervisors are not extensively trained in the science of educational supervision; typically these supervisors are experienced teachers who are presumed to have a knowledge of supervision simply because they are experienced teachers. School principals and department heads are also supposed to supervise instruction. Supervision sometimes is that in the true sense of the term, namely a cooperative learning experience for the teacher on how concretely to effect expansive pedagogical improvement. However, sometimes supervision is simply an evaluative tool, and in a few instances it is a punitive device.

Instructional standards in Catholic elementary and secondary schools are supposed to be set by the diocesan superintendents, supervisors, principals, and department heads. Syllabi play a role here. In actual practice it is the principal who sets the standards by the degree of instructional leadership and standard-setting which he adopts. Department heads in Catholic universities set the standards. By and large, however, each teacher is so loosely supervised in Catholic schools at all levels that he or she is to all intents and purposes free to set his or her own standards. Only if a high percentage of students fails his course (as measured by standardized achievement tests or by other objective evaluative devices) will the teacher's instructional standards be reviewed by the principal.

The Program of Religious Education

On the elementary level Catholic schools normally devote from twenty to thirty minutes per day to formal religious instruction, that is religion taught as a separate subject. In secondary schools two or three class periods per week are given over to formal religious instruction. On the university level two periods per week throughout the four years is the customary requirement. In addition to formal religious instruction, there are sometimes group guidance periods and individual counseling sessions, as well as extracurricular clubs devoted to religious education.

The class in religious instruction is carried out much in the same manner as classes in the other subject areas. Religion appears to be regarded de facto as another academic subject rather than a subject whose dimensionality pervades all conduct. The pedagogical procedures are quite like those used in other subject areas. The common impression, confirmed by such on-the-spot investigators as Neuwien, is that in religion class more than in any other the students are instructed by lecturing and by telling, with much less discussion permitted. This seems particularly true of women religious teachers. Some religious institutes such as the Jesuits, however, do encourage discussion in religion class even more than they do in other classes. New trends in the teaching of religion, such as the kerygmatic approach, have produced a new spirit of religion teaching in those schools permeated by this spirit. But such trends have not substantially affected teaching methodology. There are specially prepared religion textbooks and audiovisual materials for Catholic schools. Many of the audiovisual materials are of outstanding quality. In other academic areas special textbooks have been developed to integrate the Christian dimension into the subject matter. As observed earlier in this essay, current Catholic dissatisfaction with the low quality of these textbooks has led to the substantial upgrading in some of them.

All students in Catholic colleges and universities must take course work in theology, ranging from four to eight required courses, depending on the institution. But until recently religion often was not accorded formal academic credit on the university level. However, since World War II, the theologians have been instrumental in changing the name of religion class to theology class, thus forcing Catholic university administrators to allot academic credits to these courses. However, some perceptive critics note that in a program of general, humanistic education which Catholic universities (and elementary schools and secondary schools) offer, theology must be more than a cognitive discipline; it must also include the volitional aspect of the student. In a very few instances some Catholic universities have begun introducing majors in theology. Nevertheless, inasmuch as laymen are not usually permitted to teach religion and theology in Catholic schools, surprisingly few Catholic undergraduate schools permit the student to have a major concentration in theology. Until the 1960's no Catholic university permitted a layman to attain the doctorate in theology. However, more progressive Catholic schools and universities have recently begun to permit lay persons to teach religion.

Although pertinent concrete empirical data are lacking, it is the overwhelming impression of Catholic school educators that the level and extent of preparation by teachers of religion are considerably weaker than is true of teachers in other subject areas. This applies to content preparation, to methodology preparation, and to pedagogical foundations. It is commonly believed that the reasons for the relatively poor quality of religion teachers include these points: that any priest, brother, or sister is automatically thought capable of teaching religion; that religion teachers are commonly part-time instructors, whose principal task is that of curate in a parish; that teaching religion provides a refuge for the physically infirm priests and religious and also for any religious who may have been unsuccessful at other tasks. Some laymen are permitted to teach religion; typically, however, laymen are not thought capable or worthy of teaching in this area.

On the secondary and university levels, it is safe to conclude that there is very little integration of religion and the academic areas of the curriculum. The subject-centered curricular design structurally forbids such integration; further, many of the subject teachers are either loath or overtly unwilling to perform such an integrative task. A few integration-minded teachers on the secondary level, and many on the elementary level, particularly the nuns, consciously strive to make the school truly a Catholic institution by attempting such an integration. Religion is also integrated with group guidance and counseling sessions and with certain extracurricular activities. It is not too much to say, however, that a great many Catholic schools are really carbon copies of the corresponding government school, with the simple addition of a few classes a week in religion.

The program of religious instruction is supervised very much like the program of other subject areas. On the elementary level the pastor of the parish sponsoring the school sometimes is involved in the supervision of the religious education program.

In most Catholic schools, except possibly in major Catholic universities, attendance at certain religious exercises is a part of the religious instructional program of the school. Elementary schools normally require students to attend Mass one weekday and also to go to Confession. Time is provided within the regular school day for attendance at such exercises. Almost all parishes reserve one Mass on

Sundays especially for the Catholic school children, with a sermon prepared especially for them. Some Catholic educationists have questioned the wisdom of this policy, maintaining that concrete religious formation is best developed within the context of family living and therefore children should attend Mass with their family group. Some secondary schools, but virtually no colleges, retain compulsory Mass or Confession during weekdays. Only one Catholic university (Notre Dame) has a chapel in each residence hall. Almost all secondary schools, colleges, and universities have one centrally located chapel. All Catholic schools at all levels gently urge frequent attendance at daily Mass and weekly Confession; all schools make concrete provisions for such opportunities. But few Catholic schools at any level offer a full complement of religious activities—for example, supplying lists of recommended spiritual reading, sponsoring Young Christian Student groups, and so on.

The overwhelming evidence of research has indicated that generally, though by no means invariably, government schools as a group at every level perform a total educative function superior to that of Catholic schools. (This of course, does not mean that individual Catholic schools may not perform a superior educative function than individual government schools.) Studies indicated that graduates from Catholic secondary schools have not performed academically as well as graduates from government secondary schools (Lee; Koos; Hill). More abundant evidence has been uncovered to indicate that Catholic schools are not having their commensurate impact upon American society at large. Catholic schools are producing far less than their proportionate share of scientists, intellectuals, and cultural leaders (Ellis). Graduates of Catholic universities seem to prefer to enter the lucrative professions of medicine, law, and politics, rather than to pursue financially less rewarding but more influential intellectual careers (O'Dea).

The evidence seems to indicate that Catholic schools at all levels do not appear to have a significant impact in substantially improving the deeper religious attitudes and conduct patterns of their students (Lee and Pallone). The degree of religiousness of a youth's parents and also the educational level he attains have been found to be more important predictors of the degree of his future religious behavior as an adult than is the fact that he attended a Catholic school (Greeley and Rossi).

The empirical investigations conclude that attendance at Catholic schools does not appear to alter significantly the attitudes and concepts of social justice of the students in these schools. Products of Catholic schools share most of the racial and ethnic prejudices of non-Catholics from government schools (Fichter). One large-scale study found that there was no significant difference in the development of social conscience between matched Catholic students attending Catholic and government schools (Greeley and Rossi).

Although sometimes conflicting, the body of the research seems to show that Catholic schools are not motivating their students to learn to a high degree the basic knowledge and attitudes of their religion (Lee and Pallone).

The studies found that the Catholic school is not providing its students with the proper measure of charity. One massive study discovered that the two most important areas of personal religious concern for students in Catholic schools are abstinence from meat on Friday and birth control (Greeley and Rossi). In short, the studies seem to indicate that Catholic schooling induces Catholic youth to attend religious services more frequently than does non-Catholic schooling; however, there is little or no evidence to indicate that Catholic schooling makes the students more Christian.

Despite the absence of empirical data, one way or another, it is the overwhelming impression that the vast majority—but by no means all—of the current apostolic and militant Catholic laymen tend to be graduates of Catholic schools, particularly from Catholic universities, and most notably transfers from seminaries. Yet it is interesting also that these same laymen tend to constitute the core of the critics of Catholic education.

The relation of the Catholic school to the parish is closest in parish elementary and parish secondary schools. In such instances, the pastor is frequently the school principal. It is true that the pastor nearly always controls the funds and the general management of the school. Yet these schools typically are not closely related to the parish and its activities. Usually the school is run almost as a separate entity, without conscious direction toward unifying procedures into parish life or the parish community. School thrust is generally directed toward itself or to the next higher level of schooling, rather than to the parish. Often there is a clash over school policy between the pastor and the sister in charge of the school. On the secondary level, the central diocesan schools, as well as the private schools operated by religious institutes, are oriented toward themselves and not toward the parish. Religious in these schools usually tend to be more interested in the pupils' schoolwork and in recruitment of vocations to the institute rather than to the parish. Moreover, students in such schools are drawn from a great many parishes, which further complicates the task of close school-parish ties. On the university level, especially those with residence halls, the students are boarders and form their own parish community. A cardinal purpose of Catholic universities is to prepare their graduates to be parish leaders; however, in the concrete, little is done to give collegians actual leadership or intern-leadership experiences in nearby parishes.

Student Personnel
and Guidance Services

The three basic overall services essential for every school program are the instructional service, the administrative service, and the student personnel and guidance service. Student personnel services are the totality of assistances which the school gives to the pupil to aid him in developing his personality and in solving his difficulties in development. Thus the personnel services are concerned with the student's total growth as a person, in contrast to the instructional service, which is concerned primarily only with the growth of his intellect and his will. Vital subservices within the personnel-service category include the spiritual life service, the recreation service, the housing service, the food service, the health service, the remedial service, the testing service, and the vocational orientation service. All of these are carried out by a professionally prepared student personnel worker (and his assistants) employed by the school and with an office there.

The most important subservices of the personnel service are the guidance service and the counseling service (Lee and Pallone). In American education the guidance service is that personal assistance which the school gives the student in working through the various personal concerns he is undergoing at any given point in his maturation. These concerns usually center around one or more of five focal points: religious concerns or problems; personal concerns; social concerns; academic concerns; vocational concerns. The counseling service is the one-to-one personal relationship through which the student-client discusses his concerns with the professionally prepared school guidance counselor and through these discussions gains insight into problems, with the subsequent strength to work them through successfully. Guidance is also done in groups, that is one guidance worker with many students, usually with a homeroom class. Professionally prepared counselors deal with students with normal developmental problems; more serious cases are referred to the professionally trained school psychologist, school psychiatrist, or community youth agency.

Counseling is carried out in a specially equipped counselor's office. This office is equipped with two comfortable chairs, with file cabinets holding student records, and a small bookshelf with appropriate books and brochures for student perusal. Students may consult the counselor either on their own initiative or because a teacher, administrator, or parent refers them to the counselor.

Group guidance is usually done in the classroom, ordinarily during a special period set aside each week for this purpose. Specially trained counselors or teacher-counselors handle group guidance sessions.

There are very few full-time guidance counselors in government or Catholic elementary schools. The recommended counselor-to-student ratio in the secondary schools is 1 to 300. Government schools have a ratio approximating 1 to 500. Nearly three-fourths of all Catholic secondary schools have no full-time professional guidance counselor. Thus the ratio is difficult to determine. It probably is in the area of 1 to 1200. Major government universities have well-developed student personnel and counseling centers. Such are a relative rarity in Catholic colleges and universities. Cost and lack of adequate personnel are the two major reasons for the shortage. Catholic schools favor group guidance over counseling because they believe this practice will stretch the guidance dollar. Catholic schools seldom have full-time psychologists or school psychiatrists.

Professional associations play a more significant role in upgrading the quality of school guidance services than do professional associations of teachers or administrators vis-à-vis their respective memberships. The American Personnel and Guidance Association (APGA), a 1952 amalgamation of many previously existing school-related guidance groups, has been a powerful force in the improvement of the training programs, the spirit of commitment, and the professional standards of guidance workers. In addition, it has sponsored and encouraged high-level research into the school guidance program and the counseling act. In 1962 the National Catholic Guidance Conference (NCGC) was formed, in an attempt to do for the Catholic school guidance movement what APGA had done for government schools. As of 1967 NCGC had proven less professional, less high-level, and less influential than its secular counterpart. Nonetheless, NCGC has been a great help in the professionalization of Catholic school guidance services. Its quarterly journal has notably improved in quality. Another important step in the upgrading of guidance services in Catholic schools took place in 1965 with the establishment of a new National Catholic Educational Association position called Consultant for Guidance Services. Its first office-holder, Fr. G. Moreau, O.M.I., has done much to stimulate the acceleration of the guidance movement in Catholic schools.

All schools at all levels have testing programs as part of their personnel services program. These tests include standardized intelligence tests, achievement tests, aptitude tests, personality tests, and vocational interest tests. Almost all government elementary and secondary schools give their students standardized intelligence and achievement tests at designated grade intervals. About 70 per cent of Catholic elementary schools and approximately 60 per cent of Catholic secondary schools give similar tests (Neuwien). The testing program is under the direction of the guidance counselor; in schools having no counselor the principal assumes the responsibility. Generally the testing program is more inclusive and comprehensive in government schools than in Catholic schools. In recent years, however, Catholic schools have made significant advances in this area.

Discipline is traditional and still quite severe in most Catholic schools, as compared with the more liberal posture in the government schools. Indeed, one of the reasons parents commonly offer for sending their children to Catholic schools is the "strict discipline." Punishments of all sorts and expulsion are far more common in Catholic than in government schools.

Religious guidance is theoretically the conscious task of every teacher in the Catholic school, particularly at the elementary and secondary levels. At the elementary level the pastor is in charge of the religious guidance program; on the secondary and college levels it is the specially designated school chaplain who has charge of this function. The chaplain's role is to conduct religious services, to make spiritual goods available to the students, to counsel with them on religious problems, and otherwise to make religion permeate the entire school program.

The Staff of the
Catholic Schools

The number of full-time priest-teachers in Catholic schools at all levels as of 1966 totaled over 12,000. The number of full-time brother-teachers was nearly 6000, full-time sister-teachers over 104,000, and full-time lay teachers over 75,000 (Catholic Directory). Added to these is the very large number of priests who serve as chaplains and who come in from parish duties to teach part-time. Also there are innumerable religious who, because of reasons such as old age or ill health, teach only part-time. On the elementary level, nearly all full-time religious teachers are women. On the secondary level, about two-thirds of all the religious teachers are women. Virtually all lay teachers on the elementary level are women. On the secondary level, about 40 per cent of lay teachers are women. On the higher educational level, the lay staff of the major Catholic universities is almost entirely male, whereas the lay staff of the smaller Catholic women's colleges typically comprises more female than male.

Schools at all levels are increasing at a substantially higher rate than the number of religious and clerical teachers. By 1967 nearly 40 per cent of all teachers in Catholic elementary schools were lay persons, with the most rapid annual rate increase over the last decade taking place at the elementary level (NCEA). On the college level the large Catholic universities have an overwhelming number of lay faculty, in contrast to religious or clerical teachers. In 1963, 70 per cent of all Catholic college and university teachers were laymen (NCWC). The University of Notre Dame, considered by many secular and Catholic educators as the finest American Catholic university, clearly is in the lead in the trend toward lay participation and control of Catholic universities. By 1967, 90 per cent of all department heads, 75 per cent of all deans, and 40 per cent of all vice presidents at Notre Dame were laymen. In contrast, the small Catholic women's colleges —which are the most numerous of separate Catholic institutions of higher learning—usually have slightly more religious faculty, especially sisters, than lay faculty. Virtually without exception, almost all higher echelon administrators in these colleges are female religious. In 1963 only 19 per cent of all lay college teachers were in Catholic women's colleges. Advocates of lay participation in and control of Catholic schools at all levels, such as the dynamic Father Neil Mc-Cluskey, S.J., note that clerical and religious presence in a Catholic school does not necessarily connote clerical and religious control of a Catholic school.

In the government schools at all levels, the administrators, the teachers, and the guidance workers must first meet specified experience and university training requirements before they can be hired to fill a designated school post. Such training normally consists of undergraduate and graduate university course work in designated subjects and pedagogical areas appropriate to their type and level of service. Virtually all government school personnel have bacholor's degrees; in many states they are also required to have master's degrees.

In Catholic schools university degrees and specified course work are not enforced requisites. Appointment by one's ecclesiastical or religious superior is the typical way in which a school obtains its staff. The Notre Dame Study of Catholic education revealed that an astoundingly high percentage of Catholic elementary schoolteachers did not graduate from college: 69 per cent of the laywomen; 48 per cent of the laymen; 44 per cent of the sisters; 38 per cent of the brothers; 25 per cent of the priests. Approximately one-third of the brothers, sisters, and laymen, and one-half of the laywomen had only two years of college education (Neuwien).

Most government schools require their elementary schoolteachers not only to be college graduates but also to complete a minimum of thirty academic credits in pedagogical courses in undergraduate universities in order to qualify for a license to teach. Less than 5 per cent of all Catholic elementary schoolteachers meet the last stipulation of this requirement. Indeed, 80 per cent of all priests and laywomen, and half of all brothers, sisters, and laymen, have had no courses in pedagogy (Neuwien). On the secondary level, the situation is much better as far as the staff having college degrees; however, a high percentage of Catholic secondary schoolteachers do not have the requisite university undergraduate and graduate course work in pedagogy. (The usual state requirement is eighteen hours of undergraduate course work in education). Although the guidance situation is rapidly improving in Catholic secondary schools, three-fourths of these schools do not have one full-time guidance counselor. On the university level the small Catholic colleges have a very high percentage of professors without the doctorate and often teaching outside their areas of specialization. In the major Catholic universities the situation is considerably better, although generally even here the faculties are usually not as outstanding as those of the better major secular universities. Faculties of Catholic universities publish far fewer books and scholarly articles than do the faculties of secular universities (Donovan).

Almost all teachers in government elementary and secondary schools spent their undergraduate years as full-time university students. Until the 1940's lay and religious (but not clerical) teachers at Catholic schools often began teaching immediately upon graduating from secondary school. If they did eventually graduate from a Catholic university, it was usually by attending summer school or evening courses, a process which meant that the teacher typically went to the university from twelve to twenty years before receiving the bachelor's degree. This scandalous situation is rapidly disappearing and soon will be extinct. However, after the bachelor's degree, government and Catholic schoolteachers today go immediately into the profession, completing their master's degree in summer school or in evening courses. Prodded by forward-looking Catholic educationists, some of the more mature institutes of women religious, seeing the inadequacy of part-time graduate-school work, are beginning to send their sisters full-time to graduate school.

Teacher aides are people who assist the teacher in the noninstructional duties of the classroom, for example, clerical work, certain aspects of classroom management, and so forth. The first teacher-aide plan was adopted in 1952 in the government schools of Bay City, Michigan, under a five-year grant from the Ford Foundation. The chief advantage of the teacher-aide plan is that the teacher is free to devote more time to each student and to better teaching since he or she is relieved of noninstructional duties. Since 1952 the use of teacher aides has been growing very rapidly in both government and Catholic elementary schools. By 1965, 25 per cent of Catholic elementary schools had a teacher-aide program (NCEA).

The normal class load for teachers in Catholic schools at all levels tends to be greater than for their counterparts in comparable government schools. However, the situation is rapidly improving. On the elementary level, the typical teacher load is a steady teaching assignment throughout the school day, with time off when specialist teachers in art, music, and sometimes the natural sciences conduct the classes. Such specialists are not common in Catholic elementary schools. On the secondary level five periods is the normal load in government schools, with six and sometimes more being typical in Catholic schools. Professors in secular universities typically have a nine to twelve hour week in undergraduate divisions, with graduate school professors teaching from six to nine hours per week. In Catholic colleges and universities the comparable loads typically are twelve to fifteen hours and nine to twelve hours, respectively.

Generally speaking, there is more academic freedom for professors and students at government schools than in Catholic schools at all levels. At the Catholic elementary and secondary levels, students are frequently expelled for behavior which would not be regarded as extreme in the corresponding government school. Catholic schoolpeople believe such strictness keeps standards high. Teachers in Catholic elementary and secondary schools have less freedom of expression and behavior than their counterparts in the government school, but the difference is not tremendously wide since government school-teachers are also often quite restricted. It is at the university level that the differences between Catholic and government schools in academic freedom of professor and student are most marked. Studies have found there is not a high degree of academic freedom for professors in Catholic colleges and universities to speak out on controversial issues (Lazarsfeld). This is particularly true of the small Catholic women's colleges operated by women religious, whose behavior requirements for the students are very rigid, especially as regards the sexual sphere. However, tremendous strides have been made in recent years in widening academic freedom for professors and students in Catholic colleges and universities. In general the effects of Vatican Council II have made themselves felt in Catholic schools at every level. Consequently greater freedom for teachers and students may be expected in the years ahead.

There are no strong Catholic teacher associations as there are in the government schools. The National Catholic Educational Association is basically a discussion group, which until recently has done little to help the workaday teacher in the Catholic school. Its secular counterpart, the National Education Association, has been very vigorous in promoting and working for both higher professional standards and for teacher welfare in government schools. A rival secular teachers' group to the NEA is the American Federation of Teachers, which has been militant in winning substantial improvement in salaries and working conditions for government school personnel. Catholic school officials do not encourage their staffs to join either the NEA or the AFT. On the university level the secular professional organization, the American Association of University Professors (AAUP), has been active in protecting the rights of and advancing the welfare of university professors. AAUP's membership is open to professors at both Catholic and non-Catholic universities. A large number of the major Catholic universities have AAUP chapters on campus; in some other Catholic colleges, particularly the smaller ones, an AAUP chapter is forbidden by the administration. Most dioceses have their local Catholic Teachers Association, which is typically designed to have an annual Communion Breakfast and engage in charitable works favored by the bishop.

The Parents
and the
Catholic School

Both the Roman Catholic Church and American educationists have strongly stated that the primary responsibility for the education of the child resides in its parents. They have gone on record stating that it is consequently the parents' supreme right—a right which cannot in justice be taken away from them—to form the basic policy of the school. Notwithstanding, American Catholic schools at all levels give the parents virtually no voice in the determination of school policy.

Parental contact with the Catholic school is sporadic and often on an individual basis. Such contact usually occurs when the time arrives to pay the student's tuition; when a teacher asks a parent to visit the school to discuss the reasons for a particular student's poor academic or behavioral performance; when the school needs to raise money by cake sales and bazaars, and parents' help in providing the manpower is required; when meetings of an existing association of parents and teachers are scheduled. Catholic schools at all levels typically schedule parents' nights or "open school days" when parents can visit the schools, chat with the teachers, and visit classrooms. However, these activities are usually for the purpose of public relations or for interpreting the school to the parents; only rarely are they to involve parents deeply in formulating school policy or participating deeply in the work of the school.

Fully 25 per cent of all Catholic elementary and secondary schools do not have any form of parent-teacher association, even for fundraising. There is a national organization called the National Home and School Service (founded in 1960) which is intended to facilitate the establishment of branch chapters in all Catholic elementary and secondary schools. Surprisingly, the NHSS has no data on the percentage of Catholic elementary and secondary schools which have affiliated chapters. However, Mealey, an NCCW official, estimated the 1966 percentage at about fifty. The chapters meet with the teachers and school officials several times a year. The NHSS is not affiliated with the influential National Congress of Parents and Teachers (NCPT), which coordinates parent-teacher associations in government schools. Unlike the NCPT the NHSS specifically excludes as the purpose of the organization any role of the parents in making or helping to form school policy. The NHSS is more of a social organization of parents, an organization intended by school officials to help them implement certain aspects of school policy (usually disciplinary matters) and raise funds for the school. Of interest is that the parent organization of NHSS is not, as would be expected, the National Catholic Educational Association. Rather NHSS is affiliated with the National Council of Catholic Men and the National Council of Catholic Women.

Special Educational Problems
Facing Catholic Schools
in the United States

Throughout this essay, many problems confronting American Catholic education can readily be discerned by even the most casual reader. In this concluding section, attention will be restricted to only a few of these problems—recalling all the while that: first, this short treatment touches only on a few of the problems; second, that this treatment merely sketches rather than plumbs the depth of the problems; the third, that this treatment presumes familiarity with the basic contours of the problems as delineated in the previous sections of this essay.

The first and most serious of all the problems confronting American Catholic education is an ontological one: Should American Catholic schools continue to exist? This question, considered almost blasphemous by clergy and religious until a few years ago, is still being discussed in something less than the open forum. But it is being more widely talked about than ever before. A massive, carefully conducted scientific investigation conducted in 1965 by a theologically conservative priest-sociologist concluded that "there is no evidence that Catholic schools have been necessary for the survival of American Catholicism" (Greeley and Rossi).

Any private school, that is nongovernment school, is by its very nature a protest school. A nongovernment school is an institutional protest that the government school is failing to provide something essential which can only be received in a private school. Consequently a private school can exist legitimately only if it performs its total educative function better than does the government school. Two elements are involved in this concept. First, if in the perform-

ance of its total educative function the private school is either inferior
to or merely as good as the government school, it should not continue
to exist. The basis for this conclusion is Ockham's razor: "Beings
should not be multiplied without necessity." Also adduced in support
of this conclusion is the hallowed principle of subsidiarity: A being
of a higher ontological order (in this case the Church) should not
perform functions which a being of a lower ontological order (in this
case the government) can perform equally as well. The second of the
two elements involved in the legitimacy of the Catholic school's existence is that it must perform the total educative function better than
the government school. Thus, for example, if it only performs the
task of teaching religion better than does the government school,
then the other subjects or areas of educative experience should be
left to the government, with the Church merely operating schools of
religion (instead of the present system of operating complete schools).

The previous sections of this essay have shown that not only is
the Catholic school typically not performing its total educative function better than or even equal to that of the government schools, but
even more, it is deficient in teaching the students a high degree of
religious knowledge, attitudes, and overt behavior.

Several solutions have been advanced by Catholic educators to
solve the Catholic school problem. One solution, the classic one used
by Catholic school officials, is to augment the Catholic school effort
to the extent that the hierarchy's announced goal of "every Catholic
child in a Catholic school" will be fulfilled. But even the most opti-
mistic of Catholic schoolpeople realize that this will never come to
pass for a variety of reasons. Further, in view of fostering optimal personal development for each child or youth, it is preferable for some
Catholic students to attend a non-Catholic school.

Another solution frequently advanced is that of keeping the status
quo. However, this solution is also inadequate, in view of the swelling
Catholic population of school age.

Still another solution is to abandon Catholic schools altogether.
This solution seems simplistic. The consistent teaching of the popes
has been for a flourishing, vigorous, religiously oriented Catholic
school system. The fifteen-minute Sunday sermon is not really adequate to insert the religious dimension into every aspect of the daily
lives of the faithful. Such insertion is far more possible of realization
per modum the Catholic school program, which calls for twenty to
forty hours per week (depending on the grade level) of integrated
Catholic education. Surely the home is vital in the religious forma-

tion of the child; however, the professionally minded Catholic school, being a structured learning environment, can more systematically help the student fuse the City of God with the City of Man than can the relatively untrained parent or friend in an unstructured environment.

The present writer believes that the solution lies in reinvesting personnel and money to prune away those branches of the Catholic school system which are inefficient when viewed from the Church's purpose in operating schools. Specifically, all elementary schools should be abandoned; Catholic nursery schools should be inaugurated; Catholic secondary schooling should begin at the age of puberty; Catholic universities as they are now should be dismantled and re-structured into Catholic colleges within the nearby secular university of stature. The reason for discontinuing Catholic elementary schools is the empirically proven fact that the attitudes and values of children from six to fourteen years of age (who attend elementary school) are almost totally parent-derived, with the school providing little influence. The Catholic school exists far more to provide basic attitudes and values than to teach the student to read and write or to be a nuclear physicist. Hence, specifically, Catholic schooling is unnecessary at an age when school makes no deep value or attitudinal impact. By going into the nursery school apostolate—which psychoanalytic research has shown is a period of tremendous ingestion of attitudes and values from an institution—the Church would derive rich fruits from its school effort. It is during early childhood and again in the seven or so years following puberty, that values and attitudes are the most forcefully learned; hence the reason for the Church also to move aggressively into establishing the five-year Catholic secondary school program. On the university level, Catholic colleges just cannot compete with the major secular universities. By becoming affiliated colleges within the major secular university, Catholic higher education can come of age. Students would be enrolled in the Catholic college, and would be free to take most of their classes in any college within the total university. At those school levels which the Church would retain, the highest degree of professionalization should be the touchstone. New pedagogical and organizational structures must be pioneered and implemented. Such structures must be profoundly new and not merely superficial alterations of the present outmoded structures. Some prophets of doom call for the wholesale abandonment of the entire Catholic school system because it has failed. In response, the present writer asserts that the Catholic school system, optimally organized to pivot-point levels and ontologically based structures, has not failed because it has never been tried.

A second major problem confronting the entire American Catholic school system is that of professionalization. The majority of Catholic schoolpeople, particularly the nuns, do not seem fully to perceive education as a profession. Rather, education is viewed solely as an apostolic concern, something which requires chiefly dedication, with some degree of knowledge of what one is teaching. But piety, or dedication for that matter, is no substitute for competence and technique. One does not become a good teacher because one is assigned to teach by one's religious superior. Nor does one become a good administrator principally because one has been relatively effective as a classroom teacher for a quarter of a century. The grace of Orders or of vows does not automatically make one a competent guidance counselor.

Forward-looking Catholic educationists have noted that to secure the necessary ingredient of professionalism in Catholic education, a new mentality must pervade Catholic schoolpeople. Education must be approached as an art-science which must be learned and constantly renewed. Competence must be continuously sharpened and honed. Not all religious should be permitted to teach or to be administrators. Rigorous selection devices should be employed to insure that only the psychologically, scholastically, and technically proficient will be admitted to both the teaching ranks and to the various hierarchies within it. Schoolwork must be regarded as a career choice, not as merely presiding over a classroom doing one's duty for God's kingdom. The constitutions of religious institutes should be tailored to meet the professional demands of teaching, and not vice-versa, something which has ruined professionalism in Catholic schools. Catholic school officials should cease to regard government-suggested professional standards for school personnel as necessary evils which must be met for appearance sake; such officials should embrace these suggestions as tools to make their schools more professional. Catholic schoolpeople should be completely prepared professionally before being assigned; these people should not be sent to their positions only partially trained, as is sometimes the case now. Further, vigorous inservice programs for significant professional upgrading should be introduced.

A third major problem is the area of lay-clergy and lay-religious relations in Catholic schools. Despite the ringing pronouncements from the hierarchy, the clergy, and the religious there is little doubt— as evidenced by the concrete actions of these persons—that the layman in Catholic schools is regarded as a necessary evil, something to be endured until the religiovocation shortage is alleviated. Laymen have really no place to go within the Catholic school structure. There are virtually no lay principals of Catholic elementary or secondary schools, or lay presidents of Catholic colleges and universities. A few laymen have risen to the post of assistant superintendent, but these positions do not entail very much power. The few laymen who do occupy relatively high (but not powerful) positions in the Catholic schools or universities and in the National Catholic Educational Association are, with some notable exceptions, caterers and aides to the clergy or hierarchy.

The majority of perceptive Catholic educationists concur that laymen should be able to rise to any position within the Catholic school system. They should not be discriminated against because of their canonical status. Talent and professional competence should be the criteria for placement and advancement.

Even more fundamental than this, the Catholic school system should be regarded as basically a lay concern rather than a clerical province. After all, teaching mathematics or administering a school is not really priestly work. A layman can perform these functions as well as, and perhaps better than, a priest. As competent laymen are recruited for Catholic school work, priests should withdraw from this arena and return to the direct pastoral ministry. By his sacramentally transformed nature, a priest is a pastoral apostle who has been given special powers for mediating in a unique manner between God and man. Hence the direct pastoral ministry is the chief and indeed the only real function of the priest—a pivotal fact noted by the Scriptures (cf. Heb. 5:1), the ordination ceremony, and St. Thomas Aquinas (S.T. Sup. q. 37, a. 2). Priests are in school work now because of an emergency; there were for centuries few competent laymen available to enter this vineyard. But now the situation is rapidly changing, so that soon the priests will be able to return to that for which they were ordained. It is the more progressive and thoughtful among the clergy who are the most vocal that the priesthood be returned to the priests. Some, such as Father Schleck, C.S.C., believe that one of the reasons for the present unhappy vocation crisis is that young men do not wish to give their lives to teaching, a post which they can perform just as well if not better from the vantage point—with all its material, social, and interpersonal advantages—of a layman. Young men wishing to be priests desire to become sacramental mediators between God and man. The current blurring of the distinctiveness of the priesthood only serves to extinguish the spark of a priestly vocation in the mind and heart of the questing young man. Many apostolic young American priests ardently desire to leave teaching for the direct pastoral ministry and to turn over administration and instruction to brothers, sisters, and laymen. This does not mean priests will abandon the Catholic school apostolate, however; rather they will remain in the school as guidance counselors, a post exquisitely suited to the pastoral and sacramental role of the priest.

A host of other problems present themselves for attention. But the problems are as many as the space is short. Hence only a brief enumeration of problems and suggestions will be possible. Much more skillful financial management must be utilized in Catholic schools. It has been reliably estimated that millions of dollars are wasted every year by Catholic school administrators who have no budgets, who fail to utilize sound accounting and managerial procedures, who inadequately supervise plant maintenance (Seidl). Research in the teaching of catechetics will have to be augmented. Demonstration laboratories should be inaugurated toward this end. Experimentation should not only proceed as far as content goes but, just as important, on the process of teaching catechetics. The Catholic school curricula must be reorganized to integrate religion into all areas of the Catholic school program in such a way that the students will see God mingled intimately with all of life. The guidance program will have to be modernized and professionalized. And much more will have to be done on all fronts.

If American Catholic schools are beset with many critical problems, they are faced with an even more shining future. The field is ripe for the harvest. With the use of the most modern educational tools, with the assistance of highly professional workers, the harvest can be limitless. With proper planting and watering, surely God will give the increase.

Selected Bibliography

Burns, J. A., C.S.C., and Bernard J. Kohlbrenner. A History of Catholic Education in the United States. New York: Benziger, 1937.
(Though somewhat dated, this work is the best single-volume history of American Catholic education at all levels.)

Greeley, Andrew M., and Peter H. Rossi. *The Education of Catholic Americans.* Chicago: Aldine, 1966.
(One of the most comprehensive research investigations ever undertaken on the religious effects of Catholic schooling.)

Hassenger, Robert, ed. *The Shape of Catholic Higher Education.* Chicago: University of Chicago Press, 1967.
(A series of scholarly essays reporting empirical and conceptual researches into the various sectors and dimensions of Catholic colleges and universities.)

Lee, James Michael, *Principles and Methods of Secondary Education.* New York: McGraw-Hill Catholic Series in Education, 1963.
(The best textbook in its area, with discussion of the basic organization, principles, and research evidence on American government and Catholic secondary schools.)

Lee, James Michael, and Nathaniel J. Pallone, *Guidance and Counseling in Schools.* New York: McGraw-Hill Catholic Series in Education, 1966.
(The only textbook which treats of guidance and counseling in Catholic and public schools at all levels.)

McCluskey, Neil G., S.J. *Catholic Viewpoint in Education,* 2nd ed. Garden City, New York: Doubleday Image, 1959.
(A conservative-oriented monograph in defense of the American Catholic school system.)

McCoy, Raymond F. *American School Administration: Public and Catholic.* New York: McGraw-Hill Catholic Series in Education, 1961.
(A textbook which gives principles and practices of school administration in both Catholic as well as government schools.)

National Catholic Educational Association, *Bulletins.* Washington: NCEA, annually.
(Reports of annual conventions and occasional reports of research.)

Neuwien, Reginald A., ed. *Catholic Schools in Action: A Report of the Notre Dame Study of Catholic Elementary and Secondary Schools in the United States.* Notre Dame, Ind.: University of Notre Dame Press, 1966.
(Despite its many shortcomings, the official report of the most massive research on the American Catholic common school ever undertaken.)

Power, Edward J. *Education for American Democracy,* 2nd ed. New York: McGraw-Hill Catholic Series in Education, 1965.
(A standard textbook of high quality giving an overview of the basic features of the American government and Catholic school systems.)

Power, Edward J. *A History of Catholic Higher Education in the United States.* Milwaukee: Bruce, 1958.
(The best one-volume history of American Catholic colleges and universities.)

Appendix

Appendix

This appendix gives the basic outline
which each essay scrupulously follows.

TITLE OF SECTION AND SUBSECTION OF EACH ESSAY

I. A brief history of Catholic schools in (country)

II. The Purpose of Catholic education in (country)
    A. The stated purpose
    B. The real purpose

III. Relationship of Catholic schools with government schools (except in financial matters involving present fiscal support)
    A. Government school legislation which has affected Catholic schools
    B. Comparison of status of Catholic schools with government schools

IV. The present form of Catholic schools in (country)
    A. To organizational level (school system qua system)
        1. Preschool level, elementary level, secondary level, higher education, adult education, confraternity, etc.
            a. Articulation and cooperation of schools at different levels
        2. Differentiated school patterns
            a. Basis on which student admitted into one of the differentiated patterns
                (1) Compulsory education—length and type
                (2) Examinations and other selection devices to gain admission
        3. Control structure of Catholic school system
            a. Governance of schools
            b. Administrative setup of schools in terms of personnel
            c. Clerical control of education
                (1) Degree
                (2) Signs of change
    B. Some statistics on Catholic schools
        1. Table indicating the following:
            a. Number of Catholic schools in the country at each level, as compared with number of government schools

      b. Absolute number of students in Catholic schools at each level
         (1) Absolute number of students of all denominations in government schools
      c. The size of Catholic schools in terms of pupil enrollment at each level
         (1) The median enrollment per school
         (2) The median number of students in a classroom
    2. The school year
    3. The school day:
      a. Length of the school day at each level
      b. Divisions of the school day
    4. The school building, its appearance, new trends in school architecture

V. Financial support of Catholic schools
  A. Type of support—blanket funds, funds allocated on basis of enrollment, funds only given in special situations, teachers' salaries paid, etc.
  B. Percentage of total Catholic school budget financed by state
  C. Financial status of school personnel, especially salaries, salary increment based on service and/or skill, financial fringe benefits, health insurance and pensions, for example

VI. The curriculum
  A. Elements of—that is the typical subjects and/or educational experiences received by students at each level
    1. Subjects taken
    2. Required and elective courses
    3. Extracurricular activities
  B. The curricular design used
  C. Curricular innovations since World War II
    1. Source of these innovations—state, Church, teachers' committees, students
    2. Research taking place, both in the experimental and theoretical levels, on curricular innovation
  D. The syllabus
    1. Its existence
    2. Its structure
    3. The degree to which it must be followed rigorously
    4. The source and the content of the syllabus, that is the result solely of experts in subject areas, or made up by teachers of the course, or the result of teacher-student planning, etc.
  E. "Bookish" curriculum or one related to life problems

TITLE OF SECTION AND SUBSECTION OF EACH ESSAY

VII. Instruction
    A. The methods of teaching used, lecture, discussion, role-playing, panels, audiovisual devices
      1. The approximate percentage of time the teacher at each level allocates to the various methods
    B. The place of homework, field trips, supplementary readings, textbooks, audiovisual aids, etc. in the teacher's repertoire of instruction
    C. Motivation
    D. The relative emphasis of cooperation vs. competition in the typical classroom at each level
    E. Evaluation of student learning
      1. Nature of evaluation, that is as part of learning or as something which comes after it, as continuous or sporadic
      2. The manner in which evaluation is carried out
      3. The composition of achievement tests
        a. Standardized or teacher-constructed
        b. Degree of objective and subjective questions in each test
    F. Method of reporting evaluation of learning
      1. Report card to parents
      2. Parent-teacher conferences to discuss report card
      3. Teacher-student conferences to discuss report card
    G. Supervision of instruction
      1. Who does it—state inspector, religious community
      2. The nature of the supervisory act—solely prophylactic to eliminate teaching mistakes, a learning experience for teacher, a punitive device, etc.
    H. The establishment and maintenance of instructional standards
      1. The person responsible for such establishment and maintenance
      2. The type and frequency of review

VIII. The program of religious education
    A. Percentage of the school day devoted to religious instruction at each level
    B. The manner in which religious instruction is carried out, e.g. similar to other classes in methodology with content in religion
      1. The principal pedagogical methods used in religious instruction at each level
        a. Percentage of class time devoted to each
    C. The quality of religious instructors compared with instructors in other academic areas of the school
      1. Level and extent of preparation of religious instruction, both

in content and in professional education foundations (e.g. curriculum study and educational psychology) and in methodology

D. Extent to which religion is integrated into the other areas of the school program
E. The supervision of religious instruction
F. Attendance at religious exercises, such as confession, and mass, as a part of the religious instructional program of the school at all levels
G. Results of Catholic schooling compared with government schooling (as found by research evidence)
   1. Academic preparation
   2. Faithfulness in attendance at religious exercises
   3. Level of Christianity
H. Relation of school to parish at each level

IX. Pupil personnel and guidance services
A. Brief outline of the organized pupil personnel and guidance service program
B. Group guidance and counseling
C. The testing program: organization, types of tests given, etc.
D. Discipline: its theory and practice
E. Religious guidance
   1. The role of the chaplain in the religious guidance program

X. The staff
A. The number of priests, nuns, brothers, and laymen teaching at each level
B. The professional preparation of administration guidance personnel and teachers
C. Academic freedom for teachers, students, and administrators
   1. Censorship and reprisals
D. Teachers' associations

XI. The parents and the school
A. Contact of the parents with the school (administration, teacher, guidance personnel)
   1. Nature of this contact
   2. Extent of this contact
   3. Purpose of this contact

XII. Special educational problems facing Catholic schools in (country) (with indications of possible solutions to these problems)

Profiles of
Contributors

Profiles of
Contributors

Didier J. Piveteau is Professor of Catechesis and Education at the Institut Catholique de Paris. He is also Editor-in-Chief of *Orientations,* one of France's leading journals on Catholic education. A member of the Brothers of the Christian Schools, Doctor Didier has also served as Dean of Studies at St. Genes High School. Currently also Lecturer in Education for American Catholic agencies in Europe, Brother Didier has twice been a Fulbright scholar, and three times acted as the official French delegate to the International Conference on American Studies held annually in Salzburg, Austria. Moreover, he has been a grantee of the British Council and of the Swedish government. He is also Director of Education of CODIAM, a French government organization for promoting schooling in French-speaking Negro Africa. Books by this French educationist include a series of textbooks for Catholic schools (Ligel, 1952–1962), *Actualité des langues vivantes* (Ligel, 1953), and *Equilibre affectif et sexuel de l'Ecolier* (Centre Cath. Educ., 1962). He is a co-editor of *Le Prêtre educateur* (Maine, 1964). Doctor Didier also is currently a translator for the journal *Concilium;* he has also translated various books into French. His articles have appeared in numerous journals, including *Le Maison Dieu; Pédagogie; Catechistes; Orientations;* and *La Famille Éducatrice.*

Franz Pöggeler is Professor Ordinarius and Dean of the Pädagogische Hochschule Rheinland, located in Cologne. A specialist in Catholic higher and adult education, Dean Pöggeler also holds licenses to teach on the secondary school level. Dr. Pöggeler's academic career included Assistant Lecturer in Education at the University of Marburg, Assistant Lecturer in Education at the University of Hamburg, First Lecturer in Education and Research Director of the German Institute of Education at Münster, and Professor Extraordinarius of Education at the Pädagogische Hochschule Rheinland. Dean Pöggeler was an Exchange Lecturer at the University of Bristol, England. He is General Secretary and Director of the Institute of Adult Education, a branch of the German Institute of Education, Münster. Professor Pöggeler has been President of the Committee on Pedagogical Processes of the Association of German Catholic Teachers. He is presently President of the Friederich Wilhelm Foerster Gesellschaft, Director of the Academy for the Study of Youth Problms, and also founder and Director of the Archives of the History of Education based jointly in

England and in Germany. Dean Pöggeler is Research Adviser to the Federal Ministry of Family and Youth, headquartered in Bonn. Professor Pöggeler has authored over ten scholarly books on education, including *Einführung in die Andragogik* (Henn, 1957); *Die Pädagogik Friederich Wilhelm Foersters* (Herder, 1957); *Methoden der Erwachsenenbildung* (Fromm, 1962), subsequently appearing in a second and third edition; *Katholische Erwachsenenbildung 1918–1945* (Kosel, 1965); *Der Mensch in Mündigkeit und Reife* (Schoningh, 1964), released in a second German edition in 1965 and translated into Dutch under the title *De Mens As Wollwassem* (Antwerp, 1966); *Inhalt der Erwachsenenbildung* (Herder, 1965). Dean Pöggeler's articles have appeared in a host of scholarly and religious journals, including *Erwachsenenbildung*; *Vierteljahraschrift für Wissenschaftliche Pädagogik*; *Pädagogische Welt*; *Katholische Frauenbildung*; and *Caritas*.

Josephus J. Gielen is a Professor of Education and Director of the Institute for the Study of Education at the Catholic University of Nijmegen. He has taught in Dutch schools at all levels, from primary through university. He has been inspector, and later head inspector of primary education; also Secretary of the Board of Education of The Netherlands. Dr. Gielen served a term as a member of the Tweede Kamerlid (House of Representatives), and is currently Eerste Kamerlid (Senator) with a specialization in educational affairs. He also served as the Vice-President of Katholieke Volkspartij (Catholic Peoples' Party). Professor Gielen's civil decorations include Grand Officier De La Legion D'Honneur and also Ridder in De Orde Van De Nederlandse Leeuw (Knight of the Order of the Dutch Lion). He is the author of numerous textbooks and scholarly works in education, including *De Wandelende Jood in volkskunde en letterkunde* (Spiegel, 1931); *Moderne wereldliteratuur* (deHaan, 1952); *Handleidung bij de Nederlandse letterkunde*, 5th ed. (Purmerend, 1954); *Het sociale in opvoeding en opvoedkunde*, 2nd ed. (Bosch, 1965); senior authorship of *Leerboek ener opvoedkunde*, 4th ed. (Bosch, 1965); *Woordkunst*, 24th ed. (Wolters, 1965); *Belangrijke Letterkundige werken*, Vol. 1, 9th ed.; Vol. 2, 9th ed.; Vol. 3, 11th ed. (Purmerend, 1966); senior authorship of *Grondbeginselen ener opvoedkunde*, 10th ed. (Bosch, 1966); *Naar een nieuwe katholieke school* (Bosch, 1966). His articles have appeared in such professional journals as *Tijdschrift voor opvoedkunde r.k.*; *Opvoeding, Onderwijs en Gezondheidsleer*; and *Pädagogische Studien*. Professor Gielen was assisted in his essay in the present volume by his son, Dr. W. J. G. M. Gielen, Assistant Director of the Institute for the Study of Education at the Catholic University of Nijmegen. The younger Dr. Gielen, a specialist in school law, school organization, and the economics of education, has published articles in *Katholiek Staatkundig Maandschrift, Politiek, De Tijd*; and *Onderwijs, Opvoeding en Gezondheidszorg*.

Vincenzo Sinistrero, is Professor of Comparative Education at the Advanced Institute of Education, Pontificium Athenaeum Salesianum (Rome), of which he was formerly the Dean. Father Sinistrero has held a wide variety of teaching and administrative offices in Salesian educational institutions at all levels. He has been Ecclesiastical Consultor to the Catholic Educational Office in Italy, a member of the Vatican delegation to the UNESCO Assembly, educational representative of the Holy See to the First International Conference of the Union Mondiale Organismes Sauvegarde Enfance et Adolescence (UMOSEA), and delegate of the Vatican to the Fifth World Congress of the Association International Educateurs Jeunes Inadaptes (AIEJI). A former Vice-President of the Office International Enseignement Catholique (OIEC), Professor Sinistrero has also been a member of various commissions of the Ministry of Public Instruction and of the Ministry of Work. Doctor Sinistrero is currently President of the Commission for School Legislation of the Federation of Institures Dependent on Ecclesiastical Authority (FIDAE). Scholarly books by this Italian educationist include *I problemi del pensiero* (SEI, 1938), *Verso la Liberta mediante la Parita* (SEI, 1947), *Problemi attuali della scuola* (SEI, 1956), *La scuola cattolica* (SEI, 1961), *Scuola e formazione professionale nel mondo* (Las, 1963), *La politica scolastica 1945–1965 e la scuola cattolica* (FIDAE, 1966), and *Il Vaticano II e l'Educazione—Testi e commento* (LDC, 1967). Father Sinistrero has written over 150 articles in various education journals, including *Orientamenti Pedagogicil; Salesianum; Vita e Pensiero; La Scuola e L'Uomo; Docete.*

John P. White is Senior Lecturer in English and Acting Head of the English Department at St. Mary's College of Education of the Institute of Education, University of London. He is a specialist in the teaching of English in Britain's school system. His professional career began in 1955 in King's School, Somerset. Professor White also was Lecturer in English Literature at the Delegacy of Extra-Mural Studies, Oxford University. At St. Mary's he both teaches the structural and methodological processes of the teaching of English, and also spends considerable time in English secondary schools to supervise instruction. Professor White also served as Lecturer in English Literature to the Workers' Educational Association as well as Lecturer and Chairman of Conferences for Teachers at the Eckersley School of English for Foreigners at Oxford University. He is currently lecturer for and member of The Catholic Marriage Advisory Council (London Branch). Professor White's articles have appeared in a number of important professional and religious journals, including *Catholic Teachers Journal; The Tablet; New Blackfriars; New Outlook;* and *The University of London Institute of Education Bulletin,* of which he is a corresponding editor. He also has been commissioned to prepare two books, one in teaching of language and the other on the writings of Samuel Beckett.

James Michael Lee, a specialist in catechetics, the teaching process, and on American Catholic education in general, is Head of the Department of Education at the University of Notre Dame. He has taught in the New York City government school system on the secondary school level as well as in the adult education program. Doctor Lee has also been Lecturer in Education in the School of Education at Seton Hall University (N. J.), Lecturer in Education in the Graduate School of Hunter College (N. Y.), and Assistant Professor of Education at St. Joseph College (Conn.). He and two Catholic sociologists were instrumental in receiving a $100,000 grant from the United States Government to institute and then evaluate an educational program for disadvantaged children and youth. Doctor Lee is special consultant for a national research project on seminaries sponsored by the American hierarchy through its Center of Applied Research on the Apostolate (CARA), and also is a project consultant for the United States Government's Office of Education. Professor Lee's books include *Principles and Methods of Secondary Education* (McGraw-Hill Catholic Series in Education, 1963); senior authorship of *Guidance and Counseling in Schools: Foundations and Processes* (McGraw-Hill Catholic Series in Education, 1966); senior editorship of and major contributor to *Seminary Education in a Time of Change* (Fides, 1965), which was later translated into French; senior editorship of and contributor to *Readings in Guidance and Counseling* (Sheed and Ward, 1966). His articles have appeared in leading educational and religious journals, including *Catholic Educational Review; National Catholic Guidance Conference Journal; School Executive; Review for Religious;* and *The Catholic World.*